THE GANGS C

The book is dedicated to my mam, Bella.

THE GANGS OF LIVERPOOL

From the Cornermen to the High Rip:
The Mobs That Terrorised a City

Mick Macilwee

MILO BOOKS

First published in May 2006 by Milo Books
This edition published in 2007 by Milo Books

ISBN 978 1 903854 60 0

Typeset by e-type

Printed in Great Britain by CPD

MILO BOOKS LTD
The Old Weighbridge
Station Road
Wrea Green
Lancs PR4 2PH
www.milobooks.com

Contents

Acknowledgements

Illustrations:
The author wishes to thank the following for permission to use images from their collections:

Ruth Hobbins of Liverpool Libraries for reproducing photographs from the Records Office collection: Tithebarn Street (1925); Kirkdale Gaol (1832); Clarke Aspinall; Thomas Stamford Raffles; Entrance to Walton Gaol; Maiden's Green (1935); Naylor Street (1935); Prussia Street (1930); Major Greig; Highfield Street (1900); Eldon Vaults (1910); Dale Street Magistrates Court; Tithebarn Street (1915); Whittle Street (1902); Silvester Street (1897); Boundary Street (1897); Ford Street (1897); Walton Road (1899); St George's Hall (1906); William Brown Street (1897).

The photographs of the Vernon Arms and the cornernmen outside the Goat Public House are courtesy of the Walker Cain Archive at Merseyside Records Office.

Alan Hayhurst for the photograph of a holding cell in St George's Hall (from Alan Hayhurst, *Lancashire Murders*, Stroud: Sutton Publishing, 2004).

Kate McNichol of Merseyside Police for the photograph of Athol Street Bridewell.

Home Office Prison Department for the photograph of two juvenile vandals.

Paul Brennan for the photograph of Blackstone Street.

Jim Rawsthorn for the photograph of Samuel Morgan.

The following images came from the cited publications:

Justice Day. (Arthur Day, *John C.F.S. Day: His Forbears and Himself: A Biographical Study By One Of His Sons*, London: Heath Cranton Ltd, 1916)

The North Dispensary. (Thomas Herbert Bickerton, *Medical History of Liverpool from the Earliest Days to the Year 1920*, London: Murray, 1936)

A Multiple Hanging. (William Calcraft, *Life and Recollections of William Calcraft*, 1870)

Sir William Nott-Bower. (Sir William Nott-Bower, *Fifty-Two Years a Policeman*, London: Edward Arnold, 1926)

Justice Butt. (*The Graphic*, 1892)

A Remedy for Ruffians. (*Punch*, September 10, 1898)

Kicking assault on a policeman. (*The Illustrated Police News*)

ACKNOWLEDGEMENTS

The author also thanks the following for permission to include quotations:

Colin Wilkinson from Bluecoat Press for permission to quote from Freddy O'Connor, *A Pub On Every Corner, vol. 4: Scotland Road, Everton, Anfield*, Liverpool: Bluecoat Press, 2001 and Richard Whittington-Egan, *Echoes*, Liverpool: Bluecoat Press, 2002.

Chris Walker from Trinity Mirror North West & North Wales for permission to quote from the *Liverpool Echo*.

Quotation from Hippolyte Taine's *Notes on England*, translated by Edward Hyams. Copyright 1957 Thames & Hudson Ltd. Reproduced by kind permission of Thames & Hudson Ltd.

Continuum Books for permission to quote from Rob Sindall, *Street Violence in the Nineteenth Century: Media Panic or Real Danger?*, Leicester: Leicester University Press, 1990.

Liverpool University Press for permission to quote from P.J. Waller, *Democracy and Sectarianism: A Political and Social History of Liverpool, 1868–1939*, Liverpool: Liverpool University Press, 1981.

Quotations from the following books are reproduced by kind permission of Oxford University Press:

Harry Hendrick, *Images of Youth: Age, Class and the Male Youth Problem, 1880–1920*, Oxford: Clarendon Press, 1990.

Leon Radzinowicz and Roger Hood, A *History of English Criminal Law and its Administration from 1750, vol. 5: The Emergence of Criminal Policy in Victorian and Edward England*, London: Stevens & Sons, reprinted by Clarendon Press, 1990. The author has been unable to contact Stevens & Sons but has obtained permission from Clarendon Press.

Quotations from Geoffrey Pearson, *Hooligan: A History of Respectable Fears*, London: Macmillan, 1983, reproduced with permission of Palgrave Macmillan.

Thanks to Peter Walsh for having faith in the project, our Ste for all the computer related bits, and the library staff at Liverpool Records Office, JMU Document Delivery and Aldham Robarts Learning Resource Centre for their help in obtaining material.

Every effort has been made to contact the copyright holders of the material included in this book. In instances where this has not proved possible, particularly with some of the old images, apologies are offered to those concerned. Any omissions will be rectified on notification.

List of Illustrations

Map of Tithebarn Street
Women selling crockery (1900)
Tithebarn Street (1915)
Highfield Street (1900)
The scene of Morgan's murder (1925)
Samuel Morgan
Prussia Street (1930)
Boundary Terrace (1897)
Maiden's Green (1935)
Naylor Street (1935)
Cornermen outside The Goat (1908)
Girl Singing (1900)
William Brown Street (1897)
Kicking assault on a policeman
St George's Hall (1906)
Vernon Chambers
Kirkdale Gaol (1832)
A multiple hanging
Whittle Street (1902)
The North Dispensary
Walton Road (1899)
Clarke Aspinall
Ford Street (1897)
Young cornerman (1910)
Juvenile vandals (1899)
Boys reading
Blackstone Street
Holding cell
Justice Butt
Map of the worst area of High Rip violence
Athol Street Bridewell
Dale Street Police Court
Silvester Street (1897)
Walton Gaol
Navvies
A remedy for ruffians
Thomas Stamford Raffles
Justice Day
Major Greig
Sir William Nott-Bower

Gangs of Victorian Liverpool

1860s
Hibernians

1870s
Cornermen

1880s
Blackstone Street Gang
Lemon Street Gang
Housebreakers' Gang
High Rip
Logwood
Finnon Haddie
Dead Rabbits
Regent Street Gang
Roach Guards

About the Author

Dr Michael Macilwee has an MA in Victorian Literature and a PhD in American Literature and has contributed to numerous academic journals. A librarian at Liverpool John Moores University, he has conducted detailed research into the Merseyside underworld. *Gangs of Liverpool* is his first book.

Preface

ONE MORNING IN 1886, readers of the *Daily Post* opened their newspapers to the headline "Savage Liverpool". The editorial beneath it was a scathing attack on that city's apparent moral extremes: "The highest type of civilisation and the lowest type of savagery are to be found in Liverpool, existing side by side; and in no city in the world can a more startling contrast of the two races of mankind – the civilised and the uncivilised – be found."[1]

It was as if Liverpool suffered a dual personality, with good and evil existing together in some sociological form of Jekyll and Hyde schizophrenia. This was the same year that Robert Louis Stevenson had published his disturbing tale of the respectable Dr Jekyll, a man forced to confront the dark, malevolent side of his own character.[2]

In a similar spirit of self-examination, the newspaper felt compelled to inform its readers as "to what depths some of their fellow citizens are capable of sinking". There followed a series of revelations about a gang of ruffians who were openly terrorising the community. The article opened up a public debate about street crime, law and justice, as concerned readers sent in letters describing their own shocking experiences of violence, theft and intimidation. The correspondents' responses to the crime wave were both as civilised and as savage as the city itself. Some advocated humane social solutions, while others were vociferous in their support of brutal physical punishments for those responsible for crime.

That debate continues to this day. Hardly a week goes by without the publication of some newspaper editorial highlighting the problem of street crime. Whatever the official statistics might indicate, everybody's experience of crime seems to be that the number of offences is going up and that the situation is getting worse. My local newspaper, the *Liverpool Echo*, includes a steady trickle of letters from people from various parts of the city, all of whom with similar horror stories to tell of rampaging youths, anti-social behaviour and vandalism.

Members of the public, for their part, want tougher measures to combat crime, including both longer gaol sentences and harsher regimes in prison. They seek the return of corporal punishment and hanging. People cry out for more police on the beat and for officers to be more pro-active in their pursuit of criminals. They want the streets cleared of yobs. The city council is urged to do more to prevent crime, by providing youth clubs, for example. There are calls for the government to bring in tougher legislation. Parents are denounced for the behaviour of their offspring. Magistrates and judges are blamed for handing down lenient sentences to criminals.

Yet these responses to crime are nothing new. Every point just made has its origins in the Victorian debate about criminal justice. This book will focus on gang activity on Liverpool's streets and how the press and public reacted to it, particularly two major outbreaks of brutal mob violence. The first case, known as the "Tithebarn Street outrage", is dealt with in some depth, as it was perhaps the first major reported case of a street-gang murder in Liverpool and provides an interesting example of how the criminal justice system worked. In 1874, an innocent, respectable man was beaten to death by a group of youths as he walked to his home in a city centre street after a Bank Holiday trip to the Wirral.

The second outbreak of violence on Liverpool's streets has become part of local folklore. Between 1884–86, the so-called "High Rip" gang gained increasing notoriety for committing murder, extortion and violent robbery. Newspapers, led by the *Daily Post*, couldn't publish enough bloodthirsty tales of the gang. Typical headlines included "High Rip Terrorism", "High Ripping in Marybone", "The High Rip Outrage at Aintree": they were headlines guaranteed to keep readers fixated on Liverpool's savage underworld.

In addition to looking at these two major outbreaks of violence, this book also examines various other manifestations of gang crime, such as bare-knuckle fights, juvenile disorder and sectarian feuds, finishing with an overview of gang activity in the rest of the country, particularly in Manchester and London.

A word must be said about the sources used in research. The information about the crimes and social conditions has largely been gleaned from contemporary newspaper and journal reports. Today in Liverpool, only one evening and one morning newspaper cover the whole city, the *Echo* and the *Daily Post* respectively. In Victorian times, the city reader was spoilt for choice. There were, at various times, the *Daily Post*, *Daily Courier* and *Liverpool Mercury*, which were all quality dailies. The *Evening Express* and *Liverpool Echo* were more popular titles. There was also the *Liverpool Mail* and *Liverpool Daily Albion*. The *Liverpool Telegraph Shipping Gazette* had a maritime slant. In addition, there were also many local journals, including the *Liverpool Journal*, *Liverpool Review*, *Liverpool Citizen* and *Liverpool Town Crier*. The *Porcupine* was a satirical journal of current events while *Plain Talk* was a Christian periodical. All these publications were consulted during the writing of this book. Suffice it to say, they do not all agree with each other either in their reporting or in their opinion of events.

Please bear in mind that the viewpoints expressed in this book are often those of journalists and editors and their middle-class readers. One has to be wary of the political bias and party affiliations of certain editors. Some have an obvious axe to grind against the town council or against the police authority, for example. As for the people who wrote to the newspapers, it is clear from some of the letters that the authors included taxpayers and ratepayers who were in regular employment, who were able to read and write and who were able to afford a daily paper. Their comments often express the values and prejudices of their social standing.

However, the characters involved in the various crimes – as victims, assailants and witnesses – were largely drawn from the lower classes, most likely people with very little education and who were forced to scrape a living from day to day. The middle classes mainly saw such people as a social problem that needed to be tackled.

Nevertheless, in looking at how the press and public responded to the terror on Liverpool's streets, it will be seen that people's attitudes to law and order haven't changed over the years. The Victorians thought that they, too, were living in desperate, lawless times and they also wanted something done about it. The concerns that drove angry nineteenth-century Liverpudlians to write letters of complaint to their local newspapers are the same issues that motivate present-day inhabitants of the city to highlight their own troubled experiences of anti-social behaviour. Interestingly, the tough solutions to crime proposed by today's newspaper correspondents are often the very same solutions offered by the Victorians all those years ago.

CHAPTER 1

The Tithebarn Street Outrage

AT 2 P.M. ON the Monday Bank Holiday of August 3, 1874, twenty-six-year-old Richard Morgan and his twenty-three-year-old wife Alice took a short boat ride across the River Mersey. They were heading for the Druids' Gala at New Ferry Gardens on the Wirral, and a day out by the beach. Like the better-known New Brighton, New Ferry was a popular tourist destination for Liverpudlians, particularly those of the poorer classes. Its sea, sand and gaudy attractions were a welcome relief from the stinking courts and alleys of the town.

In festive mood, Alice Morgan drank a bottle of porter going across to the gala and another one when she got there. After an enjoyable day in glorious weather, the couple returned to the landing stage at Liverpool for about 9 p.m., where they met Richard's older brother Samuel, who was twenty-nine.

The Morgans couldn't have picked a better day for their holiday treat, but the merriment was to be short-lived: "It was a lovely evening, a perfect finish to a perfect day. A constant stream of holidaymakers was pouring up from the direction of the river. The refrain of a song or the strains of a concertina broke upon the ear. All was mirth and good fellowship, yet within the space of a few minutes one of the tired but happy holidaymakers was to be hurried into eternity without a moment's preparation."[1]

The two Morgan brothers lived close together, Richard and Alice in 10 Court, Leeds Street, and Samuel in 12 Court. It was a slum area, but the Morgans, like many there, were law-abiding, hard-working people. Richard and Alice had been married for thirteen months, after an eight-month engagement. Richard was a porter in the service of Mr

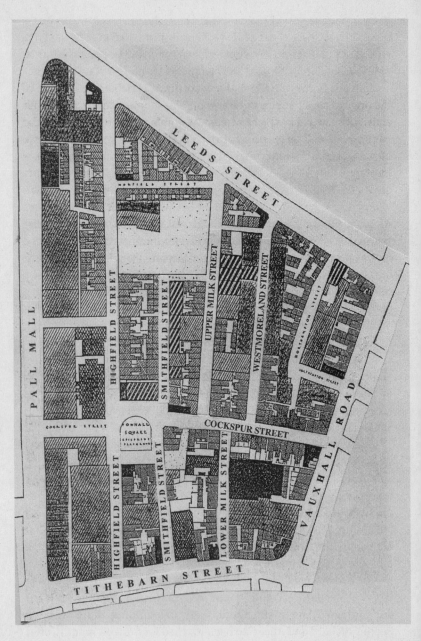

Map of Tithebarn Street area.

Peate, a shopkeeper of Richmond Street in the town centre. He was a powerfully strong, low-set man, weighing just over twelve stone, and was an industrious, respectable worker, having never missed a day's work to illness. Samuel, who worked as a carter, was bigger and equally robust.

To reach home, the trio had to walk down Tithebarn Street, one of the original seven streets of Liverpool. This thoroughfare bristled with activity, but was also a place where two worlds met, a microcosm of the city itself. To walk its length was to pass from the prosperity of the centre of one of the world's great seaports to some of the most appalling slums in Europe. The Liverpool of the late Victorian era was a place of both great wealth and utter poverty, and in the Tithebarn Street district rich and poor confronted each other daily in what contemporary observers saw as a clash of the civilised and the savage. The American novelist Nathaniel Hawthorne, who had been an American consul in Liverpool in the 1850s, reported his own shocking experience of Tithebarn Street:

> I never saw ... nor imagined ... what squalor there is in the inhabitants
> of these streets as seen along the sidewalks. Women with young figures,
> but old and wrinkled countenances; young girls without any maiden
> neatness and trimness, barefooted with dirty legs. Women of all ages,

Women selling crockery at Paddy's Market, 1900

even elderly, go along with great, bare, ugly feet, many have baskets and other burthens on their heads. All along the street, with their wares at the edge of the sidewalk and their own seats fairly in the carriageway, you see women with fruit to sell, or combs and cheap jewellery, or coarse crockery, or oysters, or the devil knows what, and sometimes the woman is sewing meanwhile.[2]

At one end, Chapel Street connected Tithebarn Street to the landing stage and docks. Here was the gateway to the New World of America, and the magnificent portal to Liverpool for immigrants arriving from other countries. Passing eastwards along Tithebarn Street there were grand offices, such as the Clarendon Buildings and Commerce Buildings, housing cotton brokers, merchants and businessmen. Halfway down the street stood the Exchange Station, built in the 1840s. This was a grand and massively expensive building, one of the architectural marvels of Liverpool (it would be replaced by the present structure between 1884 and 1888).

At the other end, Tithebarn Street forks into Marybone and Great Crosshall Street, leading to the Vauxhall and Scotland wards. Together with Exchange ward, these two districts formed perhaps the most densely over-populated area in the country, if not Europe. It was in the Vauxhall ward that most of the characters connected to ensuing events lived.

At one end of Tithebarn Street, therefore, was the river leading to the wide-open space of the sea, generating an optimistic sense of opportunity and adventure. At the other end was stagnation, the claustrophobia of cramped living and a bitter resignation to poverty. In the space of a five-minute walk down Tithebarn Street, the Victorian pedestrian could pass from hope to despair.

In August 1874, Richard Morgan did not even make it that far. After he and his wife met Samuel, the trio strolled slowly down Chapel Street. They were all perfectly sober as they headed for home. However, just after 9 p.m., they decided to turn into a public house in Chapel Street for a final drink to cap the day. Morgan had two pennyworth of whisky mixed with a bottle of ginger beer while his wife and brother each had a glass of ale. They then went quietly on their way home along the northern side of Tithebarn Street. Alice was in the centre, her husband, wearing a sealskin cap, kept to the inside and

Tithebarn Street (1915). Looking towards the River Mersey.

Highfield Street (1900). One of the side streets leading from Tithebarn Street.

Samuel walked near to the road. They passed the Exchange Station, crossed Pall Mall and then Highfield Street. At about 9.25 p.m., Mrs Morgan made a brief visit to the tobacconists at 79 Tithebarn Street. The owner of the shop, David Ellis, had earlier seen the Morgans at the gala.

At the corner of Lower Milk Street, four or five lads stood outside a spruce beer shop. Spruce beer was a cheap alcoholic drink made by boiling spruce leaves and twigs with sugar.

At this point, the footpath was wide and the party had plenty of room to pass the youths. Although it was dusk, there was plenty of light from two alehouses and a lamp at the corner of the street. Samuel Morgan walked first, a few yards in front of his brother and sister-in-law, and passed the lads. As Richard approached the group, however, a youth roughly grabbed his coat sleeve and pulled him back. He then demanded money in a very aggressive manner.

"Hey, young man! Give us sixpence. We are short of sixpence for a quart of ale."

Richard Morgan responded in kind, with a question, "Hey, young man, where do you work?" or words to the effect that the youth should work to pay for his own beer.

The scene of Morgan's murder (1925). The "Spruce Beer Shop" has become a dining rooms.

The lad's reply was menacing. "We work at knocking down such men as you to take it off you when we can."

Upon hearing such a threat, Alice Morgan intervened: "Go on and knock somebody else down; don't knock him down. Come on, get away from them. You'll get nothing out of him."

"It's a good job you have got a woman with you," said one of the youths, implying that he was going to let the incident pass. But as the words were spoken, Richard Morgan was smacked behind the ear with a stunning punch. He stumbled helplessly into the road and fell on his side. He never spoke again or uttered a single sound.

Samuel Morgan retaliated at once, knocking the assailant down. To summon help, one of the ruffians whistled and two or three colleagues, perhaps more, joined the group. A youth ran at Samuel, but was immediately knocked down by him. Nevertheless, the same lad got up and joined the first attacker in viciously kicking Richard's ribs. Alice heroically threw herself on top of her husband in a vain bid to protect him. Another youth sprinted over from the public-house corner and took a running kick at Alice. He parted her from her husband before targeting Richard's lifeless body, kicking it two or three times in the stomach and side.

As the attacker tried to kick his victim, he fell on top of him and instead began choking Richard with both hands for about two minutes. Bravely, Alice tried to get the assailant off her husband, but he struck her on the side of the head, leaving her deaf in one ear. The other ruffians continued the kicking while simultaneously fighting with Samuel. One lad took off his belt and "scutched" Richard with it.

"Murder!" cried Alice. "Police!"

Attracted by the screams, a crowd assembled – yet they cheered the attackers on. Mr Ellis, now putting up the shutters to his shop, heard the disturbance but, as was the case with other shop owners, thought it was an everyday street brawl and did not take much notice. How large the crowd grew is uncertain. Estimates by witnesses would vary between a "few", "thirty to forty", and "a hundred" people. So far as the spectators took any part in the row it was, incredibly, against the Morgans rather than in support of them. The crowd certainly did nothing to help them, other than to hold Samuel Morgan back; they even attacked him for interfering.

Samuel fought bravely with the three principal attackers to keep them from Richard. As he wrestled with one lad, the others continued the kicking. At one point, Samuel got beside his prostrate brother, shielding him between his legs and knocking the youths down two or three times. Samuel himself was knocked down in the melee.

To cries of "give him it, give him it" from one female spectator, the kicking of Richard Morgan continued. At one point there were about seven men booting his body. Despite his brother's valiant efforts, Morgan was kicked "like a ball" from one side of Tithebarn Street to the other, a distance of about forty feet. He ended up at Macfie's sugar warehouse, opposite the public house.

Such was the ferocity of the attack some people shouted: "The man is kicked to death ... there is a man killed." Eventually a policeman approached and one of the attackers shouted, "Hec, Hec," (or "Nix, Nix" according to some reports) which means to run away. This was accompanied by cries from the youths of "Back out, back out ... back down into Lower Milk Street." One of the lads, after stuffing Morgan's sealskin cap into his jacket, fled with the others.

Samuel followed them down Lower Milk Street but soon lost sight of them. He rushed back to Tithebarn Street, where he found his brother's mud-bespattered body being picked up by three or four men and placed on the steps of the warehouse. Somebody had got some brandy or water for him, but he was unable to drink it. Although the whole episode lasted up to ten minutes, the fight itself was thought to have been over in about three minutes.

A policeman reached the scene just after the men had fled. At about 9.50 p.m., PC Adam Green was in Vauxhall Road guarding some cotton that had been burnt in a warehouse fire. He was approached by two women and told to have a look at the victim of an attack in the street around the corner. However, he had been told by his inspector not to leave the cotton until all was quiet. When he eventually arrived at the scene, PC Green found Morgan lying on the steps with his head resting on his shoulder. At first he thought the man had suffered a fit. Under the constable's direction, several men carried the body to the North Dispensary in Vauxhall Road.

After Samuel Morgan found his brother being picked up, he went into Vauxhall Road. Here, he saw one of the attackers, later identified as Michael Mullen, and punched him two or three times, knocking him over the bale of burnt cotton. Even though at this point Samuel was unaware that his brother was dead, he angrily accused Mullen of murder. Samuel continued to thump Mullen until he dodged around the cotton and escaped into the crowd.

On returning to Tithebarn Street, Samuel saw the three main attackers standing at the corner of Cheapside. When they caught sight of Morgan, they again ran away. He pursued them and finally, in Smithfield Street, overtook one of the ruffians, later identified as John McCrave. Aided by a man called Samuel Lipson, Morgan caught the culprit by the muffler, but he

Samuel Morgan. The brave brother of the Tithebarn Street victim.

pulled out a knife and threatened to use it. Somebody then grabbed Samuel from behind and put a knee to the small of his back, disabling him. The crowd that followed the chase were probably supporters of McCrave, but it is also possible that at least some of the people who then closed round Samuel and dragged him away did so in order to protect him from being stabbed. Nevertheless, McCrave was again able to escape.

Samuel doggedly followed the youth through Pownall Square, but McCrave dodged round a lamppost and his pursuer slipped and fell. Full of adrenalin, Morgan jumped up and continued the pursuit. After chasing McCrave down a dark narrow street into a yard, Samuel was prevented from going any further by a menacing group of women who blocked his way.

A dejected Samuel then went the short distance home, where he discovered the tragic news. A Dr Corscadden had examined Richard's body at the North Dispensary, and pronounced life extinct. The deceased had then been taken home to Leeds Street to await a coroner's inquest. The body was shockingly cut and bruised and the whole of the back and one side were reported to be "black and blue". There also appeared to be a stab wound on the left side of the neck, as if caused by the point of a pocket knife. The right thigh was reported to have suffered two similar wounds.

There was a knock at the door. Some boys told Samuel that McCrave was again in Tithebarn Street, and driven by a sense of justice for his brother, Morgan again set out. He found the culprit standing with a young woman at the corner of Vauxhall Road and Tithebarn Street. It was about 10 p.m. when he finally confronted McCrave and handed him over to a fire-policeman called John Lewis.

Morgan told Lewis that he was certain that McCrave was the man who had kicked his brother. On hearing this, McCrave boasted to Morgan, "I have witnesses enough to prove I didn't do it." Lewis admitted that he could not interfere as he was on special fire duty, so he handed the prisoner to another policeman, Adam Green, who was then returning along Vauxhall Road. On being apprehended, McCrave stated, "I know nothing of it. If he is dead it will be murder." Samuel accompanied the pair to the bridewell, where McCrave pleaded his innocence, denying that he was in the row and maintaining that they had got the wrong man.

During the night and the following day, Inspector Wood and several detectives searched around the tightly packed cellar and court dwellings of Prussia Street for the other attackers. This was the squalid slum area near to where McCrave lived. However, two of the other lads were not so naïve as to head back to their home turf. Their sights were set firmly outside Liverpool.

On Tuesday, August 4, Detective Hale charged John McCrave with the murder of Richard Morgan. In answer to the charge, the prisoner put names to his accomplices: "It was not me that kicked him. I was fighting with the other man. Mullen and Campbell were fighting with him when I came up. The two men and the woman knocked me down and I was drunk at the time." Hale also told McCrave that a boy had found Richard Morgan's cap hastily stuffed under a shutter near to where he lived. McCrave admitted, "Yes, I had that cap, and I picked it up in the street and thought it was my own."

The legal process began to roll into action the moment John McCrave was arrested. The first hearing was on August 5 at Liverpool Police Court in Dale Street, where McCrave was formally charged with the wilful murder of Richard Morgan. The prosecuting solicitor stated that he had four additional witnesses who all clearly identified the

Prussia Street (1930). Morgan's cap was hidden under a shutter

prisoner as one of the attackers. McCrave admitted that he fought with "them" before someone shouted, "Police!" and then he ran away. However, he claimed that he had never owned a knife in all his life. Denying the charge, McCrave was remanded until Monday, August 10

RICHARD MORGAN was buried on Saturday afternoon, August 8, at the Smithdown Road cemetery. The funeral cortege, consisting of a hearse, two mourning coaches and several cabs, started from the family home in Leeds Street, a short distance from the scene of the murder, just after 2 p.m. As the coffin was removed from the court into the street, a crowd of people, mostly women, loudly expressed both their commiseration for Mrs Morgan and their condemnation of the wicked ruffians who had murdered her husband.

Although no disturbance took place, several neighbours followed the hearse for some distance. As bystanders in Tithebarn Street, Moorfields and Dale Street discovered whose body was being carried to the grave, the procession was regarded with great interest.

At the cemetery, while several funeral parties awaited the chaplain, they were caught in a drenching shower, but none of the mourners sought shelter. Richard Morgan's aunt loudly lamented the fate of her nephew who, she sobbed, had been "murdered for sixpence". Finally the widow, who had up to this point remained stoic in her grief, at last gave way and fainted. Upon recovering, she was led away to the mourning coach. As the chaplain had by this time arrived, the church service was concluded.

Alice Morgan's plight touched the hearts of the both public and the press. The coroner had already given her a sovereign from the poor box towards the cost of the funeral. Later, a newspaper correspondent was so moved after seeing her in the witness box at the committal proceedings that he suggested a fund be set up: "The sight of the poor woman, recounting the circumstances under which her husband was brutally kicked to death, made me ask myself, has society done anything to alleviate her sorrow? ... Morgan was a sacrifice to the lawlessness of Liverpool, shall Liverpool do nothing to help his widow in her affliction?"[3] The writer acknowledged that the replacement of her loss was impossible, but argued that the public should still do something to keep her from poverty. The newspaper itself added, "We can only say that all our information regarding Mrs Morgan is to her credit, and that she appears to be poor and respectable. If anyone, moved by our correspondent's appeal, thinks well to send a subscription to our office on her behalf, we will see that it is properly applied."

After the trial, *The Times* was in agreement. The newspaper urged that a public fund be set up to help Mrs Morgan. Indeed, as future events unfolded, the poor woman needed all the help that she could get. Samuel Morgan was also recommended for some financial reward for his tenacity and bravery.

The wicked actions of a small group of lads from the back slums and alleys of Liverpool had made their mark on the national public consciousness. For this was seen as no ordinary murder. Not only London-based newspapers and journals but also government ministers at the highest level, right up to the Home Secretary, would become involved in debating the crime. One of Britain's foremost writers and critics, John Ruskin, was so affected by the murder that he quoted a passage from the *Daily Telegraph* in his book *Fors Clavigera*: "In all the pages of Dr Livingstone's experience among the Negroes of

Africa, there is no single instance approaching this Liverpool story, in savagery of mind and body, in bestiality of heart and act."[4]

The case would become a *cause célèbre*, placing the harsh gleam of the national spotlight on the dark corners of the town and its ruthless criminal underworld. But who were these ruffians who had caused such a nationwide scandal?

CHAPTER 2

The Cornermen

WITH JOHN McCrave having implicated his friends, the police now had the names of the three main culprits. Two of them were familiar faces. All three were undersized youths of light build and make, roughly about the same height, with narrow shoulders and drooping heads. None one of them had yet developed any muscles, indicating that they had never done a hard day's work. Their misspent lives could be summed up in three words – ignorance, drink and crime.

John McCrave, also known as "Quinn", was twenty years old. He had a more determined look than his companions and was more steeped in criminal activity. He was regarded as one of the worst of what were then known as the "dangerous classes", a pest to the law-abiding residents of the community. He was a source of endless trouble to both police and magistrates. McCrave was described by the police as a notoriously bad character and was well known to the inhabitants of Marybone by the nickname "Holy Fly", a title he had received partly through his pious aversion to swearing and partly owing to his rapid flights in and out of prison. He embodied the two extremes of the civilised and the savage, the saint and the sinner. A parish priest reported that McCrave's friends had often mocked him for refusing to use bad language. However, his religious beliefs never seemed to deter him from indulging in violence and robbery; nor did they keep him out of the cells.

Indeed, when McCrave attacked Morgan, he had not long been released from gaol for knocking down a man and taking his money. In all he had been incarcerated seventeen times for various offences. As early as 1869, when he was under sixteen years of age, he was held for

Boundary Terrace (1897). It was such appalling housing conditions that drove many youths and men to gather on street corners.

three days for an assault. In January 1870, he served a similar sentence for being drunk and disorderly. In the same year he twice returned to prison: for a month for "being a suspected person" and for six months for stealing a knife and money; so much for him having never possessed a knife. In 1871, McCrave was imprisoned on six separate occasions: he was gaoled twice for seven days for being drunk and disorderly and twice for fourteen days; he also received a month for fighting; in October of that year he served a further three months for again being a suspected person. In 1872, McCrave was convicted five times for drunkenness and received various terms of imprisonment: seven days, fourteen days and three separate spells of one month. In May 1873, he was again sent to gaol for a month for drunkenness.

Five months later, he was tried at the Borough Sessions and was sentenced to nine months' imprisonment with hard labour for attacking and robbing Charles Norton. On Saturday, October 4, the elderly victim had been walking along Hatton Garden when McCrave and two associates jumped out of an alley, knocked him down and took a purse containing ten shillings from his pocket. McCrave had therefore only been out of prison for about two weeks before the Tithebarn Street murder.

McCrave's family lived in Maiden's Green, off Prussia Street. Its name may have conjured pictures of a rural idyll, but the street was a narrow alley, inspiring the following lines of local verse:

Maiden's Green (1935). Home of John McCrave.

Can *this* be Maiden's Green!
Here where these dingy dwellings rise,
Was this a pastoral paradise?[1]

Liverpool had changed. The past, with its romantic sense of nature, space, youthful innocence and promise, had been lost in the name of progress. The growth of the docks and its industries had transformed a verdant landscape into a series of congested ghettos where the stunted, starved inhabitants, all of who were old before their time, lived a meagre day-to-day existence.

McCrave was well built, despite his small stature. Just under middle size and with an oval face and closely cropped hair, he had the look of a hardened ruffian. Indeed, his brothers and sisters were also steeped in criminality. At the coroner's inquest, Samuel Lipson revealed that McCrave's sister, Mary, had threatened another witness outside the court. She was supposed to have warned a young boy called Bernard McCarthy, "Don't you go against him or I will kill you." McCarthy, however, interrupted: "I did not say that. It was because I found the sealskin cap that belonged to the deceased man she said she would kill me: 'For finding that I will kill you.' But on seeing Detective Officer Hale coming up just then, she said, 'I will give you a shilling for finding that.'"

It also seems likely that the callous female who had shouted, "Give him it," as Richard Morgan was being kicked was Mary McCrave. In the 1881 Census, she was listed as an unmarried inmate at the "Female Convict Prison" Knaphill Woking in Surrey. By then she had been in prison herself for a dreadful crime (see Chapter 7).

John McCrave was classed as a labourer, although he did little or no work: "He was one of those contemptible wretches who are not ashamed to live upon the miserable earnings gained by levying contributions upon prostitutes whose aider and protector he was."[2] He was what is today known as a pimp. Liverpool's status as a seaport meant that there was a regular demand for prostitutes. Many were young Irish girls desperate for money. In 1871, the police estimated that there were 830 brothels in the town.

The two accomplices identified by McCrave were Michael Mullen and Peter Campbell. Mullen, aged seventeen but looking more like fifteen, was a typical example of the Marybone and Bevington Bush rough. He was described as being of "repulsive appearance". Mullen had been convicted twice before the murder of Richard Morgan. At the January 1872 Sessions, when he was little more than fourteen, he had been found guilty of being involved in a mugging where an old man had been beaten up and robbed of his watch. For this Mullen was imprisoned for twelve months. He also served a month's term for an assault on a policeman. Mullen, by occupation a carter, sometimes stayed with McCrave and also with his own mother, a poor woman living in a court in Naylor Street, off Vauxhall Road. Like many other impoverished women, she earned a pittance by trudging the streets selling cheap wares from a basket.

Campbell, also known as "Miggy" or "Midge", was a mild-looking nineteen-year-old. The tallest of the trio and more proportionally built, he was described as having an "aristocratic appearance, finely chiselled features and almost gentlemanly bearing". Though never before convicted, he was not altogether unknown to the police, having once been charged with a theft of which he was later acquitted.

Naylor Street (1935). Where Michael Mullen was raised.

Campbell had lived with his mother and two sisters in a cellar off Leeds Street, near to the Morgans. In the 1860s, Hippolyte Taine, a French philosopher and literary critic, visited the area and was deeply shocked by what he saw:

What a spectacle! In the neighbourhood of Leeds Street there are fifteen or twenty streets with ropes stretched across them where rags and underwear were hung to dry. Every stairway swarms with children, five or six to a step, the eldest nursing the baby; their faces are pale, their hair whitish and tousled, the rags they wear are full of holes, they have neither shoes nor stockings and they are all vilely dirty. Their faces and limbs seemed to be encrusted with dirt and soot. In one street alone there must have been about 200 children sprawling and fighting... Livid, bearded old women came out of gin shops: their reeling gait, dismal eyes and fixed idiot grin are indescribable. They look as if their features had been slowly corroded by vitriol.[3]

Despite living in a slum part of the town, Campbell's family was respectably connected. Mrs Campbell was a widow. Her husband had been a master of a ship, which many years earlier had sailed from Liverpool and was never heard of again. Since then, Mrs Campbell had gained a living for herself in an honest and industrious way. In the midst of the squalor, she had brought up her family well, with one of her daughters holding the position of forewoman in the stationery department of Russell's printing firm in Moorfields.

However, bad associations had carried Peter Campbell away entirely. He had always been a great trouble to his mother, spending much of his time at John McCrave's house, owing to his relationship with McCrave's seventeen-year-old sister, Mary. The couple had attempted to marry, but had been stopped at the church by Mrs Campbell. Since then they had cohabitated and had a child together. It was felt that Mary McCrave had helped lead Campbell astray. It was a fact in his favour, nonetheless, that, at the time of the murder, Campbell was in regular employment as a porter, working for George Taylor, Glass Bottle Merchants, of Seel Street, and that his employer held a good opinion of him.

Campbell was therefore viewed as a slightly better class of person than his partners in crime. His friends were seen as the lowest of the low, a species commonly known as "Cornermen".

THE PERPETRATORS of the Tithebarn Street outrage belonged to an impoverished underworld where drunken violence was a feature of daily life. These youths lived by their wits on the streets. The main goal in life of these "Cornermen" was to scrape together enough money to buy beer:

> They were given up to every form of misconduct, morally and socially; they preyed upon society and degraded the very instincts of society. They were Cornermen: they worked not an honest labour, but lived on depredation and outrage. The public house was their familiar haunt, and the street corners their hunting ground. Their practice was to waylay honest citizens and demand blackmail, without violence if possible, but with whatever violence might be required to extort or steal a ransom.[4]

Cornermen outside The Goat, St Andrew Street (1908).

Young girl entertaining drinkers in a Great Homer Street pub, 1900.

They were called Cornermen because they loitered outside the public houses that were invariably situated on the corner of each street. In 1874, there were 1,929 pubs, 384 beer houses and 272 off-licences listed in Liverpool, a total of 2,585 places to buy beer and spirits, or simply to stand outside waiting and hoping for the price of the next drink.[5] Then, as now, the public house was a social, economic and cultural focus of the working-class community. Here the men could meet, gossip and debate, be entertained and even learn of job vacancies from others lucky enough to be in work. Those unable to afford a drink would simply gather outside.

After the Tithebarn Street outrage, the term "Cornermen" became synonymous with scrounging, intimidation and violence. Cornermen were seen as layabouts who infested the corners of Liverpool streets, and who were up for any crime, ranging from pitch and toss to murder. Rather than work, they lived by robbery, begging and prostitution. Twelve years after the murder, the term was still in use:

The expressive phrase "Cornermen" by which this class of people is known, is of recent origin; though it is widely known locally as almost to be classic. It was invented by the late Detective Superintendent Kehoe, and was applied by him to the young fellows who some years ago kicked a man to death in Tithebarn Street. The great aim and object in life of these Cornermen is to pass their lives without working. Like the lilies of the field "they toil not, neither do they spin", and so long as they can procure food and drink, or, as they would term it in their vernacular "scran" and "booze", they are willing to commit any crime that may be requisite to accomplish their end.[6]

It wasn't just the town centre that was plagued by Cornermen. Travelling eastwards along West Derby Road, the pubs at the end of each street all had their own set of ruffians, swearing and spitting as they pleased. Any attempt by respectable passers-by to correct their behaviour would be met by verbal abuse, intimidation – or worse.

"They will block up the entire footwalk and, as a novice, you may entertain some idea that they will make way for you to pass," wrote one journalist in 1883, describing the Cornermen of Sherwood Street, off Great Howard Street, a stone's throw from the River Mersey in the Vauxhall district. "On the contrary, they will stand immovable and watch your manoeuvres to get through without one glimmer of intelligence passing across their countenances. If you are wise, you will make a circuit round in preference to running the blockade of the street corner."[7]

A question for the politicians of the day was how much of this was press exaggeration, an attempt to stir up panic about unfortunate out-of-work men who were brutalised by their own poverty? At the town council meeting on January 12, 1875, Alderman Chambres related how he had recently set out one evening from his safe, middle-class, Wallasey home on a fact-finding tour of Liverpool's seedier streets. After the murder in Tithebarn Street, he wished to see for himself whether all that had been written of the brutality of Liverpool roughs was true or not.

Like an inner-city version of an African explorer, Chambres began a brave trek through darkest Liverpool. It was raining heavily when he arrived and this probably accounted for the lack of people on the streets. Confidently carrying his purse and watch, the fifty-five-year-old proceeded alone up Park Lane and Pitt Street.

After meeting a policeman and only one drunk, he carried on to explore Paradise Street and Scotland Road, where he saw some more police officers and another single drunk. What struck Alderman

Chambres on this dark wet night was the glaring illumination from the spirit vaults. Crossing through a narrow street he arrived at Bevington Bush, where the contrast was shocking. He looked into two or three dingy courts and, from what he saw, he did not wonder that the men from these atrocious, stinking slums should go and stand under the welcoming lights of the public houses, where it at least looked warm.

Turning into Vauxhall Road, Chambres saw, under the bright light of the spirit vault windows, crowds of men, aged from sixteen to thirty-six, whom he considered to be of a dangerous character: "He did not mean 'dangerous' to people who might not speak to them, but to ill-conditioned people who, it might be, spoke the truth to these young men, which might not be very pleasurable to them."[8]

Chambres refused to judge these poor people. He was almost tempted to enter a vault for a brandy and water and therefore could not find fault with people who had a little of what he himself desired. The point that Alderman Chambres wanted to make was that he felt as safe in Liverpool as he did on the other side of the river in Cheshire, where a couple of years earlier a man had been murdered and where the culprit remained at large.

Cornermen in William Brown Street, 1897.

What Alderman Chambres was describing in Vauxhall Road, close to the murder scene, were groups of Cornermen. As he noted, the warmth and light of these open-air community centres must have been preferable to the dark, dank, fetid cellars and courts in which they lived. For a few hours, the men could escape from their small, damp, crowded homes and enjoy companionship and conviviality. Clearly not all of these people would have been intent on committing crime, but as with groups of youths a century later who congregated outside chip shops and off-licences, the men must have presented an intimidating sight, particularly for respectable people who were sometimes asked for money to buy beer.

Chambres made the point that the men did not seem dangerous to the mere passer-by, but noted that the potential for violence was there, reserved for those who rubbed them up the wrong way. Richard Morgan's awful death was testimony to how brutal a group of these men could be when somebody did not quietly pass them by but, in response to their request for money, stopped and "spoke the truth" to them.

In an article entitled "Cornermen – Move On!", a religious journal offered a sartorial description of this street brotherhood. The men usually wore ragged and dirty clothes with heavy hob-nailed boots that acted as armour. "By the use of which, in kicking his victims, he obtains the money wherewith to purchase the drink that makes him mad, and which he is madly bent upon having, though he kick an unoffending man's brains out in order to get it."[9]

This attempt to give the Cornermen a uniform singled them out as a group, making it easier to identify and ultimately demonise them, although this was probably not the journal's intention. In fact, the dress code was standard labouring-class apparel. The boots were nothing new. As far back as 1862, local journalist Hugh Shimmin offered a vivid description of Liverpool roughs: "Men of short stature, with big heads, broad, flat faces, and thick necks [with] white trousers turned up at the bottom to show their high-laced, greasy boots."[10]

The Tithebarn Street murder saw the culmination of two worrying nineteenth-century criminal trends: the growth of the Cornermen and a wider outbreak of "kicking crimes" in Lancashire, which then included Liverpool. In August 1874, the month of the murder, a total of seventeen brutal kicking cases were dealt with at the county courts

Kicking assault on a policeman.

and the tendency to boot people with iron-tipped clogs looked set to continue. In January 1875, newspapers continued to run headlines such as "Another Brutal Kicking Case at Bolton" and "Kicking at Oldham".

The murder of Richard Morgan was seen as yet another example of this vicious northern epidemic. People responded by writing letters to newspapers, giving their own horror stories of violent kicking attacks, such as the following alarming account from a resident of Wigan:

Sir – The kicking practice is still not stopped, and the repeated shouts of "Hey, hie yon, theer's two men feighting, theer be sherp do, one is purring t'ether mon's yed", bears proof of it. When the above exclamation is heard, off rushes a crowd of men, women and children, not to stop the beastly exhibition but to watch and encourage it; and a scene ensues quite ghastly enough to satisfy the shade of Nero as far as blood-spurting goes. Crack, crack, thump, whacks the iron-toed clog on the head and ribs of one of the savages. Perhaps an eye is protruded, a nose doubled up, a jaw-bone broken, front teeth gently loosened to save the trouble of lancing, or it may be a skull is split open and two or three ribs staved in, or a leg or an arm smashed to pieces. After these operations one of the "kickers" is very quiet. Then there arises a shout, "Here's th'bobby." "Bobby" comes up, "Now, what's up, what's to do?" "Oh nowt, nobbut Bill and this man's ben heving a bit of a do loike, and Bill's warmed him reight weel." They take the quiet one away, and "Bobby" goes to take Bill. Up rush five or six of these kicking bloodhounds, and if "Bobby" does not "hook" it "Bobby" gets sent sprawling on the ground with five or six gentle kisses from the clog toes to soothe him, while Bill has time to "hook" it.[11]

Whereas in the early twenty-first century the teenage uniform of the hooded top, or "hoodie", was said to characterise the yob in society, in the 1870s it was the boot that became a symbol of brutality, much as it would in the 1970s for the Skinhead or "Bovver Boy" gangs. Again, anxious Victorians sent letters to newspapers and journals offering fearsome descriptions of working-class footwear. The sole of the boot was covered with large iron nails, the heads shaped like the roof of a house and raising the actual sole about half an inch from the ground. Sometimes, in substitution of nails, an iron plate, bending around the front edge of the sole, was placed on the tip of the boot.[12]

It was against this background of poverty, squalor, drunkenness and a violent fashion for kicking people that news of the Tithebarn Street murder smashed its way into the public's consciousness.

CHAPTER 3

Manhunt

"In important cases the offenders very seldom escape."
Head Constable's Special Report Book, entry dated January 4, 1875

WITH THE POLICE busy searching for Michael Mullen and Peter Campbell, two people came forward voluntarily and independently to admit taking part in the murder. A third man also went some way towards implicating himself. Needless to say, all three were under the influence of drink when they did so.

The first was Henry Butler, a brickmaker of Buckley in North Wales. On August 6, at about 1 a.m., Butler went to Chester police station and stated to PC Diggory that, together with McCrave and Mullen, he had committed the murder in Tithebarn Street. He later explained that it was not he but McCrave who had put the boot in on Richard Morgan. Butler, who was dressed in the uniform of the Flintshire Volunteers, was accordingly locked up.

The next morning, however, having become sober, he denied any knowledge of the murder. He explained that he was a bandsman and was at Wrexham on the Monday and at Plas Teg on Tuesday; he also said that, having had a little drink, the account of the Tithebarn Street murder, which he had read about in the papers, "preyed upon his mind". He admitted that he really knew nothing about the affair. At a hearing at Chester Police Court on August 9, it was discovered, following inquiries made in Liverpool and Buckley, that Butler could not have had anything to do with the murder, as he had been in Buckley at the time. He was discharged after paying a fine for being drunk.

On Wednesday, August 12, at Crewe Police Court, Henry Poole was charged with being drunk and riotous. Two days earlier, he had been drinking at the Talbot Inn in Crewe. Sitting near to him was Mr Talbot. Poole drew attention to himself by making several contradictory statements about his birthplace, first saying that he was an Irishman and following that up by saying that he was an Englishman who had been born in Birmingham. He also boasted that he had taken part in many a "do" in Liverpool.

Becoming noisy, Poole was given into custody and Mr Talbot then told the police of his suspicions. After later being informed that he was suspected of the Tithebarn Street murder, Poole stoutly denied that he had ever been to Liverpool. On searching him, however, the police found a document proving his acquaintance with somebody living in Great Crosshall Street, near to the scene of the crime. Marks of dried blood were also visible on his vest.

The police received instructions to communicate with the Liverpool detective department. On learning that his description was to be forwarded to Liverpool, Poole became agitated. He was, however, found to be in the clear, but was still imprisoned for fourteen days with hard labour for his drunkenness.

The next person to put himself in the frame was Richard Hannah, a tall, rough-looking man. On August 29, he was brought before Mr Mansfield, the deputy stipendiary magistrate at the borough Police Court, charged with being drunk and stating that he was one of the men who murdered Richard Morgan in Tithebarn Street. On the previous evening, Hannah had been drinking in several public houses in Vauxhall Road, bragging that he had been one of those who had killed Morgan. After explaining his part in the attack to a police officer, Hannah was arrested for drunkenness. Later, he boastfully repeated his guilt to the bridewell keeper at Chisenhale Street. However, on being sent to the cells, he looked very uneasy.

In court, asked by the assistant magistrate's clerk what he had to say about his admission, Hannah explained that he had been drunk when he made it and that he was not in fact present when Morgan was killed.

It was thought advisable that the witnesses to the murder should see the prisoner. Some of the lads who had already identified McCrave came forward. With the exception of one small boy, the witnesses failed to identify Hannah as being present, and even the boy admitted that he did not see Hannah kick or do anything to Morgan. Thomas Stamford Raffles, the stipendiary magistrate, discharged the prisoner, advising him to remain sober in future.

ON THE NIGHT of the murder, the fugitive Mullen and Campbell slept at a model lodging-house in Ben Jonson Street, off Scotland Road. They left early in the morning. Since their escape, no reliable information had been obtained about their whereabouts, but it was suspected that they were keeping low until the pursuit died down. The newspapers felt that it was unlikely that they could have left the town, but if they had, they would have got no further than Manchester as, in their condition, travelling was not easy. The case was put in the hands of Detective Officers Hale and Fitzsimmons.

What in fact happened was that, the following day, Campbell and Mullen went their separate ways in pursuit of freedom. Early in the morning, Mullen woke his younger brother, Thomas, informing him that he had got into a row with "Holy Fly". Michael Mullen later stated that he had stayed in the same bed as Thomas, but it is unclear as to whether the younger boy lived in Ben Jonson Street or whether Michael made his way back to his family home in Naylor Street.

"The man we kicked last night is dead," Michael revealed to his brother. "Come and let us stow ourselves away."

Thomas then accompanied him to Victoria Dock, where they hid themselves on the American ship *Caravan*, bound for New York.

Because the murder had taken place a few minutes' walk from the docks, the police were wise to the possibility that Mullen and Campbell might attempt to leave the country. The river police were on high alert and made several swoops upon ships, not always with the right result. At the Dale Street Police Court on Saturday, August 8, a youth called Charles Kenny was placed in the dock charged with stowing himself away on board the steamer *Iberian*.

Shipping master William Mesney stated that, on Thursday, August 6, he had received instructions from the Liverpool police to search the steamer for persons connected with the Tithebarn Street murder. He went on board and made a thorough examination of every part of the ship, but could find no one answering to the description of the wanted lads. At the conclusion of his search, Mesney found Kenny concealed in the forecastle. On being hauled out of his hiding place, the lad's excuse for boarding the ship was that he had come down with his brother's bag. He was apparently very "saucy" in his attitude. The vessel was in the process of taking in coals and Mesney was able to bring the boy on deck and hand him over to another ship, which brought him ashore.

The next afternoon, Mesney again went on board the *Iberian*, just as the steamer was about to sail. He was amazed to find the same lad secreted in the same place. On being unearthed for a second time, Kenny explained that he had come on board for the good of his health, as the ship was bound for Constantinople. In court, a woman came forward to state that the boy was subject to fits of weakness and that he had been under the impression that going to sea would "make a man" of him. He was remanded for a week for further inquiries.

After leaving Victoria Dock on August 4, the *Caravan*, containing the Mullen brothers, lay in the river for a week owing to high winds. On Thursday, August 13, when the ship had finally got clear of land, three stowaways were discovered. They were transferred to the accompanying pilot boat in order to be returned to Liverpool. From there they were handed over to the British, inward-bound ship *J.G. Robinson*, returning from St Johns, New Brunswick. This vessel arrived in the Mersey, not far from New Brighton, on the morning of August 14. At 10 a.m., the ship was boarded by a detachment of river police, under the direction of Coxswain Kermode, who were taking their morning cruise on the *Livingston*.

The captain of the *J.G. Robinson* handed over the stowaways to the police. PC Whittle was alert to the fact that the *Caravan* had sailed just after the Tithebarn Street murder and thought it was his duty to go ashore to further investigate the identities of the stowaways. Upon Whittle's return, it was confirmed that two of the would-be emigrants matched the description of the wanted youths.

At the police hut, one of the lads stated his name was William Murphy of Bridge Street. The younger boy declared that he was Thomas Smith of Edgar Street. In fact, Edgar Street was the continuation of Naylor Street, his family home. It was reported that the elder youth looked twenty-three or twenty-four years of age and that the other boy looked about eighteen. This is probably a reflection of the harsh conditions that they had been hiding in, since Michael Mullen was generally thought to look younger than his seventeen years. The lads probably hadn't washed or exercised for over a week, being cooped up in some cramped hiding place, barely able to utter a sound for fear of being discovered and apprehended. It is not clear how much food the boys had eaten during their stay on the *Caravan*. They might have brought supplies with them or perhaps a seaman had secretly fed them. If the ship hadn't spent so much time in the river, it is likely that the lads would have got further out to sea before being discovered and that they might even have been able to make it to America and freedom.

The brothers were taken into custody by PC Whittle and brought to the Cheapside Bridewell, where Michael Mullen was identified by one of the witnesses as having played a major part in the kicking of Richard Morgan. When charged by Whittle with being Michael Mullen and having been involved in the murder, the lad, much disturbed, replied, "Not me." However, at the detective's office, where Mullen now tried to assume a careless demeanour, he was picked out of an identity parade by Alice Morgan, Samuel Morgan and several other witnesses. Mullen was booked on a charge of taking part in the outrage and remanded until August 15. His brother was also locked up for aiding and abetting the escape. The third stowaway, a native of America, was allowed to go.

On August 15, Michael and Thomas Mullen were brought before Mr Mansfield, deputy stipendiary magistrate, at the Police Court in Dale Street. Michael was charged with the wilful murder of Richard Morgan, and Thomas, who was initially charged for being a stowaway, was also charged as an accessory after the fact. Alice Morgan confirmed that she had identified Michael Mullen as the man who had attacked her husband. She explained that McCrave first spoke to her husband, but that it had been Mullen who had kicked him when he had been on the ground and that she had distinctly seen him do it.

Michael Mullen asked Mrs Morgan whether another young man had not knocked her husband down and thumped him. Mrs Morgan replied, "That was you, my husband was dead."

Mullen admitted that he had been present but was adamant that he had not touched the victim. He also declared that his brother had had nothing to do with it and that he knew nothing about it.

On Monday, August 17, John McCrave and Michael Mullen were placed together in the dock at Dale Street Police Court and charged with murder. The prosecutor, a Mr Davies, asked for a further remand of seven days, explaining that another man, Peter Campbell, who was connected with the murder, had not yet been caught. Detective Inspector Carlisle stated that he was confident they would be able to capture the man.

A week later, McCrave and the Mullen brothers made another appearance at Dale Street Police Court. Mr Mansfield asked if there was reasonable hope of Campbell being caught. Mr Davies replied that handbills giving Campbell's description had been extensively circulated and that detectives were doing everything necessary. In any case, however, he would only ask for another remand. Mr Mansfield declared that it would be necessary to fix a day, especially for the trial, because a great amount of care would have to be taken with the medical evidence. The prisoners were then remanded.

Before being "put down", a starving McCrave placed the thumb and first finger of his right hand into his mouth and, appealing to a poorly dressed man standing in court, begged, "Bring us some chuck – something to eat."

On Monday, September 7, McCrave, Michael and Thomas Mullen appeared before Mr Raffles at the Borough Police Court. The magistrate proposed to take the case on September 15 and therefore remanded the prisoners for another week. Once the prisoners were removed from the dock, Mr Raffles asked whether anything had been heard of Campbell. Mr Davies had to admit failure, but still remained hopeful. "We may hear something of him, for all that, when the reward is known of at the other side of the Atlantic," he said. Davies added that it was as well that these people realised they could not, without consequence, defeat justice by aiding and abetting the escape of criminals.

While McCrave and Mullen were continually being remanded, strenuous efforts were being made to bring Peter Campbell to justice. Just after the murder, one newspaper correspondent suggested a reward for the apprehension of the murderers:

Sir – Another crime has been added to the list of atrocities for which Liverpool is infamous and the murder of Richard Morgan must not go unavenged. A price must be set upon the heads of every one of the ruffians who took part in this outrage; and I would suggest that a public subscription be immediately set on foot to raise the necessary funds.[1]

On August 27, an inquest jury, despite the absence of Campbell, returned a verdict of wilful murder against the three men, even though they had not yet been tried in the criminal court. Coroner Clarke Aspinall then wrote to the Secretary of State suggesting that a sum of £100 should be offered for the capture of the missing man. The proposal was at once adopted and handbills, giving a full description of Campbell, were issued all over town and even as far as America:

He is twenty-one or twenty-two years of age, five feet six or seven inches high, proportionate build, dark brown hair, cut short, no whiskers, beard or moustache, blue or grey eyes, rather prominent and well-formed nose, pale complexion inclined to fair, rather long oval face, good forehead, the first finger of the right hand or the second of the left hand bent and stiff from a cut inside; dressed in an old shabby black frock coat, which was rather short for him, dirty striped moleskin trousers in imitation of cloth, with black stripe down the side, and a round Scotch or Bucco cap, with peak to match and knob on the top; he is of low habits, frequenting the corners of streets and low public houses, and has been in custody as a suspected character; has hitherto been employed in bottling stores. Her Majesty's Secretary of State for the Home Department, has authorised the payment of £100 to any person giving such information as will lead to the apprehension of the said Peter Campbell.

For people living on a pittance, with some not knowing where their next meal was coming from, this was a staggering amount of money – today worth about £7,200 – and must have provoked a sensation among the communities around Vauxhall and Scotland Road. Yet even this tempting financial inducement failed to have the desired effect and Campbell continued to remain at large.

In fact, he was neither in Liverpool nor attempting to flee to America. The day after the murder, he left Liverpool for Chowbent, near Bolton, where he found a job with the Combermere Coal Company. For unloading wagons, he received a daily wage of three shillings and sixpence. No doubt terrified of the ghastly fate that awaited him if he was caught, Campbell kept to himself and socialised little with his colleagues.

Nevertheless, the police got information that he had been seen in the neighbourhood of Chowbent. On September 11, officers raided Campbell's lodgings after detectives had tailed his sister. How the police came to trace Campbell to Chowbent is a story of great detective work, followed by an amazing blunder. Mrs Campbell's home in Liverpool was kept under surveillance and at midnight on a Friday a woman was seen paying the family a visit. She was Mrs Baxter, an acquaintance of the Campbell family. She lived with her husband, a collier, at Elizabeth Street in Atherton – the very place where Campbell was lodging.

On returning home in the evening by a late train from Tithebarn Street, Mrs Baxter, accompanied by Campbell's sister, was followed by Detective Jackson and another officer. With the detectives were a seafaring man and a boy, brought along for purposes of identification. On arriving at Bolton, the females took a cab to Atherton, a distance of six miles. The detectives, who by this time had enlisted the services of Superintendent Holgate and two of the county police from Bolton, quickly followed them in another cab.

Having arrived at their destination, the women informed Campbell that a plan had been devised for getting him away, either to Melbourne or America, and that he must make ready for leaving Atherton in a cab in a few minutes. By this time, the police were closely watching the premises' back and front.

At this point accounts differ as to what happened next. One version is that Detective Jackson, having gained entrance by the front door, instantly seized a man called Hughes, who was another lodger in Baxter's house. The superintendent from Bolton meanwhile took hold of Hughes's brother. A violent fight followed, the brothers putting up the most determined resistance. Hearing the struggle going on in the lower rooms, the constables stationed behind the house instantly burst open the door to help their colleagues. In the melee, which went on in pitch darkness after the candle had been knocked over and extinguished, Campbell raced downstairs and out of the front door, which had been left unguarded.

However, it was also reported that Campbell's sister went to the house with an unidentified male. Holgate and Jackson rushed in at the front door and each seized a man. Jackson immediately proceeded to manacle his prisoner who, with an exclamation of astonishment, told him that he had got the wrong man. The prisoner pointed to a third person in the room, declaring that he was Campbell. The lad was near the lobby at the time, and before the police could rectify their mistake, he made a sudden bolt for the door. Under cover of pitch darkness, he managed to escape. It seems that Jackson had seized the tenant of the house, while Superintendent Holgate had, in the excitement, actually grabbed the throat of the man who had accompanied Campbell's sister.

The officers were devastated. Campbell was nowhere to be found, despite the most thorough search of the district by an increased squad of police. Detectives even descended various pits in search of him, without any luck.

After fleeing Chowbent, Campbell took great risks to return to Liverpool. Considering that he faced the death penalty if caught, the decision to visit his old haunts, particularly while a substantial reward was being offered for news of his whereabouts, seemed almost suicidal. On Saturday, September 12, Campbell's movements were traced. During the evening he was seen in the company of Mary McCrave, the sister of Holy Fly and the mother of his child. Campbell appears to have made up his mind to stay all night. Perhaps it was to see his baby that he had returned to Liverpool. His intention may also have been to dodge about the town until Tuesday morning with a view to boarding a Melbourne clipper that was due to sail.

After drinking together, Campbell and McCrave were seen to visit 4 House, 9 Court, Gascoyne Street, off Vauxhall Road. A criminal named Talbot lived there; in October 1873, he had been sentenced to imprisonment for robbing a man's watch. Talbot, as will be seen in a later chapter, came to an unfortunate end, not entirely unrelated to his association with one of his lodgers.

Campbell visited Talbot at about ten on Saturday night. The people in the neighbourhood, having heard of the reward, were on constant lookout for him and his presence was quickly made known to the police. At about 1 a.m. on Sunday, September 13, a person – the newspapers stated that they were bound to suppress the sex for the sake of the informant – went to the detective office in Dale Street and asked to see Detectives Hale and Fitzsimmons. Neither of those officers was available and the person was asked about the nature of the business. However, the informant remained tight-lipped, refusing to reveal why the detectives were required except in the presence of the officers themselves. Hale and Fitzsimmons were duly sent for and, on their arrival, were told that Campbell was in Gascoyne Street.

Detectives Boyes, Fitzsimmons, Hale and Grubb, with Inspector Kerrin and William James, a night clerk from the detective office, rushed to the street. The house was surrounded and admittance demanded but refused. After they warned the inmates that the door would be forced, it was eventually opened. Hale and Boyes dashed upstairs while the other officers remained below in the kitchen. In the top room the officers found Mary McCrave in bed with a child. There were also a man's clothes discarded on the floor, leading the detectives to believe that their prey was not far away.

On descending to a room on the second floor, Detective Hale saw a figure, probably Talbot, lying on a bed. The bed itself was suspiciously bulky. Hale asked whether Campbell was in the house, but the man denied all knowledge of him. However, from the uncomfortable position in which Talbot was lying, Detective Hale suspected that the fellow had something under him besides the mattress on which he was lying. Without saying anything to the man, Hale thrust his hand underneath the bed, where it came in contact with an arm.

"Come from under the bed," Hale ordered.

Campbell was pulled out naked and the detective immediately recognised him as the wanted man. He offered no resistance, muttering, "All right. I'll go quietly." After letting him dress, the officers took him to the detective office, where he was charged with being connected with McCrave and Mullen in the murder. Campbell was adamant: "I was there at the time, but I was not near the man. It was Mullen and McCrave that were fighting with him."

On September 14, Campbell was placed among a line-up of a dozen other men at the bridewell. Alice Morgan and several other witnesses immediately pointed him out, but Samuel Morgan failed to identify him. Morgan explained later in court, "I did not at first identify Campbell in the lock-up because I think he had got thinner in the features." It was the first time that Morgan had seen Campbell since the fateful Bank Holiday and the lad's harsh experience of life on the run may well have affected his appearance.

The next day, at the Dale Street Police Court, Campbell, McCrave and the Mullen brothers were brought up before Mr Raffles. Mr Davies, prosecuting, said that the only evidence he would offer would be against Campbell. He then asked that the prisoners be remanded until the next day when the case would be gone into thoroughly. He added that, with reference to Thomas Mullen, he did not intend to proceed further against him. The magistrate duly dismissed the lad with the rebuke, "You see you have suffered some weeks' imprisonment for interfering with the police in the discharge of their duty and in aiding and abetting your brother in effecting his escape; and you have very properly been punished for that. At the same time, your offence is perfectly different from that of the other prisoners and you may be discharged."

Before leaving the dock, Thomas shook hands with the other three prisoners and kissed them. They, in turn, made an attempt to cry.

Whoever told the authorities of Campbell's whereabouts remains a mystery. However, not one person, but three, eventually received the reward. In February 1875, Coroner Clarke Aspinall wrote to the Home Secretary requesting the money in order to forward it to the claimants. In reply, A.F.O. Liddell, from the Home Office, asked Mr Aspinall to "favour him with a statement of the manner in which it is proposed to divide the reward and the reasons for it." On April 7, in response to Mr Aspinall's letter, the Home Office stated that the Treasury had agreed to split the reward as follows: £40 for "the man", £20 for "the woman" and £40 for the "second woman".[2] Perhaps two of the claimants were a married couple. No names were mentioned and so the identity of the informants remained a secret shared by the coroner and the detectives concerned.

Whoever earned the reward, three lucky people from the slums of Liverpool would have found their lives transformed. Meanwhile, at St George's Hall, three other people were about to have their own lives destroyed.

CHAPTER 4

The Black Assize

ON DECEMBER 15, 1874, in the Crown Court of the Liverpool Assizes at St George's Hall, the three youths went on trial for the Tithebarn Street murder before Mr Justice Mellor. Such was the notoriety of this particular case that the event was labelled "the Black Assize".

There was huge public interest in the fate of the lads. Throughout the proceedings, which began daily 10.15 a.m. and finished at 8 p.m., the courtroom was full. All available seats in the galleries were filled with spectators, including a few fashionably dressed women. Even the corridors leading to the courts were packed. Anticipating a big crowd, the High Sheriff issued an order restricting admission and thereby preventing an inconvenient crush in the court, something that had been a feature of many previous murder cases.

Although it was a bitterly cold day, a large crowd, made up of those who had been unable to gain admission, remained camped on the steps in front of St George's Hall, eagerly questioning anybody who came from the court.

The indictment charged John McCrave, Michael Mullen and Peter Campbell with having, on August 3 last, feloniously, wilfully and of malice aforethought killed one Richard Morgan. Mr Leofric Temple, Q.C., and Mr McConnell were counsel for the prosecution. Mr Cottingham defended Campbell; Dr Commins appeared for McCrave; and Mr Shee represented Mullen. Each of the men pleaded not guilty.

Mr Temple, in opening the case, asked the jury that if they had heard or read anything of what had been called the Tithebarn Street kicking case, they should banish it from their minds. He instructed them merely to listen to the evidence that would be placed before them, and to give their verdict upon that and that only. He was sure, he said, that they would have no prejudice one way or the other, but that they would weigh the facts as proved, fairly, calmly and considerately.

The prosecution brought no less than thirteen witnesses to prove their case, some of them children as young as fourteen who bravely testified against the accused. Yet the witnesses differed as to who they thought had delivered the first blow. Some were sure that it had been McCrave; others were certain that it had been Mullen. Almost all agreed that it had been Campbell who lay on Morgan's body and tried to strangle him.

The three doctors who had examined the body at the inquest were called individually. The first to appear was Dr Corscadden, who saw the deceased when he was brought to the North Dispensary. The doctor did not find any marks of blows under the left ear of any kind. He considered that the deceased's heart was a little enlarged and very fat. Both sides of the heart were partially empty, a fact that he could not reconcile with a healthy condition, although he admitted that the "deceased was a strong built man and I would have expected him to have lived for many years".

St George's Hall (1906).

   The defence tried to discount claims that Morgan had been kicked across the street. Since he weighed just over twelve stone, it was suggested that this was impossible. Explaining a bruise found on Morgan's left side, Dr Corscadden said it was quite possible for a kick or a blow under the backbone and ribs to produce nervous shock. Dr Commins, acting for McCrave, seized upon this information by suggesting that the mark had been caused accidentally by an awkward fall, which might then have triggered the fatal shock. Dr Commins kept pressing Dr Corscadden to admit that Morgan's body showed little physical evidence of a beating. The defence even suggested that the overweight Mrs Morgan might herself have accidentally killed her husband when she jumped on his body to save him from the kicks.

   However, it was generally agreed by all three doctors that Morgan died from shock as a result of the violence he had suffered.

   The trial was not without its lighter moments. A young witness, a ragged street urchin called Bernard McCarthy, a boy smart in intelligence but not in appearance, was involved in a misunderstanding over the defence's use of the word "struck", here meaning a kick rather than a blow with the hand. This caused some amusement in court.

Dr Commins: Can you tell me where any kick struck him?

McCarthy: Oh, that won't do. How could it strike him?

Dr Commins: Come, come, you need not be saucy; you have come here to speak the truth.

McCarthy: Oh, yes, I came here to speak the truth, but not to be puzzled out of it.

Dr Commins: I ask where did any kick strike him?

McCarthy: How can a kick strike him? They did not strike him – they kicked him.

   If this little incident had occurred during any other trial, the boy's smart reply and resolute demeanour would have caused laughter, but on the occasion of such a solemn murder trial, the hilarity was carefully suppressed.

   At the previous committal proceedings, McCrave had exhibited anger and impatience throughout. When Samuel Morgan was asked whether Richard started the fight, he had replied, "My brother never struck a blow," at which point McCrave, the devout ruffian, remarked,

"This is but an earthly judge; there is another Judge looking at this case." When Mrs Morgan's sworn evidence was being read over, she was offered a seat. At this kind act, McCrave, his features writhing with passion, spat out, "Why is she not made to stand the same as us?" Continuing her evidence, Mrs Morgan described how her husband had been kicked across the street. A smiling McCrave interrupted her: "It would require a great deal of kicking to kick a man across the street." He turned to Mullen, who also laughed.

Mullen, for his part, was argumentative throughout the committal. He accused a policeman of "putting things into the witness's head". As Mrs Morgan recounted the conversation between the accused and her husband, just before the first blow was struck, Mullen again interrupted her: "It is not fair play, your worship. I have taken notice that during the woman's evidence that man [pointing to an official in the court] is telling the witness what to say." His flippancy and defiance eventually earned him a rebuke from the magistrate. Such was Mullen's display of confidence, even arrogance, that some in the court felt that he would "die game" should it come to that.

However, at the assizes, McCrave and Mullen adopted a different attitude. They didn't appear to be interested in the case, and were remarkably cool and indifferent throughout the entire trial. They hardly noticed each other and appeared to take little interest in what the witnesses were saying. They never showed that they were affected by what was happening around them in any way, even when Mrs Morgan gave her evidence with sobs and tears, which moved everybody else in the court deeply.

The expression on McCrave's face displayed little awareness of the enormity of the crime for which he had been charged, although at times, particularly when questioning the brother of the murdered man, he betrayed slight signs of nervousness. Preoccupied chiefly with chewing a lump of tobacco, he looked quite happy and reckless of the consequences: his only anxiety appearing to be to learn his fate as quickly as possible.

Mullen had lost weight, but wore the same clothes as he had done on the night of the murder. His behaviour amounted to sullenness. He hung over the dock-rail like a heavy-headed but big, bad-tempered boy, apparently taking little interest in what was going on. He turned round occasionally to yawn or to look about the court in search of friends.

Campbell seemed to be the only one aware of the perilous position he was in. He seldom took his eyes from a witness until they had left the box and only then so that he could fix them on the next witness, with the same steady gaze. He smiled occasionally, however. When Samuel Morgan was asked a question about whether or not he had knocked Campbell down, the latter could barely suppress a defiant laugh that seemed to say, "I should like to see him do it."

In his summing up, Judge Mellor made the following points. The defence had attempted to prove that Morgan suffered from heart disease, but in order to prove a murder it was not necessary that the victim should be free from disease. People could not be allowed to speculate as to whether a man was healthy or not and if the jury was satisfied that his death did not result from natural causes, but from violence inflicted that night, even though they might not be able to distinguish the fatal blow, if they then found that it was done by one of them with a common design, they were all equally guilty.

The jury retired to consider their verdict at 7.30 p.m. They were absent for only fifteen minutes before returning to their places in the box. It was only at this point that the prisoners appeared to show any concern with the proceedings. They all looked anxiously in the direction of the jury box as each juror entered. McCrave whispered something to Mullen. Silence was proclaimed while the Clerk of Arraigns put to the foreman the question of whether or not they had agreed upon their verdicts. They had.

The first verdict was on "Holy Fly" McCrave. He heard the word "guilty", and seemed to take it calmly, but was still unable to conceal a shudder. On the second guilty verdict, Mullen tried hard to suppress his tears, but soon recovered his composure. As Campbell too was found guilty he appeared dejected, but brightened up on hearing that the jury had recommended him for mercy. McCrave turned to Mullen and in a broken voice cried, "Oh! It's Campbell." At the recommendation, a burst of sensation and astonishment resounded around the courtroom. It was evident that Campbell, who had a meek and inoffensive appearance, had gained the sympathy of the jury and spectators. Campbell was heard to say that he "hoped he would get off". The other prisoners appeared bewildered at the verdict, for they were apparently under the impression that they too would get off with at least something short of a murder conviction.

Silence was demanded. The judge placed the black cap upon his head and, in solemn tones, read the dread sentence of the law – death. "May God in his infinite mercy grant you that pardon which I have no power to give," he concluded. At this point the terror-stricken Mullen placed his hands in his hair and broke down into a fit of sobbing. He then roared out as if in agony and pleaded to his brother, "Tom, come down and see me!" Justice Mellor concluded by warning Campbell not to buoy himself up with the hope of receiving royal clemency.

The prisoners were then removed from the dock. McCrave bid, "Good bye, old boy," to somebody. Then, addressing a crowd at the back of the court, he warned young men to "mind and keep from drink". Campbell's face twitched nervously and there were tears in his eyes as he turned around to ask the judge if he could see his mother. He was about to say something further when the warders rushed him away with the other prisoners.

Immediately after the death sentence had been passed, a woman's shriek was heard in the corridor. A basket girl knew exactly what was meant by the cry. She rushed screaming away down the steps of St George's Hall, half maddened with grief, repeating over and over in a loud voice, "They are all three sentenced." Among those assembled outside the court was the distressed figure of the mother of one of the condemned lads. With bitter grief she declared that it was too bad for three men to be hanged for the death of one and that the jury were no gentlemen for doing it.

At the back of the hall, a large number of people had collected, waiting to see the prison van transport the three youths to the gaol. Several women cried out messages and farewells, which they hoped would reach the ears of the lads within. The van was followed for some distance by a number of the prisoners' friends, who loudly shouted lamentations. This caused great excitement and commotion in the neighbourhood of Lime Street, and perhaps it was as well that the van was well guarded.

The lads were sent to Kirkdale House of Correction, where they would be kept until three Sundays had elapsed before execution, as was the custom with condemned criminals. The prison was a circular building with two huge wings and with a chapel in the centre. From 1819, until it closed in 1892, it was one of the largest gaols in the country, able to house up to 800 prisoners. The conditions were squalid and the regime extremely tough. According to one local historian, "Throughout its history, Kirkdale had the highest rate of death of any prison in the British Isles."[1]

On arrival, McCrave, Mullen and Campbell were placed in separate cells and had a warder assigned to stay with each of them day and night. All social contact between the condemned youths ceased the moment they entered the prison. Able to wear their own clothes, rather than the prison uniform, they were said to be very respectful to the chief warder, Mr Hyslop, and to the other prison officials. For their part, the lads made no mention of their crime, although outside the prison walls half of Liverpool was talking of nothing else.

PETER CAMPBELL'S supporters lost no time in acting upon the jury's recommendation for mercy. Strenuous efforts were made to obtain a commutation of the sentence. Three separate petitions on behalf of Campbell were forwarded to Richard Assheton Cross, the Home Secretary. Father Doyle, of St Bridget's Catholic Chapel, Bevington Hill, also organised a more general petition aimed at all three condemned lads.

Such a recommendation from the jury was influential but by no means decisive. Between 1861 and 1881, sixty-eight of the 243 murderers who were thus recommended were nevertheless executed.[2] Various factors weighed heavily with the Home Secretary, who was responsible for relaying the decision. These included the support of the trial judge, evidence of intent to kill, insanity, drunkenness, the level of provocation and the youth or even old age of the prisoner. Proof of previous good character was another favourable factor. Indeed, Campbell's fate finally rested with the opinions others held of him.

Mr Ponton, Campbell's solicitor, managed to obtain upwards of 400 names in his support. These included signatures of Roman Catholic priests and ministers of other denominations, a number of tradesmen to whom Campbell was known while in the employment of Mr Taylor, the medical witnesses at the trial, together with other influential people.

As grounds for clemency, the petition alleged that the evidence of Campbell having taken part in the fight had been conflicting and that even assuming that he had been present at any time, the evidence

Vernon Chambers. The Dale Street office of Mr Ponton,
Peter Campbell's solicitor.

proved Morgan had died from the effects of a blow received before
Campbell had got involved. The appeal also pointed out that, before
the outrage, Campbell had displayed a good character. The petition
also made reference to the condemned lad's youth.

The firm of A. & D. Russell, the employer of Campbell's sister,
organised the second petition. This was also forwarded with a decent
number of signatures attached. Finally, Mr George Taylor, Campbell's
employer, forwarded a letter praising his former employee's sobriety,
diligence and general inoffensiveness.

Father Doyle drew up an appeal, almost blaming Morgan himself
for provoking the fatal attack:

To the Right Hon. R.A. Cross, Secretary of State for the Home
Department. The petition of the undersigned respectfully showeth
that the three young lads, under sentence of death for the wilful
murder of Richard Morgan, in Tithebarn Street, Liverpool, deserve the
consideration of her Majesty's clemency. The evidence does not show
any previous malice, not such violence as was necessary to take away
the life of a healthy person such as the deceased appeared to be. The

condemned could not be aware that Morgan's life could be so easily taken away, and it is probable that the deceased would not have been assaulted at all had he not given a contemptuous answer to an appeal made to him by a youth not drunk enough to be insensible to rebuke, and not sober enough to take it meekly.

The petitions were forwarded to the Home Office on December 24. As day after day passed and no news of a reprieve came, supporters of the prisoners began to give up hope that mercy would be extended to them. Campbell's sister and mother were plunged into despair. Mrs Campbell attended Mr Ponton's Dale Street office daily, bewailing the terrible fate that awaited her son. She habitually asked whether a reprieve had yet arrived and pleaded that something more should be done to "save her poor boy's life". She declared that he was not a bad boy. Far from being a "corner loafer", as he had been represented in the press, he was industrious, steady and kind to her and had never lost a day through sickness since he had been at work. She blamed his plight on his relationship with McCrave's sister.

Despite the petitions raised to save the lives of all three prisoners, only one was successful. The news came at a late stage in proceedings and had no doubt been delayed by the Christmas break. On the morning of Saturday, January 2, two days before the planned executions, Captain Gibbs, the governor of the gaol, received a letter from the Home Secretary directing that Campbell be reprieved, chiefly on account of his previous good character. Instead, he had his sentence commuted to penal servitude for life, which normally meant twenty years.

The press was largely against the reprieve. It was argued that the decision was a mistake that "would seriously impair the calculated warning intended to be conveyed by the fate of the other two".[3] Another newspaper wrote:

No one for a moment will regret that the unhappy man's life has been spared; but, beyond the fact of his having led a rather better life than the others, it is difficult to make a distinction between his degree of guilt and that of the two men who yesterday morning forfeited their lives for the same murder in which he was proved, without the shadow of a doubt, to have equally taken act and part ... though Campbell's life has been spared, his future existence on this earth will be one which, in many people's minds, is even worse than immediate death at the hands of the executioner.[4]

What life must have been like for Campbell can hardly be imagined. The relief at being spared death must have quickly turned to despair at the prospect of spending years in prison. Basil Thomson, a Victorian prison governor, described how he had once announced the good news of a reprieve to another murderer at Liverpool in the 1890s. Seeing the man shortly after, back in an ordinary cell, Thomson was shocked: "Never have I seen such a change ... a few minutes before he had been in a class by himself; now he was just one among a thousand. They had clipped his hair to a pattern, and with his own clothing he seemed to have cast off every link that bound him to the past. He was the most dejected man in the prison."[5]

The 1891 census shows Campbell as an inmate sixteen years into his sentence at Portland Prison in Dorset, far away from both his family and his friends. Given the atrocious conditions of most prisons at the time, he might well have suffered a worse fate than his colleagues.

McCrave and Mullen were to be hanged, along with another criminal, William Worthington, who had been convicted of murdering his wife. Originally from Scarisbrick, in Lancashire, Worthington was a thirty-three-year-old former bricklayer who was earning his living on the barge *Eda*, trading between Liverpool and Wigan. With his heavy muscular frame, black beard, moustache and whiskers, he was every newspaper editor's stereotype of a violent criminal: "A man more nearly approaching to a brute there probably never lived in a civilised community."[6]

After a few drinks with his wife in Vauxhall Road, Worthington started hitting her and had to be warned by a policeman. The beating was renewed on the barge the following morning. He kicked his wife in the side and stomach so hard that he splintered the bone of her stays. He also hit her with a poker, breaking a bone in her hand.

In a perversely belated gesture of kindness, Worthington gave his sick wife £5 to seek medical care. However, she fled to a house in Ivy Street off Falkner Street, for a week before making a journey to Wigan to see her sister. It was there that she finally died as a result of her terrible internal injuries. At the post mortem, doctors found that her shattered ribs had penetrated her lungs.

Worthington, a poorly educated man, tried to vindicate himself by explaining that his wife, who suffered from pleuro-pneumonia, was already very ill and that she would have died anyway. At his trial, the defence even argued that Worthington, in giving his wife the money to see a doctor, had no intention of killing her. It was also asserted that Mrs Worthington herself had been guilty of negligence in not seeking medical attention sooner. Indeed, it was argued that the journey to Wigan had only aggravated her injuries. Worthington was nevertheless convicted and sentenced by Justice Mellor to be hanged. The jury added a recommendation to mercy.

Worthington's mother and wife were Protestants; his father, on the other hand, was a Catholic. Worthington had been baptised, but that was "about it". He was not confirmed, he had never attended a Roman Catholic church and nor had he received confession before his conviction. Father Bonte, the Roman Catholic prison chaplain, remarked, "He cares more for his belly than his soul."

When Campbell received notice of his reprieve, Worthington asked piteously, "Is there none for me?" He refused to accept the terrible fate that awaited him, right up to the last minute. Father Bonte added that Worthington had no intelligence at all and that he was "only half a man".

In addition to the press hostility that followed Campbell's reprieve, public opinion also ran very high against all three convicted youths. It was declared that if a certain section of the community had got hold of them, the executions at Kirkdale would never have taken place at all: that the lads would have been torn limb from limb. People who normally would not have harmed a fly eagerly supported an alternative proposal: that the three lads should be flogged to death instead of being hanged.

CHAPTER 5

Execution

IT WAS GENERALLY expected that the friends and relatives of John McCrave and Michael Mullen would hold wakes. This had certainly been the case some months earlier when Thomas Corrigan had been hanged for murdering his mother. However, on visiting the murderers' haunts on the night before the execution, journalists could find no evidence of such a tribute being paid to the lads. Perhaps this was as a result of the sensible advice of the Roman Catholic priests and McCrave's sister. However, candles had been purchased for the wakes and many of the men's friends were disappointed that the drinking party had been cancelled. The police reported that the area of Tithebarn Street, Prussia Street and Pall Mall appeared very orderly on the eve of the hanging, with the Cornermen and other ruffians being remarkably quiet.

On both the morning and evening of Sunday, January 3, the day before the execution, Mullen, McCrave and Worthington attended divine service in the Roman Catholic chapel of the prison. Father Bonte preached the usual sermon for the dying, following which Mullen and Worthington received Holy Communion. McCrave and Mullen asked Father Bonte to request the Roman Catholic inmates of the prison to offer up a prayer on their behalf to St Joseph, the patron saint of a happy death. On the same day, the Reverend Mr Piggott, the prison's Episcopal chaplain, preached a sermon that contained special references to the men under sentence of death. He took for his text the twelfth verse of the seventy-ninth Psalm: "O let the sorrowful sighing of the prisoners come before thee: according to the greatness of thy power, preserve thou those that are appointed to die."

Every day since the passing of the sentence, the Protestant inmates had offered heartfelt prayers for the eternal welfare of the condemned men.

In 1888, fourteen years after the murder, a series of journal articles describing famous executions was published. The following is an account of McCrave's final night, related by one of the warders, whose job it was to guard him in the condemned cell:

McCrave was always asking me if the hangman had arrived. The night before his execution he went off in a doze about 9 o'clock and, as he lay on the bed, I sat on a chair watching him.

He had been asleep some time, with his face turned down on the pillow, when, all at once, he awoke and jumped straight up in the bed with a shriek that nearly froze the blood in my veins. His hair fairly stood on end, the perspiration rolled down his white face, and his eyes seemed nearly coming out of his head. "I saw him. I saw him," he stammered. "He came to the grating when I was asleep, and he looked at me. Oh! oh! oh! Don't let him touch me!" and he sprang to me and hid his face on my shoulder. "Who came, my lad?" I asked, as I tried to soothe him. "The hangman," and he sobbed like a child. "I know it was him. A man with long whiskers. I saw his face, and I saw his eyes."

I pooh-poohed the idea and did my best to soothe the lad. At last he went off to sleep; but he kept on waking up all through the night and crying out: "He was looking at me! He was looking at me!"

And do you know, the [warder] concluded, I found out in the morning it was quite right. "Mr Anderson" *had* been at the wicket looking at him, just out of curiosity, at the very time the lad said. But how the dickens McCrave could have seen him when he was fast asleep with his face on the pillow, I never could make out.[1]

The hangman appointed to carry out the executions was a rather mysterious figure. "Mr Anderson" was one of several of his aliases. At Kirkdale, he particularly requested that the prison officials did not divulge his name to journalists. He was described as "a middle-sized man, closely shaven, with very sharp features and keen, deep-set eyes".[2] He arrived at the gaol on Sunday evening, well attired in a black overcoat, a black velvet waistcoat and a semi-clerical wide-awake hat with a white cambric handkerchief protruding from his left breast pocket.

All kinds of rumours circulated about the identity of the new Jack Ketch (the name of a famous hangman). He was referred to by prison officials as Mr A.B.C., alias Mr Henderson, alias Mr Evans. Some thought that he was a gentleman of fortune who had a love for his hideous trade. Others reckoned that he was a surgeon labouring in the interests of science. It was felt that he had some knowledge of anatomy, but from where nobody would hazard a guess. Others thought him to be a farmer from South Wales who was known as the "gentleman amateur", although this enigmatic man preferred to be called "Calcraft's assistant".

The leading hangman in the mid-nineteenth century was William Calcraft. He was Britain's longest-serving executioner, working for forty-five years, from 1829 until his retirement in 1874 at the age of seventy-three. During the latter part of his career, an assistant sometimes accompanied him. So enthusiastic was he for the profession that this protégé followed the veteran executioner throughout the country freely rendering his services for the "pure love of the thing".

Calcraft was an incompetent hangman at the best of times and his meagre skills deteriorated as he got older. His last execution at Kirkdale was so badly handled that his services were dispensed with. During the hanging of James Connor, in August 1873, the rope snapped, causing the poor man, masked and pinioned, to fall two or three feet to the ground. Believing that he should now be spared death, the injured Connor was devastated to discover that, eight minutes later, he would have to go through the ghastly process a second time. With a drop of only eight inches, Connor twitched and struggled to a hard death.

With Calcraft no longer welcome in Liverpool, it was generally supposed that another hangman, William Marwood, would carry out the executions, but "Calcraft's assistant" looked set to become Calcraft's successor. The man was Robert Evans of Carmarthen, "a dilettante of the scaffold, though he claimed to be moved by 'humane motives'".[3] He was the son of a lawyer and had received medical training, although he never practised. His other sobriquet was the "medical executioner". As well as acting as an "assistant", Evans also became chief executioner whenever he was required to perform the role. The general opinion was that he had a remarkable talent as a hangman. On his first visit to Kirkdale, his systematic fixing of the rope and the excellent terms upon which he appeared to be with himself after the event left anyone who saw him in no doubt that he was no common hangman. He was believed to have executed Thomas Corrigan in a very scientific manner.

On Evans' last visit to Kirkdale, however, it was understood that, as a result of his aloofness towards the prison officials, his services would no longer be required. Nevertheless, he returned for the hanging of McCrave, Mullen and Worthington and seemed to have conquered any antipathy towards the prison staff. He was justly regarded as the legitimate successor to the veteran Calcraft.

However, despite the success of his work at Kirkdale on January 4, that office was conferred, the following year, on William Marwood of Horncastle, who continued to officiate almost to the day of his death in 1883. It was Marwood who perfected what was known as "the long drop". Rather than have the victim slowly strangled at the end of the rope, the drop meant that the vertebrae were dislocated, causing instantaneous death.

Evans himself retired into anonymity, although both his appearance and manner made a lasting impression on the people of Liverpool. As local historian Tod Sloan observed, "He left behind him

Kirkdale Gaol (1832).

a reputation and a sensation of fear that few men have ever achieved in influencing the outlook of Liverpool people. 'Mr Anderson will get you' became a constant warning given by parents to misbehaving children, and nearly all of them grew up believing it."[4]

The Kirkdale scaffold was a small, but stout, compact structure, with a single crossbeam above that had been lengthened to accommodate the three prisoners. Three ropes, four or five feet in length, were attached to the beam by short chains. The ropes were coiled awaiting use, with the nooses ready to adjust. The scaffold was a little higher than normal, although the fall was to be of the usual length – about two-and-a-half feet. However, at the last execution at Kirkdale, where Marwood had officiated, the drop had been over five feet.

The morning of January 3, 1875, was cold, foggy and miserable. The spell of frost, which reached its climax on New Year's Eve, maintained its grip on the ground and created treacherous travel conditions near to the prison. Both the moon and stars remained hidden and there barely appeared to be any sign of morning. The scene was as still as death, save for the occasional ghostly clanking of keys heard from within the closed doorway and the footsteps of a few policemen under the prison walls.

Although executions were held privately, a number of people still flocked to the gaol, content to wait outside for the ghastly deed to be done. Despite the atrocious weather conditions, a crowd of fifty or sixty people, split into small groups, assembled at the corner of the gaol where it was known that the scaffold had been erected. These people were largely poor and curious, and carefully scrutinised all who approached the prison. Another group of more middle-class spectators seemed to be waiting for the raising of the black flag, signalling that the condemned had been executed. A group of journalists also stood under cover of almost total darkness, awaiting entrance to the gaol.

This was not a big crowd. At previous hangings there had been 200 to 300 people assembled, morbidly waiting for the black flag to ascend. Indeed, when executions had been public events they had been almost been as popular as FA Cup finals are today. When John Gleeson, the notorious mass murderer, was hanged outside Kirkdale in 1849, the crowd was estimated to be between 50,000 and 100,000. Many of them had travelled on special trains laid on for the occasion. The low turnout for the Tithebarn Street murderers owed perhaps to the darkness of the morning, which made the black flag invisible.

At about 7.45 a.m., the sky began to brighten a little overhead. This raised hopes among the journalists that the impending spectacle would not be shrouded from view.

By this time the procedures were already well under way. Mullen and McCrave rose at 5.30 a.m., dressed and waited with resignation in their respective cells in silent meditation. Father Bonte visited them at 6.45 a.m. He later described the lads as being fully prepared to meet their fate. After mass, they returned to their cells for breakfast, consisting of bread and a thin gruel called "skilly". Worthington, the man who cared "more for his belly", was the only one who touched it. The prisoners were then hurried from their cells across an open court to what was known as the "reception room". Care was taken to prevent the condemned men from seeing the scaffold, even though the black beams and dark drapery of the ghastly structure must have been almost invisible in the dim light that shrouded the yard. The closing scene was almost at hand. McCrave and Mullen shook hands before turning to shake hands with Worthington. They then engaged in yet more prayers with Father Bonte, before being introduced to the hangman.

Before they made their way to the scaffold, the prisoners' arms were pinioned. This involved fixing a broad leather body-belt around the waist. On each side of the belt was an arm strap, an inch-and-a-half wide, which was used to clasp the condemned man's arms at the elbow. Another strap fastened the wrists to the belt in front. Immediately before the execution the prisoner's legs were also pinioned with a two-inch strap below the knees.

At 7.50 a.m., a voice was heard at the prison gates. "Now, gentlemen, step this way, please," was the invitation from a gaoler, who threw open a small door in the gateway to admit a group of selected journalists. Once they were inside, they found themselves under a broad, spacious archway. For a short time, the reporters were kept standing in this gas-lit arcade, waiting to be led across the gaol grounds to the scaffold. The generally gloomy yard looked even darker and more dreary than usual. The dim outline of the black painted uprights and crossbeam was becoming faintly visible through the mist at a few yards' distance.

Nevertheless, at 7.55 a.m. the fog remained so thick that it seemed doubtful whether much of the hanging would be seen. A warder lit a gas lamp near to the steps leading to the scaffold. A faint light also glimmered from the pinioning room, revealing that the preliminary operations were already in progress.

A Multiple Hanging. A nineteenth-century illustration of a group execution by Calcraft.

A few minutes before 8 a.m., the carpenter, an elderly and portly veteran of such executions, who was wearing a thick topcoat and a heavy red muffler, climbed the steps. He stepped onto the scaffold and peered over the iron railings surrounding it before testing the treacherous platform with his weight. Satisfied with his work, he retired to the door of the pinioning room and waited until it was all over. Every precaution had been taken to avoid anything unseemly. Some chairs were placed on the scaffold in case the men gave way during their trying ordeal.

The funeral dirge from the bell tower continued to toll its slow, measured death knell, sending at each stroke an involuntary shiver through the frames of those gathered, even those hardened to the sound of the dreadful chime. At this moment, hundreds of prisoners were bent in prayer in their cells. At the tolling of the bell, all the inmates, at the request of Father Bonte, offered up prayers in unison. The wish was carried out, but as one newspaper pondered, "Whether the solemn warning of that tolling bell sank into many hearts we know not, but it certainly penetrated deep into every quadrangle and every cell of the great gaol."[5]

The prison clock began to strike eight and the death bell, which had been tolling for a quarter of an hour, rang out a few sharp, rapid strokes, announcing to the murderers that their hour had come. It was slowly starting to become light and the surrounding objects were vaguely distinguishable. The door of the reception room was flung open and, in a quick procession, the condemned men emerged from the reception room and ascended the thirty steps to the "old pinioning room". The solitary gas lamp shed a sickly yellow gleam over the group, but they were lost again in an instant, vanishing through the doorway at the head of the steps. They reappeared almost immediately through a door that led out onto the scaffold.

The burly frame of chief warder, Mr Hyslop, headed the group. Worthington and the executioner followed. Next came Mullen and after him McCrave, each prisoner accompanied by a warder on either side. In the midst of the trio was Father Bonte, wearing a surplice, stole and biretta and reading the litany for the dying. The deputy undersheriff and the governor made up the remainder of the procession. As he approached the scaffold steps, McCrave asked Father Bonte, as his last request, to visit his sister to caution her against leading a sinful life and to warn her to repent. Sadly, as will be seen later, the message failed to have any effect on the young woman.

Mullen appeared calmer and looked resigned but extremely pale. Although he had broken down in tears at the trial, he remained stoic in his final moments. In the grey dawn, he was easily recognisable by his white jacket, the very coat that he had worn on the night of the murder and which had helped identify him as one of the murderers. McCrave alone had a terror-stricken appearance, his face twitching nervously. As he caught sight of the scaffold, he looked as though he would faint.

On reaching the platform, Worthington was the first to be conducted under the beam. The executioner placed a white hood or cap over his face and then adjusted the rope round his neck. While the executioner was thus engaged, all three men kept offering prayers for divine mercy and made the responses to the "Litany for a Soul Departing", which was being recited by Father Bonte.

Just before reaching the platform, Mullen and McCrave kissed each other and bade each other goodbye. Mullen was next brought onto the scaffold and the executioner performed the same sad preparations for him as he had done for Worthington. Mullen showed no signs of fear and submitted passively to the attentions of the hangman. He conducted himself more quietly than Worthington had done and did not utter the responses as frequently or as loudly. Perhaps his were mental prayers.

Although no journalists at the time reported the incident, in the 1888 account of the execution, related by one of the warders present, Mullen is supposed to have urged the executioner, as the cap was being pulled over his face, to "Snap me off quick!" This was seen as "a good index to his stubborn, relentless character". The prediction that he would "die game" seems correct.

McCrave was the last to appear under the beam and he also prayed earnestly, calling upon God to be merciful to him a wretched sinner. On being brought onto the drop, he looked fearfully up at the rope before the white cap was placed over his face. As the noose was adjusted round his neck, he trembled violently. In a tremulous and intense voice he begged, "Oh Lord Jesus, have mercy on me. O God, be merciful unto me a sinner. Oh my sweet Jesus, forgive me. Lord Jesus forgive me. Christ have mercy on me. Sweet Jesus, do save my soul tonight. Sweet Jesus, have mercy on me this morning. Lord be merciful to me, a wretched sinner." His voice was said to have been so loud that it must have been heard outside the prison walls.

Having placed the ropes and caps upon the men, the executioner then pinioned their legs. Checking that all was complete, he then shook hands with each of them and bade them a final goodbye. The chaplain now withdrew from the scaffold. McCrave, in a loud voice, continued to beg frantically to be saved, while Mullen stood silently with his hands clasped.

They were still busy in prayer when, on a signal from the hangman, the warders and others quietly moved back off the trapdoor. At exactly 8.05 a.m., the executioner drew the bolt and the men were launched into eternity. The heavy platform fell with a thud upon its hinges, leaving the three bodies suspended in mid-air. As the drop fell, there was an exclamation of "Oh!" from one of the men, but the sound was frozen still in the chilly air, cut short by the sharp snapping of a neck. Richard Morgan's murder had been avenged.

A journalist, not present at the Kirkdale execution, but a veteran eye-witness of many other hangings, reported what normally happened at the fatal moment: "The white cap fitted closely to his face and the thin white linen took a momentary stain as if a bag of black-berries had been bruised, and had suddenly exuded the juice of the fruit. It sagged a moment later, and assumed its natural hue."[6]

Death in each case seemed to be instantaneous. Owing to Mullen's rope having a twist in it, his body whirled round twice. The other two bodies spun round nearly half a circle. As Worthington twitched convulsively, the hangman, with help from some warders, put forth his hands to steady the swaying bodies. After about a minute the three men were hanging motionless, in the same position facing towards the east, the head of each dropping over the left shoulder. The white cap of Mullen, when the drop fell, was jerked partly off his face, exposing the chin up to the mouth, but his features were placid.

All was now still. Those in the bare, bleak prison yard below who had withdrawn to a safe distance to avoid witnessing the drop scene and hearing the dull thud of the falling bodies at too close a proximity could see little on the scaffold but the three white caps which stood out in stark contrast to the surrounding darkness. The upper part of the bodies remained visible above the drapery. The black flag, from a pole attached to a ventilating shaft, was raised to inform the outside world that the sentence of the law had been carried out.

As with all executed criminals, the bodies were left hanging on the gallows for an hour. This was to make sure that they were dead before being taken down. At 9 a.m., several warders and prisoners ascended the scaffold stairs while the executioner, in the presence of Dr Hendry, the acting surgeon, unhooked the ropes by which the men were suspended. The prisoners then carried the three bodies into the pinioning room behind the scaffold, where they were laid upon their backs on the bare floor to await an inquest into their deaths.

The corpses must have looked a most ghastly spectacle, with the white caps still over their heads. When the caps were removed, the faces of the men were not in any way discoloured and only Mullen's neck seemed to have suffered abrasion from the turning of his body after the drop. A quiet, placid look was settled on each face, as if they had passed away in a peaceful sleep. On Worthington's feet was a pair of huge hob-nailed boots with soles half-an-inch thick, the very boots that he had used to kick his wife and which had helped send him to the gallows.

While the inquest was proceeding, a group of prisoners dug graves in the southwest corner of the yard – reserved for the burial of the bodies of executed criminals. The remains of the three men were afterwards placed in shells and covered in quick lime. There was no religious service.

Just before the inquest began, two or three women and a considerable number of children from the Vauxhall Road and Tithebarn Street area waited in the yard in front of the session-house, which adjoined the prison. The group of more middle-class spectators was gazing intently at some object. When asked by a journalist what it was, a respectable-looking woman revealed that it was the black flag, adding that they came from Horncastle, Lincolnshire, the home town of the executioner Marwood, who, she mistakenly thought, had acted as hangman. The women could hardly be convinced that Marwood was not on duty on this occasion. When they were assured that this was the case, they appeared, if not angry, then at least disappointed that Horncastle had not had the honour of providing the executioner. These women had travelled about 160 miles to witness an event that, in any case, was hidden from view. It seems that Marwood was what today would be termed a "celebrity hangman", and that he had quite a large following in Horncastle, where he still worked as a cobbler.

A number of people, including one or two women, lingered outside the prison for half an hour after the execution and appeared to be deeply engaged in discussions about the Tithebarn Street murder. An old lady, the mother of one of the condemned men, alternated continually between kneeling on the cold, damp ground and raising herself up, only to throw herself back to the ground in a paroxysm of grief. She flung her yellow, withered arms aloft and sobbed, "Och, hone, my own poor darling boy. Oh, they're going to strangle my only lad. Holy Mother of God, save him, save him. Let me in till I kiss his poor face. Och, hone, the darling I've bore and suckled, and loved, to be choked. My God, my God, my God."[7]

Members of the borough police force were on duty in the neighbourhood of the gaol but, on that particular morning, their services were not required.

CHAPTER 6

Why Was the Murder so Shocking?

"FIGHTING FOR LIFE, Dad Who Tackled 'Hoodies'" ran the *Daily Express* front-page headline of May 2005. Several other national newspapers carried the shocking story. A gang of drunken youths had attacked and severely injured a respectable man. The lads wore a distinctive uniform of hooded tops. The assault came days after the Prime Minister has supported a ban on such clothing, because it helps hide the face of the wearer. Some shopping centres had already enforced the ban and the nation is led to believe that all youths wearing hoods and baseball caps are potential criminals. Panic was in the air.

The media has always thrived on a good scandal or sensational story. Throughout the twentieth century, a steady stream of "folk devils" have been put forward for condemnation. In the 1950s it was the Teddy Boys; in the 1960s it was the Mods and Rockers; in the 1970s it was the turn of the Skinheads, followed by the Punks. In 2005 it was the "Hoodies".

The great dangers to the nineteenth-century public included Liverpool's High Rip gang, the Scuttlers in Manchester, the Peaky Blinders of Birmingham and the Hooligans of London. However, one of the earliest media panics about a youth sub-culture centred on the criminal activities of Liverpool's Cornermen. The murder of Richard Morgan by these "loafers" caused a nationwide sensation and raised concerns about justice, policing, law and disorder that are as relevant today as they were over 130 years ago.

Yet the national panic prompted by the murder of Richard Morgan wasn't simply a media-generated one. There was a great deal of genuine concern and horror over what had happened to an innocent man. The crime led to much soul-searching among the Liverpool population. This was echoed in the public's anger and concern over the death of the toddler Jamie Bulger over 100 years later. In both cases, people began to question what was happening to the city; the moral condition of a generation of young people came under the spotlight. Liverpool itself was demonised in the press.

The Tithebarn Street murder generated a great deal of press outrage and much of it was to the detriment of the town of Liverpool. The crime sparked a public debate about gangs and street violence that went on to cover issues of unemployment, housing conditions, punishment, police efficiency and political will. It seems particularly ironic when people nowadays look back to the past and imagine a crime-free golden age when society knew how to deal firmly with criminals. For some it might come as a surprise to learn that the Victorians had their own version of the "Hoodies" and that they had a similar problem with binge drinking.

The press raised three main issues. First, the criminality of Liverpool people was exposed, sparking a heated debate about the solution to the problem of lawlessness. Secondly, the appalling behaviour of the crowd of spectators during the murder of Richard Morgan was heavily criticised. Finally, the lack of police presence, together with a suspected police policy of non-interference when it came to incidents of street brawls, provoked a political storm.

From the outset, the attack on Morgan was presented as no ordinary murder: it was viewed as a new chapter in the history of crime, as if a nadir of depravity had been reached. The case struck a chord with newspapers and their predominantly middle-class readership: "The bad pre-eminence which Liverpool enjoys for brutal and murderous outrages has received another illustration."[1] It was "one of the most dastardly street outrages of the century". It was also "a scene of reckless brutality which will forever remain a black spot on the annals of Liverpool".[2] "A more atrocious deed than the kicking to death of Richard Morgan has never been committed in the open streets of a great English town."[3] "The tragedy in Tithebarn Street came like a thunderclap and eclipsed in brutality all other offences of the kind."[4] Twelve years after the murder, the crime was judged to have been "as cruel and cold-blooded an outrage as has ever stained our local annals of crime".[5]

74

A notable aspect of the media coverage of the Tithebarn Street murder was that the southern press, particularly *The Times* and *Spectator*, saw an opportunity to have a go at their northern rivals. As crime historian John Archer has pointed out, "London-based newspapers were quick to play up this fact that the northern cities and towns seemed to be more violent than anywhere else. *The Times* and others dwelt in particular on crimes of violence. The phrase 'it's tough up North' came into common usage. Headlines like 'Lawless Lancashire' and 'Lawless Liverpool' were common, and not without good cause."[6] Another crime historian, Rob Sindall, remarks, "A certain mythology was created stereotyping Lancastrians as brutal on a par with Scottish miserliness or Irish stupidity."[7] Such press reporting can be seen as an early example of the media-bashing the city received.

But it wasn't just the city of Liverpool that was on the receiving end of the unfavourable press; newspapers were also quick to point out the scale of the crime problem in the county of Lancashire as a whole. "It is not surprising that *The Times* should be proclaiming to the country the disgrace of our present assize calendar. The Tithebarn Street kicking case, the St Helens outrage, the Cliviger atrocity, the Worthington wife-murder, and the killing of Mary Garvey ... are all crimes the blackness of which could hardly be exceeded."[8]

The St Helens outrage was exceptionally savage. A group of young colliers, shouting, "Kill the whole Irish lot", had smashed their way into the home of a seventy-four-year-old man. After throwing quicklime into the face of his wife, the gang beat up the old man, completely destroying his eyeball in the process. As the vitreous remains poured out, the men filled the empty socket with hot lime and, for added measure, forced some more up his nostrils and down his throat. The poor man survived, but apparently went insane. The perpetrators received twenty years' imprisonment.

The Cliviger case happened just outside Burnley. Two colliers, aged sixteen and twenty, came across a drunken woman propped up against a gate, unable to stand. The pair proceeded to rape her, while a group of friends, aged between thirteen and nineteen, stood by and watched. One bystander admitted that he saw no harm in it, while another even confessed that he thought it was good fun. The poor, insensible woman was then taken to a secluded place and abandoned on the cold, wet ground, where she subsequently died from exposure. The lads responsible were convicted and sentenced to fifteen years' imprisonment.

Yet if Lancashire, and Liverpool in particular, was so crime-ridden, why did the Tithebarn Street outrage alone attract so much press coverage? The youth of the attackers was one major point of concern. Several newspapers commented on the fact that seventeen-year-old Mullen was only a boy. Such was the lawlessness among Liverpool's youngsters that society had been required to hang a child: "And yet it seems a terrible thing to bring the hangman into our midst for the purposes of extinguishing life in these youths, one of whom is only seventeen years of age, while the eldest is a year short of legal manhood. In the eye of the law, in one sense, they are 'infants', in another sense they are criminals guilty of the worst crime provided for in the statute book."[9]

Yet it was not unusual for youths to be hanged. In 1887, in Suffolk, another boy of seventeen called Joseph Morley was executed for murdering the wife of a man with whom he was lodging. He had sliced her throat with a razor as she lay on the bed. It was not until 1888 that the Home Office established a convention that youths under eighteen years of age should not be executed. In 1910, an unsuccessful attempt was made to increase the minimum age to twenty-one. It was not until 1933 that the Children and Young Persons Act finally abolished the death penalty for youths under the age of eighteen.

There were a number of other reasons why Richard Morgan's murder became so notorious. In the nineteenth century, Liverpool certainly had a reputation as a violent town. It was known as "the black spot on the Mersey" although others felt that a better description would be "the bloody spot on the Mersey".[10] The area around the docks was a hunting ground for gangs of robbers, who preyed on the many foreign seamen who drank in the local pubs. These men would often be carrying large sums of money, having been paid off after long voyages. Blind drunk from a night on the town, or stumbling along dark alleys in search of prostitutes, they were easy pickings. Yet although they were robbed and beaten, they were rarely murdered and even if they were, such crimes in the "lower parts" of the town did not seem to affect respectable members of the general public, which is more than can be said for the murder of Richard Morgan.

Despite the levels of crime in Liverpool, people were normally able to walk the major streets of the town without being molested by strangers. The very location of the murder – on a street where businessmen, middle-class commuters, town councillors and impoverished peasants passed each other daily – meant that the crime affected everybody, the civilised and the so-called uncivilised. The fatal attack on Richard Morgan could not be passed off as something that had simply happened in the dingy courts, far away from middle-class attention. It was argued that if people dared to venture into the slums and back streets of the rough parts of town then they had to take the risk, but in the main streets, especially in one leading from a railway station, pedestrians could reasonably expect safety. The fear for respectable people, and one that was much highlighted and stirred up by the press, was that a crime such as the Tithebarn Street murder could happen to anybody at any time.

Another disturbing feature of this murder was that the victim apparently did not know his attackers: "The crime betrayed a barbarity exceptional even for the Lancashire savage, for the man attacked was in no way a companion of his murderers; he had not been drinking or quarrelling with them; he had never seen the men before."[11] Such was the middle classes' anxiety over the random nature of the crime that the main topic of conversation among businessmen on the Liverpool Exchange was that Richard Morgan must have known his attackers or that they must have had some grudge against him. However, his widow and brother denied any knowledge of the gang.

It is a fact that most murderers know their victim. This is reflected in domestic killings, such as in the Worthington case, and drunken arguments between friends that occasionally erupt into fatal violence. A list of the murderers executed at Kirkdale in the ten years prior to the Tithebarn Street murder illustrates the point; it will be noted that the condemned are not all from Liverpool but from the wider area of Lancashire:

1864 Luke Charles, ex-policeman, for the murder of his wife at Pendleton
1864 James Clitheroe for the murder of girlfriend Mary Woods at St Helens
1865 Hugh Brown for the murder of Thomas McCarthy in Crump Street
1866 Thomas Grime for the murder of workmate James Barton at Wigan

1867 Henry Farrington for the murder of his wife at Leigh

1870 John Gregson for the murder of his wife at Wigan

1872 Richard Spencer for the murder of his girlfriend in Gregson Street

1873 James Connor for the murder of James Gaffney at Mill Street, Toxteth

1874 Thomas Corrigan for the murder of his mother at Chisenhale Street

1874 Henry Flanagan for the murder of his aunt in Bent Street

1874 Mary Williams for the murder of neighbour Nicholas Manning at Bootle

Of course, these examples do not include incidents where the murderers were never caught, but the cases nevertheless indicate that the murders were largely one-on-one crimes and, for the most part, that the attackers knew their victims. Not one of the men had been hanged for a gang killing.

People usually have a reason, however feeble, for murder or brutality. Revenge, robbery, jealousy or an uncontrolled temper: all the usual reasons for homicide were seemingly missing in the Tithebarn Street case. The attack on Richard Morgan had been unnecessary and the level of violence used after he had fallen was both gratuitous and outrageous. If the gang had left Morgan alone after the first fatal punch, it could have been argued that they did not mean to kill him. However, the prolonged kicking of their insensible victim proved their murderous intention beyond doubt.

Richard Morgan had never been a threat to his attackers. With the exception of his sealskin cap, his murderers did not even attempt to steal from him, even though they had certainly wanted money. Only one witness, John Thompson, suggested that Richard Morgan appeared "to want to argue something out". This might have provoked the attack, but it was generally felt that Morgan had done nothing to deserve his beating. His attackers might have been drinking, but they were not thought to be so drunk that they did not know what they were doing. Morgan's attacker, it was said, "acted from sheer love of brutality, the pleasure of feeling his own power to kill".[12]

Part of the tragedy of the murder was that Richard Morgan was a respectable, hard-working man. He was described as a "steady and faithful servant and a light-hearted generous youth".[13] For the newspapers, his murder signalled an assault on the concept of respectability, an attack perpetrated by the very opposite of everything that the industrious and sober Morgan represented: a violent mob of drunken, work-shy scroungers.

Morgan was certainly a cut above his killers, who were portrayed as loafers, unemployed idlers, men who significantly lacked even the muscles normally developed by honest manual labour. Indeed, part of the reason that Campbell alone escaped the gallows seems to be that, unlike Mullen and McCrave, he came from a good family and was in regular employment. The petitions raised in his favour all stressed the respectability of his mother and the employed status of his sisters, in order to distance Campbell from the low, brutal character that had been attached to his companions.

Morgan's death signalled the passing of a very English sense of propriety: "It was almost the boast of an Englishman, no matter of what degree he might be, that he would never see a man kicked when down; but the numerous instances of kicking by Cornermen recently brought to light would lead us to the conclusion that from among the lower-classes, at all events, that spirit of fair play had departed."[14]

The public was led to believe that the murder of Richard Morgan threatened the nation's sense of moral identity. Centuries of ethical tradition were now at implicit risk of being violently displaced by an alien culture, particularly since those largely seen as responsible for these kicking outrages were not even English, but foreigners from Ireland.

Indeed, the Irish method of fighting was much criticised by Englishmen. In London, a rubbish carter spoke to the journalist and sociologist Henry Mayhew about the lack of gentlemanly conduct in Irish fisticuffs: "Fair fights!, sir ... the Irishes don't stand up to you like men. They don't fight like Christians, sir, not a bit of it. They kick and scratch and bite and tear like devils, or cats, or women. They're soon settled if you can get an honest knock at them, but it isn't easy."[15]

As well as signalling the loss of a golden age of English good behaviour, however mythical that may have been, there were a number of other factors that made the Tithebarn Street murder unique and dangerous. The above reference to "the lower-classes" displays a middle-class anxiety about a threat to social stability. It was felt that those in authority – such as the police and the courts – were failing to keep control over these lower orders. Middle-class society could just about accept that individuals ill-treated and murdered other individuals, who were, they thought, usually of the same class, but when ruffians started forming gangs and attacking respectable people who were minding their own business, then the threat became, understandably, more intense.

The fear of the mob was never far from the surface, as can be seen in the press reaction to the behaviour of those who had looked on as the murder was taking place. Three people were convicted of the Tithebarn Street murder, yet many more were implicated, either directly or indirectly, in the crime. The assault happened at 9.30 p.m. Public houses remained open until 11 p.m., so there would have been plenty of people about to witness the crime, but they did nothing to help.

There were, of course, a number of good reasons for not interfering in a Liverpool street brawl. At the committal proceedings, a witness called Samuel Lipson was asked why he did not interfere when he saw Morgan being ill-treated. "I didn't do anything," he replied. "There were no people about there, and I might have got into trouble myself. They are rough-looking fellows, and I would have been nowhere among them." At the assizes, he added, "What was the use of interfering with a lot of men like them? Why should I get killed myself?"

People also ran the risk of arrest by the police, either by being mistaken for the assailant or for taking the law into their own hands. Onlookers were also afraid of having to appear in court as witnesses. In his summing up at trial, Judge Mellor put forward his own theory of why the crowd had not intervened. He proposed that if the spectators had only come up at the moment when Samuel Morgan knocked down Mullen or McCrave, then they might have thought that Samuel was the primary attacker. The crowd's sympathies might then have pointed the other way.

Yet the passivity of the spectators only told half the story. For some, the onlookers did not intervene out of understandable concern for their own safety, but mostly out of a sense of apathy; one that had been borne of their own criminality. These people lived as enemies of all authority. They instinctively sympathised with the ruffians and had become so used to violence that it no longer bothered them.

The press outrage stirred by Tithebarn Street did not centre solely on the brutal murder of Richard Morgan, but was also a response to the atrocious behaviour of the crowd. Their inaction was only a symptom of something much larger and more frighteningly dangerous. Not only were the spectators judged to have been accomplices to the murder, but the whole community was viewed as morally corrupt. Such a state of affairs was seen as "a stain on the good name of Liverpool which it is incumbent on her inhabitants to wipe away". Although *The Times* admitted that violent crime was not unique to Liverpool, what singled out the town was that such violence was "both positively approved by the brutalised population of the neighbourhood at the time, and [was] not publicly repudiated afterwards by the civilised portion of the inhabitants". *The Times* concluded, "Liverpool is a town whose leading inhabitants are negligent of their duties as citizens."[16]

Middle-class journalists could pontificate all they liked about the level and nature of crime in Liverpool. If any lessons were to be learned from the death of Richard Morgan and the execution of his attackers, then the ruffians out on the streets of the town certainly didn't learn them. For the gangs of Liverpool, it was business as usual.

CHAPTER 7

Senseless Violence

THE WEEDS HAD hardly grown on the graves of Michael Mullen and John McCrave before the mayhem on Liverpool's streets resumed with a vengeance.

On January 6, 1875, Luke Buckley appeared in court charged with assaulting a black seaman called Alexander Martin. Buckley had been part of a street-corner gang who had stopped the victim as he walked down Pellew Street, near Brownlow Hill. Buckley had asked Martin if he was going to stand him a drink. The seaman replied that he had no money, upon hearing which, one of the gang shouted, "Give it to him" – words which echoed the female spectator at Richard Morgan's murder. Martin was then punched on the shoulder. As the startled man ran away, Buckley turned to a friend and asked for a knife. Martin was chased down a passage into a court where he was trapped. He was then stabbed in the arm.

On January 16, John Rossiter and John Flynn were charged with assaulting John Shea. The previous Saturday night, the victim had been walking with his wife along Maguire Street, off Vauxhall Road, when Rossiter had come up to him, and shouted in a threatening manner, "You are the man that I want. Are you as good now as you were before?" A puzzled Shea replied, "What is this for?" Rossiter then knocked him down with a vicious swipe of his belt, while Flynn, who was wearing clogs, booted him in the body. When Shea got up, Rossiter delivered a four-inch stab wound. In court, it was revealed that the attackers had an "old spite" against Shea.

One would think that the publicity surrounding the Tithebarn Street murder, particularly given that two of the gang had been hanged, would have made people wary of using severe violence. However, it seems as though some people simply didn't care about the consequences of their actions. One such set of people weren't a gang as such, but members of a family who had a score to settle. At the same court sessions in January, Alexander Murray, his brother James and his sister Catherine were charged with wounding their father Patrick and Bridget Lawless, the woman he lived with.

One Saturday night, the sons and daughter had gone to their father's house in Paul Street, off Vauxhall Road, and had threatened to kill him for living with a woman they didn't care for. The man's siblings declared that they would "be hung for it like Mullen and the Tithebarn Street fellows". When Bridget appeared at the door, James cracked her on the head with a poker, Alexander broke two of her fingers with a hatchet and Catherine finished off the attack by smashing her with a brick. After giving their father a severe telling off, they hit him repeatedly about the face. The poor woman was seriously injured, but she eventually recovered.

Shortly after McCrave's execution, his older brother, James, waged his own reign of terror on a family with whom he lodged in Chaucer Street, off Scotland Road. In February 1875, he appeared in court charged with threatening a woman by the name of Catherine Prendergast. When told that he was no longer wanted in her house, he threatened to "do for her". He also warned that he would kick her to death and stab her husband. The poor couple was terrified of him and ended up going to the police. Fining him, the magistrate couldn't believe that McCrave had learned nothing from his brother's execution.

The Tithebarn Street murder spawned a number of other street attacks. The Fontenoy Street outrage four-and-a-half months later involved an assault on Anthony Smith, near to the bottom end of Scotland Road. On December 19, 1874, Smith had been out walking when Thomas Mulchay and a gang of "roughs" accosted him. A lad named Kilhorn asked him how much money he had, to which Smith replied, "What's that to you?" Kilhorn knocked the man down while Mulchay joined in the kicking. In a scene reminiscent of Tithebarn Street, Kilhorn took the victim's cap. Smith managed to get up and run away, but his attackers captured him and beat him to the ground once again. The terrified Smith had to take refuge in a shop. After the attack, but before his arrest, Mulchay pre-empted the argument that young thugs should be put in the army by enlisting as a private in the 20 (Foot) Regiment, stationed at Bury.

In another case from the previous December, five men had been charged with setting upon Richard Ashcroft, who lodged with a family called Forsyth in Leeson Street, Kirkdale. At 4.30 p.m. on a Saturday, Ashcroft and Samuel Forsyth were walking along Whittle Street when they passed John McKnight, Fred Averill, John Prior and Thomas Gregson, who were standing with some dogs outside an alehouse. A drunken McKnight pushed the pair and then grabbed Ashcroft by the collar, demanding some money for beer.

"Let go," cried Aschcroft. "I want to have nothing to do with you."

He pushed McKnight, who fell on the slippery ground. Averill struck Ashcroft, but he too was then knocked down. McKnight rose and attempted another punch, but was again felled. Gregson then struck Ashcroft with his belt. Averill tried to have another go, but was beaten to the floor once more. After being up and down like yo-yos, the gang eventually managed to get Ashcroft on the ground: once he was there, they kicked him almost unconscious.

Whittle Street (1902). Scene of the gang attack upon Richard Ashcroft.

A bloodied but brave Ashcroft, assisted by Forsyth, painfully made his way home, where, as if on a suicide mission, he threw off his coat and went back to have another go. McKnight, Gregson and Prior rushed at Ashcroft, again knocking him to the floor. Gregson shouted, "Let us kick the bastard while we've got him down." McKnight ran to his own house and returned with a pointed tool called an auger, crying, "You bastard, I'll kill you; I'll die for some of you yet." He then thrust the point of the auger at Ashcroft's throat. Prior and Gregson joined in by thrashing Ashcroft with the buckle end of their belts.

Forsyth's father appeared and rescued Ashcroft, but then Gregson's father appeared and also started to attack the victim. Mr Forsyth ended up on the floor on top of his dazed charge. Ashcroft was eventually taken to the Stanley Hospital where he was treated for a fractured finger, head wounds and fainting due to blood loss.

When arrested, McKnight claimed, "Ashcroft is a brother Orangeman of mine and he need not have done this. I have got the worst of it." Averill and the elder Gregson both claimed that they had been assaulted first.

The Beaufort Street outrage involved two rough-looking men, Michael Sinnott and James Rowe. William Ball, a seaman from Fontenoy Street, had been walking along Beaufort Street, Toxteth, in March 1875, when Sinnott stopped him and asked him where he was going.

"That has got nothing to do with you," replied Ball.

Sinnott then tripped him up and, while he had him on the floor, kicked him in the eye. Ball got up, but was again knocked down. This time Rowe booted him in the ribs. The attackers tried to rob the victim's watch, without success, but they did manage to take his purse, which contained five pounds and fourteen shillings. When arrested, Sinnott pleaded, "I am innocent." Rowe declared, "I'll never deny having an upright fight with him."

Also in March, Joseph Ryan was charged with attacking Edward Lynch from Upper Milk Street, not far from the scene of Richard Morgan's murder. On a Sunday afternoon, Ryan and a gang of others had pelted Lynch with cabbage stumps. The following Tuesday, Lynch had been walking along Vauxhall Road when Ryan ran across the street after him and threw a knife, which struck him in the forehead. When arrested, Ryan maintained, "We had a bit of a row, but I did not use a knife."

On April 20, 1875, at 11.30 p.m., Dennis Norton and three others approached Peter Howard in Cazneau Street, off Scotland Road. Norton asked, "Have you any money?" Howard, who was with his wife, replied that it was none of his business and, if he wanted money, he should work for it like he did. The entire incident unfolded like a re-run of the Richard Morgan murder. Howard was stunned with a punch to the side of the head. Two of the gang then grabbed him by the neck and wrestled him to the ground, where he was kicked in the eye and body. His wife jumped on him to protect him from the kicks. Just as Alice Morgan had done, she screamed, "Murder" and, "Police" but was also kicked. Two of the gang escaped, but Norton was later arrested. Fortunately the incident did not end in death.

The same could not be said of an affray on Tuesday, September 18, 1877, in which John Talbot, aged forty-three, was kicked to death by a gang. The incident began when Talbot's wife had a row with twenty-one-year-old Elisa MacIntosh in a court in Freemason's Row, which ran parallel to the Morgans' home of Leeds Street. Talbot and his wife were in the house of a man called Foley, where they were still cele-brating a christening that had taken place the previous Sunday. They were both drunk. MacIntosh came to the door of the house and swore at Mrs Talbot. Her husband went out into the court, only for another young woman to throw a glass mug at his head. Fortunately, he was wearing a hat, which cushioned his skull from injury. A lad then punched Talbot.

Incensed, Talbot went home and returned with a shovel handle. The wood had a piece of string attached to it and Talbot had carefully wrapped the cord around his wrist, so that his arm and the handle were united in one long, lethal weapon.

As Talbot re-entered the court, a man named McCrave saw that he was about to harm somebody. He grabbed hold of Talbot's handle-bearing arm and tried to cut the cord around his wrist. The knife slipped and sliced into Talbot's arm. While he was disabled, a gang including three lads and two women took the opportunity to attack Talbot. They knocked him to the ground and booted him insensible. Mrs Talbot intervened by breaking a plate over the head of one of the women, but was also knocked down and beaten. The kicking lasted for five minutes. Eventually the Talbots managed to get back to the safety of their own home.

John Talbot was in great pain, but although he complained of feeling unwell, he declined immediate medical help. As a result of the kicks to his abdomen, Talbot developed peritonitis, a condition that resulted in his death in the Workhouse Hospital a few days later.

His attackers included Elisa MacIntosh and four others: Martin Kelly, Thomas Jennings and, most amazingly, Mary McCrave and Thomas Mullen, whose brothers had been hanged for Richard Morgan's murder just three years earlier. On his deathbed, Talbot declared that McCrave and Mullen had viciously kicked him in a "dangerous part", probably a reference to his genitals. In fact, three weeks earlier, Mullen had pulled a knife on Talbot and given him another kicking, saying he would do sixteen years for him. Talbot was

The North Dispensary treated many victims of gang violence.

the man who had sheltered Peter Campbell when he had been on the run from the police. The person who held Talbot's arm to stop him using the shovel handle was McCrave's cousin. Detectives Hale and Fitzsimmons arrested the gang – the same policemen who had arrested Michael Mullen and Peter Campbell.

At trial, Mrs Talbot denied that her husband had been involved in another fight with Patrick Toomey the previous Sunday, but admitted that he did "fall" on that day. However, it was later proved that the altercation had indeed taken place. The implication was that the injuries received during the earlier brawl could have contributed to Talbot's death.

McCrave's cousin, although he must have witnessed the entire episode, claimed that he had his back turned and that he did not see who was doing the kicking. Elisa MacIntosh claimed that she had no shoes on at the time of the assault. It was also suggested that any violence used against Talbot was necessary in order to wrestle the shovel handle from him. Talbot was believed to be a violent and very strong man when drunk.

However, the prisoners were found guilty of manslaughter. Mullen and Kelly received twenty years while McCrave and MacIntosh were sentenced to ten years. Mullen was sent to HM Prison Chatham in Kent. Like Campbell, he served his time far away from his old Vauxhall Road stamping ground. In the 1901 census, Mullen was listed as an inmate of the Rice Lane Workhouse in Liverpool. He was forty-one, single and employed as a dock labourer. It is unclear what happened to the child of Mary McCrave and Peter Campbell, but it could hardly have had a more unfortunate start to life, with both parents sent to gaol for lengthy periods for having kicked two men to death.

Newspapers seemed to go cold on the Cornermen as a story after the frenzy of headlines in the mid-1870s, but attacks by them continued to make occasional headlines as some committed brutal crimes, even murder, for the most trivial of reasons. Among the Cornermen, a wrong word spoken or the mere hint of disrespect could quickly escalate into violence, especially if the men had been drinking. Richard Morgan's seemingly innocent question, "Hey! Young man. Where do you work?" was viewed as being sufficiently contemptuous to justify his murder.

The situation was made worse by the ubiquity of lethal weapons. In the nineteenth century, many men routinely carried knives – even if only a penknife – for cutting up tobacco. A seaman's sheath-knife was a tool of the trade, but was occasionally used to "mend or end" quarrels. Even if unarmed, a man could put his clothing to equally deadly uses. Boots and belts were standard uniform. When a trifling argument kicked off, the result could indeed be fatal.

In 1875, local journalist Hugh Shimmin made a revealing comment about the volatile nature of Liverpool violence: "The transition from a coarse word or a ribald jest to a kick, from a poker to a knife, is made with alarming rapidity."[1]

In July 1880, Thomas Cassidy, aged twenty-three, was tortured and killed in horrific circumstances in Kew Street, near Scotland Road. The victim, a well-built man who was habitually drunk, wasn't robbed, but he might have been targeted in revenge for something he had done. The motive remains unclear. There is conflicting evidence as to what sparked the violence, but it clearly wasn't a fair fight.

At about 7 p.m. on a Saturday evening, Michael Lydon, aged twenty, was seen to punch Cassidy in the mouth and grab him by the collar of his coat. Thomas Egerton, aged eighteen, told Lydon to "stick him", while James Curran thrashed Cassidy across the head and shoulders with the buckle end of a belt. While this was happening, John Hughes was waving a docker's hook about in a threatening manner. A crowd, some armed with belts and other weapons, stood around watching the attack. Michael Hessian was returning home when he noticed the disturbance. He asked what was going on, but Lydon, with a knife in his hand, turned and shouted, "Here's another of the bastards." Hughes then struck Hessian with the hook.

While Cassidy was on the floor, Egerton ordered, "Keep him down, now is our time to do him." Egerton then drew the knife across his victim's nose, almost severing it. As the blade sliced through his flesh, Cassidy screamed, "O my God!" He was then stabbed in both legs, including his knee and other parts of his body. Somebody in the crowd then shouted, "Run away," and the attack was brought to a close.

The injured man was taken to a house, where he lay in a pool of blood before being sent to Stanley Hospital. He clung to life for almost a month. The house surgeon revealed that Cassidy eventually died from exhaustion as a result of the continuous discharge of pus from his festering leg wounds.

Lydon, Egerton, Hughes and Curran were all initially charged with murder, but only Egerton and Lydon were ultimately tried at the assizes. The prosecution stated that there had been no provocation from the victim, nor had the parties quarrelled previously. However, Mr Segar, for the defence, called witnesses who stated that Cassidy had first attacked Egerton, knocking him down and kicking him. Egerton was supposed to have left to clean himself up and when he returned Cassidy had already been injured. Since the crowd appeared to be supporters of Egerton and Lydon, it is not surprising that the accused were able to call witnesses in their favour. The victim seems to have been alone and so there was nobody to offer an alternative version of events. It is perhaps significant that one of the witnesses against the attackers had to move from his home in Kew Street after receiving numerous threats.

There was insufficient evidence to suggest that Lydon had been the man holding Cassidy while he was stabbed and he was therefore discharged. Egerton was found not guilty of murder, but was sentenced to twenty years for manslaughter.

An example of how a wrong word could provoke vicious response from the Cornermen occurred in June 1881, when a group of friends were drinking in a public house at the corner of Camden Street and London Road. Mary McCarthy bounded in, had a quick look around and asked, "Is he here?" One of the men, who did not even know the woman, replied jokingly, "Yes he is here," and as he spoke he pushed a mustard pot along the bar towards the woman. She must have been deeply offended, for she stormed out threatening to fetch somebody.

Twenty minutes later, McCarthy returned with two men. At closing time, the woman and one her companions followed the joker and his colleague out of the pub. She pointed at him saying, "There he is." The man's friend tried to explain that the words were spoken simply in jest. McCarthy asked what it had to do with him. He replied that it had everything to do with him. She hit him and then ran off for more lads. Meanwhile, the comedian slapped McCarthy's friend and, in return, was stabbed in the stomach. His colleague was also sliced under the left ear when he tried to apprehend the knifeman. Both men ended up in hospital in a serious condition ... it hadn't even been a funny joke.

The year after Richard Morgan's death, another fatal kicking incident occurred on March 18, when James McLean, aged twenty-five, killed Moses McGrath in Walton Road. Earlier in the day, McGrath

Walton Road (1899). Scene of James McLean's fatal kicking attack on Moses McGrath.

and some of his friends had been to the Grand National steeplechase at Aintree. They had been drinking both during and after the race. As they walked home in jovial mood past Walton Church, they noticed McLean and his friend, a man called Orme, having a race along the road. Perhaps inspired by the horseracing, they tried to outrun each other, but unfortunately Orme tripped and fell. McGrath and his companions burst out laughing, but McLean approached and demanded to know what was so funny. The group ignored him and carried on walking, but McLean and Orme followed for some distance before attacking the men. McGrath was struck in the face and fell. As he lay on the floor, McLean gave him an almighty kick in the head before running away. He was captured a few minutes later hiding in a nearby public urinal.

Upon hearing that the doctor had given up all hope on McGrath, McLean sighed, "Ah, it's another hanging match; but God have mercy upon me and help me through it." McGrath, who had suffered a fracture at the base of his skull, was transferred to the Stanley Hospital and died the next day of an effusion of blood on the brain, caused by the injuries to his head.

In court, McLean's defence argued that the injury might have been caused by the fall rather than by the kick and hence it was manslaughter not murder. It was also suggested that Orme had taken some part in the affray and that he might have been guilty of the fatal blow. During the whole trial, McLean clasped his hands and moved his lips constantly, as if in prayer. After ten minutes, the jury decided on a verdict of manslaughter. The stunned McLean was sentenced to twenty years' imprisonment.

A simple misunderstanding over who was being spoken to led to the senseless death of William Grimes, a man who was himself no stranger to violence. James Young, a twenty-year-old labourer, was accused of murdering Grimes in December 1876. The victim, of Gascoyne Street off Vauxhall Road, was a sailor who had served for five years in the American navy. He had been home for two months and was preparing to go back to sea. On his way to his ship, the *Iberian*, he walked along Vauxhall Road with his brother and a man called Patrick Lynch. All three were perfectly sober. At a public house on the corner of Green Street, the group met three other men including Lawrence Shields, Simon Finnigan and a drunken Young. The two groups were strangers to each other.

"Hey Larry," shouted Finnigan.

Puzzled, William Grimes turned around and pointed out, "There's no Larry here."

"It's all the same," said Finnigan, "but if you were down at the bottom of Lightbody Street, where Frank O'Neill and those fellows live, you would not be so bleedin' smart in turning round."

"Liverpool is a big town, and I suppose a man is allowed to open his mouth," said Grimes.

Lynch added, "What are you shouting after us for? Do you know us? Perhaps you are fellows who want to kick up a row and have a fight."

"No we don't," answered Finnigan. "But you perhaps do."

Finnigan then punched Lynch. Young, who had his hands in his pockets, suddenly pulled out a clasp knife and thrust it at Grimes who leaped back, narrowly avoiding the blade. Grimes' brother shouted, "Mind the knife, Billy, for God's sake mind the knife!" Finnigan and Shields went for the brother as he was trying to rescue William. However, by now William had been stabbed twice in the lung and stomach. Finnigan and Shields ran up Green Street while Young fled towards Scotland Road.

"Billy, are you cut?" asked Grimes's brother.

"Yes, I will be in the next world in half an hour. Send for the priest."

The injured man was taken to a druggist's shop and then to the hospital, where he died the next morning.

Young was arrested on January 2, 1877. He declared he knew nothing about the murder.

At the assizes, Grimes's brother admitted that he had fought a few fights in his time, but always fairly. He also revealed that both he and his brother had been to prison a few times for assaults and for being drunk. Indeed, since William had come home from sea, both brothers had served a month's imprisonment for threatening behaviour. Patrick Lynch also spoke in court to say that he was currently serving a prison sentence for an unrelated crime.

Young's defence conceded that his client had also been to prison a few times, once for taking the rap for his friends. When he was a child, he had also served four years in a reformatory. His lawyer was of the opinion that he had no sense, although in his favour one newspaper reported that he had "a face of a somewhat higher type than of the ordinary street rough or cornerman".

Finnigan claimed that when the three men approached he was simply asking his friend Young for some money. Young replied that he hadn't got a cent. It was at this point that Finnigan turned to Lawrence Shields and joked, "Hey Larry, did you hear that?" This is what sparked the row. Finnigan claimed that he had been punched first. After the stabbing he said that he had seen Young in nearby Hornby Street. Bleeding from the nose and mouth, Young declared, "I've cut that fellow."

Young then followed Finnigan home to Tatlock Street and eventually gave the knife to Finnigan's mother, telling her to dispose of it. She threw it at the back of the fire grate, concluding, "You won't cut another with it." The dejected lad cried, "Oh, Christ! I'll be hung for taking Simon's part." Finnigan shouted, "You should have used your fists, not the knife." Young's girlfriend then entered the room pleading, "Oh, Jemmy, what have you done?"

Shields was the next to give evidence. His version differed slightly. He stated that Lynch had looked around as he was passing the group and Finnigan had asked: "What are you looking at?" Lynch and the Grimes brothers stopped and one of them replied: "I suppose we can look as long as we like." They then walked on, but soon returned to attack Finnigan and Young.

Clarke Aspinall. The Coroner held the inquests on Richard Morgan
and many other victims of gang violence.

In summing up Young's defence, his counsel referred to the "evil character" of the deceased and placed some doubt on the truthfulness of the evidence of the dead man's companions, particularly given their criminal history. He denied that Young had intended to murder his victim and pointed out that there had been some provocation from the other group. However, the jury convicted Young of murder with a recommendation to mercy.

On hearing the verdict, Young clasped his hands and pleaded, "Spare me, my Lord, spare me." As the judge solemnly read the death sentence, the convicted man continually interrupted with heart-rending appeals for mercy: "Spare me, my God, Lord have mercy upon me." He was forcibly dragged from the dock, still screaming to be saved. His prayers were answered and he was later awarded a reprieve.

There were extraordinary scenes at the wake for William Grimes. The body was brought home to his mother's house in Gascoyne Street and placed in the middle of the room. The wake continued for a full week. On the final night before the burial, the event was in full swing with a number of mourners present to pay their respects. According to one report, at 1.30 a.m. on the Sunday morning, as guests were dancing around the body, the floor suddenly collapsed at a slant and the revellers and coffin all fell towards the cellar seven feet below. None of the guests was injured, but the coffin smashed open and the body rolled out, leaving the living and the dead mangled in an undig-nified heap. One young man claimed to have been severely trampled on and had to wait until all the guests had settled down before he could climb out of the place. The situation wasn't helped by cries from the street of "the wake has fallen in" and "the house is on fire", which, although untrue, caused further panic. Police were called to quell the disturbance. Refusing to let this little mishap dampen their spirits, the family had the body placed in another coffin and the wake continued at another house in the court.

The next day the coffin was on its way to Ford Cemetery when the procession reached the precise location in Vauxhall Road where the victim had been stabbed. Some superstitious mourners thought that it would be a good idea if the coffin was taken from the hearse and placed for a few moments on the fatal spot. The police, however, refused permission, much to the disgust of the large crowd.

After the funeral, Grimes's uncle wrote to the newspapers to correct some errors in the reporting of the wake. He claimed that the guests had, in fact, been sober and that no drink had been present on the premises. He also stated that the room in which the coffin had been held was only small and that there had only been twenty people sitting around in a decent, orderly and religious manner. One side of the floor unfortunately gave way and the guests and coffin slid towards the incline. He denied that the coffin had broken open and treated the malicious accusation that there had been dancing with contempt. He also stated that no police had attended the wake. The newspaper left it to the reader to decide which of the two versions to believe.

CHAPTER 8

Bare-Knuckle Grudge Match

IN AUGUST 1875, a year after the Tithebarn Street murder, one of the most brutal prizefights ever staged in Liverpool took place at Aintree. Although such illegal fistfights involved one-to-one violence, they were nevertheless steeped in gang culture. Groups of supporters, financial backers and spectators formed quite large crowds that could be more intimidating than any single gang.

Simon Looney, from Chisenhale Street, off Vauxhall Road, was a notorious hard man around the Vauxhall area and was well known to the police. For some reason he had a grudge against John Mahoney, a fellow dock labourer from Gay Street, at the lower end of Scotland Road. Mahoney claimed that Looney would never leave him alone. On his way to and from work he was constantly approached by Looney with the offer of a fight. Mahoney was much smaller than his muscular tormentor and didn't think that he was up to it. "I am not man enough for you," he said.

At the end of July, Looney, who bore all the hallmarks of a bully, once again approached Mahoney, who was out walking with his wife. The big man informed him, "I want to fight you badly. You will have to fight me next Sunday morning."

"What is it for?" asked Mahoney.

"I'll tell you when I get you on the ground," said Looney.

Mahoney, a family man with religious principles, tried to wriggle out of a contest on the Sabbath by asking for it to take place some other time, but Looney insisted that it be on the Sunday, because he would have plenty of supporters there, who in turn would have plenty of money. Mahoney claimed never to have had a fight in his life, except for a bit of sparring practice with boxing gloves.

On the Saturday night, the police received information that a big fight was to take place just off Love Lane, Pall Mall, the next day. Two inspectors and a number of constables were given the job of preventing it. At 4.30 on Sunday morning, about 300 men assembled at the site, but they were dispersed by the police. The officers went away thinking that they had succeeded in their mission.

When the time came, Mahoney's wife, mother and brother all tried to stop him from leaving the house. However, Looney's people came for him and he reluctantly went off to fight. Halfway there, he was informed that there were police waiting for them at the venue, so he turned back home.

Later in the day, Looney sent men to the house for a second time to tell Mahoney to meet at a public house known as Dandy Pat's, off Scotland Road, at 1 p.m. When he arrived, Mahoney was then told to meet Looney at Walton Junction.

However, between 2 p.m. and 3 p.m., Inspector McConchie, who was on duty in Scotland Road, noticed a crowd of men moving towards Kirkdale. Accompanied by some other officers, the inspector followed. At the brickfields near Kirkdale, the crowd spotted the police and scattered across Westminster Road, through Breeze Hill towards Walton. The officers followed for some distance outside the boundary of the borough, before passing on information to the county constabulary.

Undeterred, the pugilists and a number of their friends obtained spring-carts and made their way to Aintree racecourse. Some county police officers, unaware of what had occurred earlier, decided to investigate the crowd. The police suspected that something illegal was going on, but found the men lying innocently on the grass. Knowing that they were under suspicion, some of the men then ran foot races to throw the police off the scent.

Looney approached Mahoney and repeated his offer of a fight. "I want you," he said, before shaking his hand.

Mahoney again enquired, "What is this about?"

"You will have to fight me now," said Looney.

"This is hard for two Irishmen to fall out like that," complained Mahoney.

But Looney was already stripped to his boots and trousers, and Mahoney claimed that the crowd now forcibly tore off his own clothes to get him ready for the contest. The biggest instigator of the fight was John Coyle.

Unable to wait any longer, preparations were then made for the bout to begin, while the police tried in vain to prevent it. The spectators, some carrying sticks, slingshots and bludgeons, defied the officers and even threatened them with violence if they broke into the ring. By now, the crowd had swelled to over 400 people. The fight, for £5 a side, began with the officers reduced to spectators, unable to do anything about it.

The scrap itself was a fair stand-up contest with no kicking. A dozen men armed with sticks and belts formed a makeshift ring. Bottle holders and seconds attended each corner. Both combatants were sober. One policeman remarked afterwards that the most brutal aspect of the fight was the atrocious behaviour of the spectators. The ring-keepers had to repeatedly beat back the crowd with their belts and sticks to maintain order.

Like David and Goliath, the men squared up to each other. Looney had the better of the first round, knocking his opponent down. However, for the next three or four rounds the points were equal. Perhaps Mahoney underestimated his own boxing skills for, as the fight progressed, he came out on top. He floored Looney and a man called Kelly had to pick him up. After five or six rounds, a concerned Kelly jumped into the ring and declared Mahoney the winner. A jubilant Mahoney agreed with the decision.

However, Coyle, who was acting as Looney's second, asked his man, "Are you licked?" The battered, but proud, Irishman replied: "No, we will have it out." Then a man named Corrance jumped into the ring and offered odds on Looney to continue the fight. Mahoney, knowing that he now had the better of his opponent, prayed for Looney's backers to come in for him. Meanwhile, the crowd threatened to knock off Mahoney's head if he gave in. Mahoney argued that he had only agreed to fight on because he wanted to finish it before the police locked them all up. The contest continued until Mahoney knocked Looney down again with an almighty blow to the chin, which rocked his head to one side. Looney's seconds picked him up, but he groaned, "I will fight no more until tomorrow."

Meanwhile, information had been sent to Bootle police station that a crowd of suspicious men had been seen making their way across the fields at the back of Walton Gaol. A body of police were sent out after the crowd, but at this point they didn't know where the men were headed or why. When they finally reached the Aintree venue, they were able to assist the officers already present. The police broke into the ring and grabbed some of the men. Five of the ringleaders were arrested, including the backers, seconds and ring-keeper. In the melee, Mahoney was carried from the ring by his friends and managed to escape along the canal.

Looney was badly injured. As he was carted away, his head hung awkwardly and he begged to be laid down because he was choking. He had a fractured jaw and nose and blood trickled from his left ear. One eye, which had a gash above it, had shut completely. He was taken to Bootle Hospital, where he remained unconscious until just after midnight, at which point he died of concussion of the brain. The bout had lasted between sixteen and twenty rounds, a total of forty ferocious minutes.

Those arrested included Michael Farraher of Newsham Street, and Joseph McCann of Chisenhale Street, who had both acted as seconds. John Coyle of Clement Street, Thomas Glennon of Bevington Street and John Jones of Maguire Street were also taken into custody, all accused of manslaughter as aiders and abettors of the fighters. All of the men came from the Vauxhall and Scotland Road areas.

Mahoney, badly injured about the face, escaped to Bootle, arriving back in Liverpool at about 9 p.m. He was warned by friends not to go home, but felt that he had done nothing wrong. The next morning he saw a newspaper placard announcing "The Prizefight at Aintree". The poster stated that a man was in a serious condition. Mahoney gave someone a shilling to go to the hospital to check on Looney's health. The man returned an hour later to say that he had seen him in the "deadhouse". To his credit, on the Monday afternoon the devastated Mahoney voluntarily gave himself up to an officer in Great Howard Street, saying, "I believe the man is dead and I want to give myself up for causing his death."

At the assizes, all the arrested men were convicted of manslaughter with Mahoney recommended for mercy. He was gaoled for four months, while the others received sentences of six weeks.

SOME PRIZEFIGHTS took place on a more amicable footing than the Looney-Mahoney bout. In November 1883, a contest took place at a mystery location within a ten-mile radius of the Liverpool Exchange. The opponents were a powerful Warrington fighter "of some notoriety" and a Manchester man. Both boxers had trained for the fight for some time: the Warrington man at Blackpool and the Manchester man at Altrincham. The Warrington fighter weighed in at thirteen stone and was five feet ten-and-a-half inches tall. His opponent was lighter and smaller at ten stone seven pounds and a mere five feet seven-and-a-half inches. However, he compensated for his physical shortcomings by possessing greater boxing skills.

The only Liverpool man present at the fight acted as a neutral referee and stakeholder. The event was properly organised, attracting a crowd of about sixty spectators, mainly from the Manchester area. The prize was £25 a side and there was also some brisk betting. The wagers opened at three to one on the Warrington man, with the odds increasing to six to one at the end of the third round, after the Manchester man had been knocked down three times in a row. The last knockdown was particularly brutal, as the fighter had been punched in the throat.

However, at the start of the fourth round, the smaller man reversed his fortunes. As with the Aintree fight, superior boxing skills triumphed over brute strength and the Manchester man went on to win a decisive victory in sixteen rounds, with the fight lasting a total of thirty-six minutes. At the end of the twelfth round, a bookmaker, who had netted several hundred pounds on the fight, offered fifty to one against the Warrington boxer, but had no takers.

The loser was severely beaten about the face and head, suffering two broken ribs. He had to be removed to a local public house where he received surgical treatment. The victor, who was none the worse for the encounter, was taken to Edge Hill station from where he returned to Manchester.

It wasn't just men who were involved in organised brawls, although the manly rules of a fair fight were generally abandoned when women heard the first bell. In August 1880, Lambert Street in Islington was the scene of a brutal conflict between two women of "the unfortunate class".

One afternoon, a journalist's attention was drawn to two large crowds; the supporters of two women who were set to engage in battle. As the opposing crowds approached, they greeted each other with verbal abuse and threatening gestures. As the groups finally met, the two women launched into each other like cats, tearing each other's hair out and scratching the skin off each other's faces. The journalist noted that the cuts looked like knife wounds rather than nail injuries. One woman had a gash that ran the whole length of her face: her nose, lips and ears were in a similarly bloody state.

Proper rounds of boxing were not observed, although after a while the fighting stopped for a moment as the women caught their breath. The brawl then continued, with each woman resuming a hold of the other's hair. Eventually one woman managed to get the other on the floor where, instead of a count of ten being taken up, the victor stooped over her opponent and repeatedly smashed her head on the pavement, rendering her unconscious.

Passers-by didn't dare interfere with the fight, although a few concerned citizens searched in vain for a policeman. The champion and her supporters retired to a nearby alehouse to celebrate the victory, leaving a couple of veteran women pugilists relating stories of their own bloody encounters, boasting of how they "got three months" now and then. The loser was left lying on the floor until she became conscious, at which point she was helped away by her friends.

CHAPTER 9

Sectarian Gangs

RELIGIOUS HOSTILITY BETWEEN Catholics and Protestants spilled into open warfare on the streets of both the north and south of Liverpool in the Victorian era. The major period covered in this book, 1874 to 1886, was a particularly turbulent time for the religious factions. Vast numbers of Irish immigrants arriving in the wake of the Great Famine (see Chapter 16, The Social Causes of Gang Violence) brought their loyalties and grievances with them in a period when the future of their troubled homeland lay in the balance, and their street conflicts reflected the wider canvas of British and Irish politics.

The Liberal leader William Ewart Gladstone became British Prime Minster in 1868 and immediately declared, "My mission is to pacify Ireland." In 1870, the Home Rule Association was formed, urging the repeal of the Act of Union with Ireland and the establishment of a parliament in Dublin with responsibilities for domestic affairs. In the 1874 election, the HRA won over fifty seats at Westminster, and six years later Charles Stewart Parnell was elected leader of the Irish parliamentary party. He quickly adopted obstructionist tactics in parliament to force the Government to attend to Irish affairs, while at the same time the secretive Fenians conducted a campaign of violence with the same goals in mind.

The Orange Order had formed in 1795, in County Armagh, to promote the continuation of British rule and Protestant supremacy. So when Gladstone, the British prime minister, declared in favour of Irish home rule in December 1885, the Orange Order enjoyed a revival and became a determined force of resistance. Gladstone's attempt to carry a Home Rule Bill through the Commons in June

1886 was defeated by thirty votes. Feelings ran high in Irish communities.

"Liverpool was peculiarly situated as regards the Irish question," recalled Head Constable William Nott-Bower. "A large district of the town was quite as Irish as any district in Dublin and 'Nationalists' and 'Orangemen' were as strongly represented and as antagonistic as in Belfast."[1] It was as if the entire Irish problem had been concentrated into a few square miles of the city, leading to inevitable eruptions of trouble and, occasionally, civil war.

The July 12 Orange celebrations, commemorating William of Orange's victory over the Roman Catholic James II at the Battle of the Boyne, were a focal point for disorder. The act of marching into areas was a show of strength that was, more often than not, met with demonstrations of territorial resistance from the Catholic community. Singing songs such as "The Boys of Wexford" or "Boyne Water" was seen as an act of gross provocation. St Patrick's Day celebrations produced a similar reaction from the Protestant side.

After the July 12 celebrations of 1877, a riot took place in Bootle. When the Orange Lodge signalled their intention to hold their annual demonstration in the area, there were justifiable fears of disorder, for there were an estimated 3,000 Irish navvies living and working in the district, almost all of them Catholics. However, on the day, the procession was well policed and passed without incident, with the Orangemen dispersing without any disturbances.

However, at 8 p.m. a Police Inspector Moss noticed 200 Irish navvies making their way southwards along the canal bank towards Bootle village. The men were marching four deep in military formation and it was obvious that they were intent on trouble. Most of the police had gone off duty at 6 p.m. and the inspector was forced to send messengers in cabs to Seaforth and Waterloo to muster the support of about fifty constables.

The Irishmen were now marching towards Liverpool and the inspector decided to telegraph Derby Road bridewell to warn them of imminent trouble. The warning was justified, since many of the Irishmen carried slingshots and it was later discovered that several of them had recently purchased revolvers. It seems that they were marching to Scotland Road to attack some Orangemen.

At Stanley Road, a squad of officers arrived just in time to intercept the men and to prevent them from entering the borough. The disappointed navvies turned back to Bootle, accompanied by Inspector Moss and thirty of his men to deter them from attacking any Orangemen on the way. As the disgruntled Irishmen marched back, their numbers increased to about 1,000 men.

Frustrated in their attempts to have a fight with their natural enemies, and peeved at being kept under constant surveillance, the navvies took their anger out on the police. The attack began in Balliol Road with stone throwing. The very first volley seriously injured three officers, who were taken to hospital. One constable had his forehead cut open to the bone and a colleague had his shin stripped of skin by a sharp brick or some other jagged weapon.

After a tense stand-off, the order was given to draw truncheons and charge the crowd. At the "double quick" the officers were soon among their adversaries. In the hand-to-hand combat that followed, several Irishmen received severe blows to the head while policemen were also hurt. After a few minutes, the navvies dispersed and took refuge in the houses of streets adjoining Derby Road, where many of them lived. They continued their attacks by throwing bricks and anything else they could lay their hands on out of the windows. Some climbed onto the roofs, from which vantage point they rained missiles on the police below.

Order was finally restored at 11.30 p.m. when several ringleaders were arrested. Public-spirited local publicans closed their doors half an hour earlier than usual but kept the gaslights burning in order for the police to see what they were doing. Inspector Moss also sent messages to many of the Orange leaders advising them to persuade their members to stay indoors. This certainly helped prevent an escalation of the disturbances. Elsewhere in Liverpool, rival groups made several attempts to burn effigies of the Pope and William III, but the police prevented them from doing so.

It had been suggested that a gang called the Hibernians was the forerunner of the more notorious High Rip (see Chapter 12).[2] The Hibernians were active in the 1860s around Wright Street and Limekiln Lane, off Scotland Road. They might have originated in the Ancient Order of the Hibernians, founded by Irish-Catholics in America to promote self-defence, social and economic justice and the cause of Irish nationalism. In Liverpool, local Hibernian societies, such as the Benevolent Hibernian Society and the Hibernian Mechanical Society, were active in the public houses serving the Catholic communities. It is highly unlikely that these organisations were involved with violence. The term "Hibernians" could simply refer to the fact that the gang was Irish. Indeed, the Hibernians were still going strong in 1878.

In August of that year, a gang, including two women, were charged with assaulting a policeman after a free fight in Wright Street involving the Hibernians and the Home Rulers. The rioting, which had carried over from the night before, required twenty policemen to regain order in the street. In court, a witness declared that the combatants did not even know the meaning of the terms Hibernian and Home Rule. In other words, they just enjoyed a punch-up.

The case recalls a trial in Manchester where an old soldier was accused of stabbing a man. As he plunged the blade into his victim, the knifeman shouted, "Take that. I'm a Fenian." The judge asked the soldier what he had to say for himself. He replied, "I've been wounded in the head, sir, and spirits drove me mad. I hadn't touched them for years till this day, and do not know what Fenianism is."

Religious differences were often a mask for plain brutality and even the distinctions between the faiths themselves started to become muddled. In March 1888, John Richards, a fourteen-year-old from Brassey Street, was walking along Upper Harrington Street in Toxteth when Michael Slaven, a year older, attacked him. Slaven jumped out of an entry and shouted, "I'll kill you and hang for you and then I'll be satisfied." He then stabbed Richards in the face, puncturing his lip. This was not the first time that Slaven had attacked Richards, having previously appeared in court for a similar assault on his victim. The magistrate asked what the quarrel had been about. Richards explained that it was because he was the only Protestant in the neighbourhood. His attacker was supposed to have said to other lads, "He's a Protestant, let's kill him." Slaven interrupted to state that he was a Protestant himself, to which his mother proudly added, "He's a real Protestant." The court erupted into laughter.

In June 1878, a group of Irishmen, motivated by "national animosity", murdered a man in Litherland. Robert Bradshaw had been walking with two friends near to the Litherland Arms Hotel when he encountered a group of about thirty Irishmen. A few words were exchanged and Bradshaw was knocked to the ground and kicked. The attackers moved off, but were followed by the victim and his friends. It seems that Bradshaw wanted to retrieve his hat, which had been taken during the assault. Meanwhile, the Irishmen had armed themselves with hedge-stakes and, during the subsequent altercation, they beat Bradshaw over the head. He died a few days later from his injuries.

The Irishmen were convicted of manslaughter after trying to claim self-defence, despite the fact that the victims had been outnumbered by ten to one. James Carney was sentenced to six years and his brother Michael to five years. Two others received twelve months. "It is sad to find in Liverpool so many cases in which brutal and ferocious violence is used without regard to personal safety or life," lamented Justice Cockburn at the assizes.

The atmosphere in Liverpool around the time of the July Orange celebrations was always volatile. While having a drink in a public house in New Quay, in July 1878, William Griffiths thought that it would be good fun to hold an orange lily in his mouth. William Coady took offence and warned, "I will go for him." Shortly after, in Bath Street, near to the docks, Coady took out a knife and stabbed Griffiths.

Wearing an orange lily was seen as a provocative act to many Catholics. Ten years earlier, the Police Court heard how a man had thrust his lily at a Catholic saying, "How do you like the smell of that?" The judge asked the Catholic how he had responded. "I did not like it at all," the man replied, "so I let him have the smell of my fist."

Songs from either faction were also seen as great incitements to violence. During the 1878 July celebrations, Orangeman James Canning murdered Catholic John Barrett, both of Tindall Street, off Scotland Road. At 11 p.m. on July 15, Canning took offence at some children in the street who were singing a derogatory song about William of Orange. He shouted "bleeding Papes" at them. A crowd congregated outside the house and a row took place. Canning's door and windows were broken and he came out carrying a poker, boasting he had "the heart's blood of an Orangeman". He waved the poker indiscriminately, assaulting a boy called Luke Sharkey. John Barrett tried to take the injured lad back to his own house, but was also beaten over the head with the poker. Barrett's skull was smashed into thirteen pieces "like a china saucer" and he died a few days later.

Whenever the newspapers reported hostility between different areas within Liverpool, the cases usually involved religious differences. One such feud centred on the historical animosity between residents in Addison Street and Hodson Street, at the bottom end of Scotland Road. Addison Street had previously been known as both Dead Man's Lane and Sick Man's Lane on account of it being the place where plague victims had been buried; a fact that speaks volumes about the dark social history of the area. It seems that an imaginary geographical and sectarian line divided the lower halves of the streets from the upper halves and the tension between the sides simmered constantly. In July 1879, a pitched battle was fought between gangs from the different halves.

It started on a Saturday as a simple dispute between two militiamen from the opposing factions, but by 5 p.m. on Monday the skirmish had escalated into a full-blown war involving at least 200 people on each side. Shops and public houses had to be closed for safety as missiles flew through the air.

As the police moved in to make arrests, Andrew Stewart and Thomas Newall beat one officer over the head with a poker. The men ran off and when they had finally been tracked down to a house, managed to climb onto the roof and run from property to property like Spring-Heeled Jacks until they were captured. John Waterson resisted arrest by cracking another policeman over the head with a poker. Yet another unfortunate constable took the full force of a brick on the head.

Policemen experienced in patrolling the area admitted that they had never seen anything like it before. Chief Superintendent Hancox brought into the court, as evidence, a cartload full of bricks and stones that had been thrown during the riot and collected after the hostilities had ceased. Stewart and Newall were remanded, while Waterson, a veteran of twelve court appearances, received three months' imprisonment with hard labour. The rest of those convicted, including quite a few women for throwing stones, received the maximum fine of forty shillings and costs with the alternative of one month's imprisonment.

On July 12, 1880, Ezra Male killed an Orangeman called Matthew Foulkes. The men lived opposite each other in Beresford Street, although they had never spoken to each other. On the fateful day, Foulkes travelled to Hale with his wife and some friends and family in a small wagon. The Orange Lodge happened to be holding a demonstration in Hale, although the Foulkes family claimed they had simply gone there for an outing rather than to celebrate.

They returned home at 7.30 p.m., and as they climbed down from their wagon, merrily sang "God Save the Queen". Three youths, incensed at the perceived provocation, threw a couple of bricks at them from the roof of Male's house opposite. Male himself was not involved. Police arrived to arrest the youths and this caused some disturbance. About 200 people gathered in the street, some of them cheering the arrest.

Mrs Foulkes and Mrs Male, who was holding a baby at the time, then began fighting in the street. Foulkes accused the other woman of being the cause of the stone throwing. She pulled at Mrs Male's hair and, in the commotion, Ezra Male ran from his house and stabbed Mrs Foulkes in the arm. Her own husband rushed out to protect her but, in the ensuing struggle, he was knifed in the ribs and stomach, with the blade ripping open a gaping wound from which his bowels spilled out. He died the next day.

Male's defence tried to argue that it was not a sectarian dispute, since Male himself was a Protestant, although his wife was Catholic. However, Male was found guilty of manslaughter and received twenty years' imprisonment.

Sectarian violence in Liverpool occasionally went beyond tit-for-tat attacks by Catholics and Orangemen. In 1881, a Fenian group tried to blow up the Town Hall and Hatton Garden police station. One bomb exploded in the lobby of the police house, where the young constables lived. Fortunately nobody was killed in the wreckage.

June 1883 brought a horrific sectarian revenge attack in which a group of "Irishmen" were subjected to unspeakable torture and disfigurement – although nobody was actually hurt. Allsop's Waxwork Museum, in Lime Street, housed a display of effigies representing the May 1882 Phoenix Park atrocity in Dublin, when the Invincibles, a splinter group of the Fenian movement, had assassinated Lord Frederick Cavendish, the Chief Secretary for Ireland, and his secretary, Thomas Henry Burke. Both men were hacked to pieces with surgical knives. Close to the wax display was another exhibit featuring James Carey, the leader of the gang who, after directing the murders, turned Queen's evidence and betrayed his fellow members, leading to five of them being hanged.

A gang of Irishmen visited the exhibition, and when they thought that nobody was looking, they smashed the figures, pulverising Carey's head to a powder before throwing it onto the pile of broken limbs and mutilated torsos of the other models. The damage to the six mannequins amounted to between two and three hundred pounds. A young boy witnessed the attack, raised the alarm and three men were arrested, while another escaped. On their way to the bridewell, one of the prisoners declared, "You can hang me now that I've settled the informer." In court, the men's defence tried to argue that the worst crime was the awful likenesses of the figures. The owner of the museum defended the models by saying that they were made from photographs. Carey was himself murdered in 1883.

In April 1886, the Nelson True Blues drum-and-flute band took a break from marching to take some refreshment at a public house in Kelvin Street, Kensington. An argument broke out between the men and when the police came to restore order William Boyd gave PC Murphy a pair of black eyes. As Boyd was being taken into custody, the crowd also attacked the police with stones, with one brick hitting the same officer on the back of the head. The mob then crushed the police into the doorway of a baker's shop in an attempt to rescue the prisoner. The police managed to escape with Boyd through the shop and out of the back, but not before another shower of bricks had shattered the window, causing twenty pounds' worth of damage.

Almost 100 years before the infamous Toxteth riots, the district was well known as a "disturbed area" on account of the religious rioting there. In 1886, at the height of the reign of the north-side High Rip gang, there was frequent fighting in Toxteth between Catholics and Orangemen. The Home Rule election campaign only heightened the tension between the groups, leading to periodic outbreaks of disorder.

On July 2, 1886, an Orange band marched from Toxteth to Lime Street, where the police turned them back. The band, accompanied by a growing crowd, returned to Toxteth, where they attempted to march past St Patrick's Church. Again the police intervened, but this time they were outnumbered by the large mob and forty-nine panes of glass in the church and school were smashed with stones. Three months earlier, a similar group had attacked the presbytery. A rumour spread that a priest from St Patrick's had been severely injured, and although without foundation the report further fanned the flames of unrest.

Outraged Catholics gained quick revenge by breaking the windows of several rival churches, including Holy Trinity, Hyslop Street Presbyterian, the Baptist Mission in Jackson Street and the Toxteth Tabernacle. Over the course of the weekend, street fights broke out all over "the lower parts" of Toxteth, resulting in fifty to sixty casualties being treated at the Southern Hospital.

On July 5, Elizabeth Molloy, a powerful, well-built woman, walloped Margaret Sibbell in Crump Street, Toxteth. Molloy, a Catholic, had a history of verbally abusing her Protestant neighbour and her children. All day, a drunken Molloy had been shouting, "We'll have Home Rule." She entered Sibbell's yard and taunted the woman: "King Billy's living – I'm waiting for you." Molloy then smacked Sibbell, beating her to the ground. The victim got up and ran indoors, but her attacker followed and again knocked her down. Molloy then jumped on Sibbell, fracturing one of her ribs. In court, Molloy tried to argue that another woman had committed the assault. However, she was found guilty and sentenced to one month's imprisonment.

Also on July 5, the disturbances continued as several hundred Catholics and Orangemen fought hand-to-hand in the largely Catholic Addison Street, off Scotland Road. Sticks, stones and bludgeons were used on the ground, while aerial bombardments were also launched as men took to the roofs to rain slates and fragments of chimney pots onto the enemy heads below.

Elsewhere, Catholic Kew Street took on Orange Bostock Street in a grudge match. The two streets run parallel to each other off Scotland Road and between 800 and 900 people took part in the disturbances, which continued night and day. Bricks rained through the air to cries of, "There's a Parnellite!" (a supporter of the Irish nationalist leader Charles Stewart Parnell). Once again, men took to the roofs to launch attacks. Slates flew back and forth between the housetops of the two streets, leaving houses nearly gutted. When John Griffin, aged seventeen, had eventually been brought down from a roof, he merely continued his bombardment at ground level.

Catherine Kidd was arrested and sent to prison for a month with hard labour for being drunk in Kew Street and for throwing stones at the back windows of houses in Bostock Street at around dawn on a

Wednesday. John Hardman also appeared in court a week later charged with stoning a policeman. A drunken Hardman had led a crowd through a passage leading from Kew Street to Bostock Street, where they threw bricks at an opposing faction. He was fined forty shillings. Mr Raffles, the stipendiary magistrate, suggested to Detective Grubb that handbills containing the details of such cases, together with the fines imposed, should be distributed throughout the affected areas in a bid to deter further trouble.

Again in July, Catholic homes in Downe Street, off Richmond Row, were besieged by a mob of between thirty and fifty young men. The gang rampaged through the street throwing stones at innocent bystanders. "We'll give you Home Rule," shouted one of them. "I'm a bleeding good Orangeman." William Turton, John W. Holt and Henry Bird were the ringleaders of the gang. Twelve men subsequently appeared in court accused of having smashed every door and window of a number of houses in the street. Once inside the premises, they had completely wrecked the homes and stolen anything of value.

Mary Gill, a Catholic woman, revealed how the gang had broken into her house and taken away a chair, two chimney ornaments and a looking-glass. Her terrified husband had taken refuge in the cellar, leaving Mrs Gill at the mercy of the mob. She decided to stay put to protect her children and was consequently kicked by the gang and hit in the forehead with a stone.

Mary Ann O'Brien stated that the gang also targeted her house. They had smashed her furniture and pictures, pulled down the outside railings and torn up the steps. They had then thrown the large stones though the windows. The only reason she could give for being attacked was that she once "went witness" against a relative of one of the attackers. A neighbour called Mary Jane Smith was also assaulted in her own home. She appeared in the witness box with her head heavily bandaged.

As the gang left Mrs Smith's house, they shouted, "Here's a bleeding house not finished yet." One of the men then threw a bucket through the window. When they had completed their orgy of vandalism, twenty panes of glass had been broken in the last house alone. Ellen McGarry shouted that she would go for the police, but the gang then chased her down the street into her own home, where they smashed all of her windows. The riot lasted for about twenty minutes.

A few weeks later, Mary Gill was attacked again for daring to give evidence against the gang. Thomas Parry, the brother of one of the men charged with the Downe Street affray, saw Mrs Gill in the street. He punched her to the ground and kicked her in the side, fracturing her ribs.

Again, in July 1886, an old woman called Bridget Connor led a contingent of about 150 Catholic youngsters from Norfolk Street to an Anglican Church school in St James' Road, Toxteth. The woman then incited the boys to commit vandalism, telling them to "run along and smash the windows". She lobbed a few bricks herself for good measure.

A gang of Catholics also attacked a shoemaker in his Mill Street workshop. Isaac W. Smythe, an Orange bandmaster, used to let part of his premises as an Orange Lodge, with a room for the band to practise. William Burke and two other youths came to the door and screamed, "You bleeding Orange bandmaster, we will burn this bleeding place down." They then forced their way inside and stabbed the man about the face and body. The police caught Burke shortly afterwards. He gave the excuse, "It's all drink." He was fined forty shillings and costs or one month's imprisonment in default.

One evening in August 1886, a band, followed by a crowd, marched through High Park Street, Toxteth, smashing the windows of the presbytery and church of Mount Carmel. It seems that for some time the Catholics had quietly submitted to having their school and church windows smashed by rowdies of the opposite faction. Initially, they protested in the press and called for greater police protection. However, on September 19, the aggrieved Catholics eventually took the law into their own hands by stoning an Orange band and breaking their instruments. It was felt that Liverpool was becoming as bad as Belfast.

On the same day, in the south of the city, a group of Socialist demonstrators took to the streets calling for a general observance of an eight-hour working day, relief works for the unemployed and other measures. As the afternoon progressed, disturbances broke out and attacks were made on the police as they tried to make arrests. With religious and political disturbances reported at one end of Liverpool and the High Rip active in the north, the whole city must have seemed on the brink of disorder and anarchy.

In October 1886, a newspaper correspondent called the "Citizen" offered information on Liverpool's gangland scene:

> We have not only the High Rippers to deal with, but three other gangs, of which I will name the "Logwood", the "Dead Rabbit", and the "Finnon Haddie" gangs. Each of these gangs has organisation and a recognised captain and sub-captain, and each gang has its own way of working. Sometimes they come into collision with each other, and then there is a general row among them, when the police, if there are any handy, may lock one or two of them up for fighting.[3]

The "Dead Rabbit" was most likely named after an infamous nine-teenth-century New York gang, later immortalised in the Martin Scorsese movie *Gangs Of New York*. The American gang was originally attached to the Roach Guards, based in the murderous Five Points district of Manhattan, but legend has it that somebody threw a dead rabbit into the middle of the room during a heated dispute between members. Some took this as an omen and formed their own break-away gang named after the animal. They then marched into battle led by somebody carrying a rabbit impaled on a spike.[4] New York, like Liverpool, had a large contingent of Irish immigrants and the name of the gang must have travelled.

The "Finnon Haddie" remains a mystery. A finnan haddie is a Scottish term for a dish of smoked haddock, originally prepared in the town of Findhorn. There might well have been some Scottish ruffians in the city. Perhaps there is also some Irish connection, possibly related to somebody called Finn or Finnon.

The High Rip and the Logwood, whose antics are chronicled later, would become the most notorious of the Liverpool gangs of the 1880s, and would terrorise the northern districts in particular. Their roots lay partly in the sectarian gangs, but also in the growing number of youth gangs emerging from the filthy ginnels of the city slums.

CHAPTER 10

Tiny Terrors and Juvenile Gangs

FROM LITTLE ACORNS grow great oaks, so the saying goes. The same could be said of gangs. Criminals have to start somewhere, and gang members such as John "Holy Fly" McCrave seem to have been born into a life of villainy. Parents in the poorer parts of Liverpool often turned a blind eye to the criminal behaviour of their offspring, particularly if they could take a share of their spoils. Others, no doubt driven by poverty and desperation, actively encouraged their children to steal. However, as they sat in court waiting for their children to be sentenced, some parents must have wondered where they had gone wrong.

There were limitless opportunities for pilfering in Victorian cities. Street traders exhibiting their wares, and shops displaying goods outside, were easy targets for a quick snatch and run. In addition, a network of pawnbrokers helped shift anything that wasn't edible. In 1880, there were 190 pawnshops in Liverpool accepting 50,000 pledges a week.

Some youngsters were also inducted into burglary by older youths, who took advantage of their small bodies by bringing them along on jobs where a child could easily squeeze through small windows and tiny spaces. Of course, theft, not violent crime, was usually the errant child's first introduction to the legal system, although there were some ruthless young tearaways who armed themselves like any adult gangster.

In 1885, Richard Hale, aged about ten, was charged with stabbing another youngster in Stanley Road, Bootle. A lad had left a shop carrying some pears in his hands. Hale snatched a pear and ran away. Twelve-year-old George Kellar witnessed the robbery and gave chase, but when he caught Hale, the boy pulled out a knife and stabbed him in the shoulder, delivering a quite serious wound. In court, Hale admitted the offence, but claimed that Kellar had previously thrashed him with a belt, an accusation that the other boy vehemently denied. At the time, Hale was on the run from the workhouse and the prosecution thought that it was futile to send him back, as he would only run away again. It was the fourth time that he had been in custody.

However, it was gangs rather than individuals that caused the vast majority of the trouble. While most of these gangs remained anonymous, they occasionally took the name of the street where they lived, such as the Lemon Street Gang. Often they comprised a couple of brothers and other relatives. Sometimes a group of young boys would run away from the parental home and live a life of absolute freedom – until they got caught.

The Lemon Street mob were just one of a number of youth or child gangs – the Blackstone Street Gang, the Regent Street Gang, the Housebreakers' and several others – that sprang up in this period. Indeed, in one single month – September 1876 – Liverpool saw a veritable juvenile crime wave. It seems that publicans in particular had become the targets for a band of tiny thieves. Young boys would look out for opportunities, quickly slip round the bar and take whatever fortune favoured them, but with the emphasis very much on cash. They usually escaped undetected. These crimes coincided with a visit to Liverpool by a group of social scientists attending a congress on crime, at which Mr Stubbs, from the Dale Street Magistrates' Office, was due to give a talk on "crime and its consequences". A newspaper suggested that the social scientists take a look at this worrying new trend among young boys.

To counter the crime wave, a squad of four experienced detectives was put on the case. After a crackdown, they arrested thirty-three boys with an average age of fourteen. Some were less than twelve, the eldest seventeen. In October 1876, the children were brought up before the magistrate in small groups and were all charged with stealing from public houses during the previous two months.

William Hudson and William Franklin, two eleven-year-olds, were accused of stealing over four pounds from a public house in High Park Street, Toxteth. One of the boys was reported to have distracted the landlady by asking for change for sixpence, while the other sneaked in and committed the robbery. They were both found guilty and sentenced to eleven days' imprisonment and five years in a reformatory.

Ford Street (1897). Children grew up in squalor. Some turned to crime to survive.

Matthew Runcie, Peter Kelly, James Coleman (alias Leggy) and George Morgan (alias Rhino) were charged with burgling a shop in Standish Street, off Marybone. A shutter was removed and a pane of glass taken out of its frame. The gang stole three pounds and were only caught after a policeman heard them making so much noise as they were arguing over their share of the spoils.

Six boys were found guilty of stealing a cashbox from a public house in Oakfield Road, Anfield, in September. Two of the gang were sentenced to ten days' prison plus five years' detention at the Birkdale Reformatory Farm. Another pair was given ten days in prison and five years on the reformatory ship *Akbar*, moored in the River Mersey. The final two were sentenced to one month's imprisonment.

Five lads were charged with taking a cashbox from a public house in Anfield Road. The boys were arrested in a model-lodging house in Richmond Road, Islington, which had become a den of thieves. Others involved came from Sawney Pope Street, Richmond Row and Oldham Street, an area, one newspaper informed its readers, where social science was something of an unknown concept.

Another group consisted of seventeen-year-old Thomas Devaney, who was believed to be the captain and leader of the "Housebreakers' Gang". His "first mate" was Thomas Crawley, aged fourteen. Three others appeared in the dock alongside them. It was remarked that two of them looked as though they were impossible to reform. Their crime sprees had been quite lucrative. The gang stole twenty pounds from a public house in Park Road, Toxteth, four pounds from William Baker's public house and twelve pounds from another public house in Richmond Row, off St Anne Street.

Another gang took historical villains as their role models. Gang members went by the pseudonyms Jack Harkaway, "Light-Fingered" Jack, Dick Turpin and other names deriving from the annals of highway robbery. Such characters were featured in popular stories published at the time, known as "penny bloods", or to their critics "penny dreadfuls". These publications were the forerunners of the comic book and provided cheap entertaining reading for the working classes. Aimed at a youthful, increasingly literate, audience, they contained lurid illustrations and brutal tales of crime and adventure. Titles included *Sweeney Todd*, *Varney the Vampire: or the Feast of Blood* and *Spring-Heeled Jack: The Terror of London*.

TINY TERRORS AND JUVENILE GANGS

It was widely felt that such immoral literature perversely stimulated and corrupted young people's imaginations. These boy burglars were on the road to becoming the future roughs of the town and it could well have been the case that a number of them went on to become the notorious "High Rippers" of the next decade. The reign of the High Rip gang would also be blamed on the pernicious influence of boys' crime and adventure stories.

The issue raised concerns in the national newspapers. In 1876, a publisher called John Macgregor complained that children seemed to prefer sensational stories to religious and morally improving literature. Of the "penny dreadfuls", he explained: "Many of them make robbery, defiance and murder the core of their tale."[1] To counteract the threat, Macgregor was pleased to announce that work was underway to produce a new children's periodical, full of incident, adventure, action and lively pictures, but with a moral tone that would elevate, rather than debase, its young readers. It is true to say, however, that boys preferred the violence and bloodshed.

In the summer of 1876, Liverpool School Board received a letter from Bridgewater School Board asking them to join them in a petition to Parliament against the publication of "impure" literature. The issue was referred to the magistrates. The Head Constable of Liverpool then wrote a report on the magazines, stating that there were sixteen such titles, containing tales of murders, suicides and highway robbery, available in the town, although none were published locally. Four of them were published for 2d and the rest for 1d. The Head Constable felt that the majority of boys who ran away from home did so under the influence of such literature.

The enchantment of "penny dreadfuls" is illustrated by an episode from April 1883. Three boys, Arthur Haley, Ernest Page and Charles Rose, from respectable families living in Frizinghall, outside the city, decided to have an adventure abroad after reading a great deal of what had been termed "cheap sensational literature". The expedition had been carefully planned. They drew up a form of oath binding each of them to keep together under all circumstances. Nothing but death itself was to separate them. One of the lads cut his wrist and, using the flowing blood as ink, each of them signed the oath, which was then buried in the garden of Haley's parents.

The boys had been saving their pocket money for months and were able to purchase three revolvers and plenty of cartridges. This left each boy with around thirty shillings. From home, they took blankets and cooking equipment. Boarding the train to Liverpool, they then crossed the Mersey to Cheshire, where they eventually arrived at Egremont. Although they had money to pay for accommodation, the boys decided to camp out on the sands. After cooking supper, they wrapped themselves in their blankets and settled down to dream of further adventures.

In the middle of the night, a suspicious policeman roused the boys. On finding they had guns, he took them into custody and confiscated the firearms, although the boys protested at this. The gang stated that they had intended to obtain berths as cabin boys on any vessel bound for the Pacific. They were then going to desert ship after locating a suitable Pacific Island where they would then have set up a kingdom of their own. The parents were contacted the next day and the adventure ended happily without any real crime being committed.

For youngsters, reading opened up a new world of adventure – and crime.

Later that year, four boys, aged fourteen and fifteen, were arrested in a boat on the shore off North Greenwich, London. The boys, from Blackfriars, told the river police that they had got lost in the fog, but aimed to sail to Gravesend. An inspection of the boys' baggage revealed a comprehensive survival kit, including a pistol, bullets, biscuits, some stationery, candles, matches, a compass, a songbook and, inevitably, a copy of *Boys' World* magazine, together with similar publications. One boy also carried his own revolver, while his friend had a letter, ready for posting, informing his mother and father that he was nipping over to Australia. The parents were flabbergasted, saying that the boys wanted for nothing at home.

However, not all children were inspired to undertake such romantic adventures. In London, in October 1877, Inspector Rowe, an off-duty policeman, was driving a small wagon accompanied by his wife. As the wagon trotted down a country lane, three lads jumped out from the trees and climbed on board. "Pull up. I am Dick Turpin," shouted fifteen-year-old Joseph Littleberry. After a short chase, Rowe seized the boy and announced, "If you are Dick Turpin, I am pleased to meet you. I am an inspector of the police."

In 1880, two fifteen-year-olds, John Thompson and William Jones, appeared in Liverpool Police Court charged with two counts of burglary. The pair first robbed Thompson's employer, a leather-merchant in Boundary Street, by hiding in the kitchen until everybody had gone home. They failed to open the safe, but escaped with some money and postage stamps. For their next crime, they targeted Jones's employer, a butcher with a shop in Stanley Road. They entered the premises through the cellar grating, but found only three shillings, which they spent on a day-trip to the other side of the Mersey. In court, the detective handed the magistrate a copy of an adventure story called *The Boys of London*, which had been found in the posses-sion of one of the prisoners. The lads admitted that they had been inspired to commit the crimes as a result of reading the book.

The influence of macabre literature was taken seriously. Before seventeen-year-old Joseph Morley was hanged in 1887 for murdering the wife of the man with whom he lodged, the lad revealed that he had been motivated to commit the crime by reading an account of a recent clerical murder in Suffolk. He admitted that reading murder stories fascinated him.

However, some boys didn't need the influence of "penny dreadfuls" in order to lead lives of crime. In October 1876, two fifteen-year-olds, John Thriepe and Robert Fulton, burgled a butcher's shop in Stanley Road and stole three pounds from the bedroom of the sleeping occupants. As they entered the premises a dog barked and one of the boys grabbed the butcher's knife. In court, he admitted that he was quite prepared to stab the animal if necessary. The boys spent the money the next day, travelling to St Helens on a "spree". It seems as though the pair lived rough in an empty house without any adult supervision.

In January 1878, four boys, aged between six and ten, appeared in court charged with various robberies. The tallest of the boys could hardly see over the dock rail, while the youngest was invisible. Three brothers, William, James and Philip Brady, together with their friend Frank Craven, had stolen a brush from a house in Edge Lane. A policeman tried to arrest them, but they ran away, although they were caught later the same day. They admitted to taking the brush and, later, to having smashed it to pieces with a hammer. The crime seems so trivial as to hardly warrant attention; the magistrate agreed and considered that it was up to the parents rather than the court to deal with such "little urchins".

However, the policeman then informed the court that two of the brothers and another member of the Craven family, aged about fifteen, had committed another burglary. The gang had stolen a quilt after breaking through the wall of a house, displaying a determination, audacity and stamina worthy of any adult "hole-in-the-wall gang". The magistrate asked the constable where the boys had been between the two robberies. "Scampering about the country," came the reply.

On searching the boys' houses more stolen items were found, demonstrating that the gang, young as they were, were already both quite prolific and successful thieves. The magistrate concluded, "It appears to me that the parents are more guilty than the children." With the exception of the six-year-old, who, it was admitted, should never have been taken into custody, the boys were remanded.

In August 1878, another band of boy burglars appeared in court. Two brothers called Martin and Joseph Clark, Thomas Peevans, Thomas Fox and John Mulligan were charged with breaking into eight offices in the town centre and stealing various sums of money. The boys were between ten and fourteen years of age. Their parents appeared in court and looked respectable. All were employed, including Mrs Clark, who had raised six children alone after her husband had left her. Martin Clark appeared to be the head of the gang and appeared to be responsible for having led the other boys astray. In one burglary they broke into an office in Cable Street, off South John Street, and stole ten pounds' worth of gold, which they shared out among themselves. As the ringleader, Martin Clark was sentenced to a spell in a reformatory, while the others were imprisoned for a week and given twelve strokes of the birch. The magistrate warned the parents that this was the last time they could expect such leniency.

Another gang of boy burglars included Irvine O'Hara, aged nine, Thomas Valentine, aged eleven, John Thompson, aged twelve, Thomas Stamford, aged thirteen, and John Turner, aged sixteen. On May 12, 1880, the boys broke into a house in Seacombe Street, off Great Homer Street, stealing coins and jewellery worth ten pounds. Valentine and Thompson were caught at the scene. When questioned, Valentine implicated Stamford, whose house, when searched, was found to contain all sorts of treasure hidden in a hole in the floor. Turner also had articles from the robbery. As he tried to pledge a watch, the suspicious pawnbroker attempted to grab hold of him and he had to flee leaving the goods behind. Valentine was sent to Toxteth Industrial School for five years. Thompson was handed a spell at Newton Reformatory Farm for the same period. Stamford received twelve strokes of the birch and the other two prisoners were discharged.

In September 1880, three youngsters, all under ten years of age, were charged with stealing six shillings from nine-year-old Ellen Smith. The girl had been sent on a message and carried the money wrapped in paper. As she passed near a windmill in Mill Street, Toxteth, she met Richard Conlin, James Clarke and his brother Matthew. Conlin put his hands over the girl's mouth to stop her screaming while James stole the money. When caught, James admitted to the theft, saying that he had spent some of the cash on sweets and two pairs of clogs for himself and his brother. In an act of poetic justice, a girl in Beaufort Street stole the clogs from the boys later the same day. Conlin also admitted that they had used some of the money to visit the theatre. Mrs Clarke admitted that her offspring were bad lads, while Conlin's mother reckoned that her boy was good sometimes. The magistrate remarked that the modus operandi of the crime suggested that the boys had been reading a Newgate Calendar, a publication listing the crimes of prisoners. The children were sent to the workhouse for a week while further enquiries were made.

Stealing children's footwear was a common crime, although it was normally carried out by adult females.

One of the strangest juvenile gangs was a group of young "child-strippers", as they were called. On April 27, 1887, four children appeared before the magistrate. Jane Pimlett, aged ten, Peter Pimlett, aged twelve, William Quirk, aged fifteen and John Quirk were all charged with having stripped other children of their boots in the neighbourhood of Commercial Road and Stanley Road, Bootle. The gang was caught after young Jane offered a pawnbroker some footwear in pledge. The man became suspicious and alerted the police. Upon their arrest, it was discovered that the youngsters had roamed the streets forcibly taking boots from any child lucky enough, or rather unlucky enough, to own a pair. They had successfully pawned four other pairs. Oddly enough, the crime is still popular today among teenagers, although it is likely to involve brand-new trainers rather than hob-nailed boots.

Perhaps the most dedicated and hardy juvenile gang came from Bootle. In December 1883, six wild, ragged-looking boys, aged between twelve and sixteen, appeared in court charged with having broken into a confectioner's in Regent Road. They had stolen five shillings' worth of sweets after breaking a valuable plate-glass shop window. The boys lived rough in a hiding place they had built among a pile of timber on some waste ground near Nelson Street. They had dug a trench, fifteen feet long, five feet wide and almost three feet deep. The pit was covered with planks, over which they heaped sand, leaving space only to crawl in and out of a narrow gap. The officers investigating the burglary found the den with a couple of thieves still in it after they had become suspicious of smoke plumes wafting from a hole in the ground. As the police approached, three boys were seen clambering out. After a short chase they were captured and taken back to their hideout where more boys were discovered. The others refused to surrender and the police had to dismantle the roof to flush them out.

The den contained a large quantity of potatoes, cabbages, a container filled with water, some cooking utensils and a glass dish stolen from the

No ASBOs for this pair of Portsmouth vandals. In 1899 they received five days' hard labour.

sweet shop. A fire was burning in a perforated bucket. The boys admitted to the robbery, saying that they had lived in the pit for some time, surviving on what they could steal. They ate quite well. Among the stolen items were a tin of corned beef, weighing fourteen pounds, and two large tins of lobster. Some of the parents appeared in court, stating that they hadn't seen their children for several weeks. The magistrate, concerned that such literature was leading young people astray, asked the arresting officers whether they had found any boys' storybooks in the den.

In January 1885, ten boys, ranging in age from nine to fifteen, appeared before Bootle Police Court charged with having stolen a box of biscuits as it was being unloaded outside a shop in Derby Road. The package weighed almost twenty pounds and was worth six shillings. The mother of one of the boys was also convicted of having knowingly received the stolen goods. She was sentenced to fourteen days' imprisonment with hard labour. Some of the boys were given between six and twelve strokes of the birch, while Robert Lowe, aged fifteen, was given fourteen days' imprisonment and two years in a reformatory. James Roach, aged twelve, was also gaoled for fourteen days, but was then sent to a reformatory for four years.

In April 1885, eleven boys, ranging in age from nine to fifteen, appeared at Bootle Police Court charged with a midnight raid on another shop in Derby Road. This time they had stolen thirty-one tins of salmon. One of the gang, ten-year-old John Fogarty, turned Queen's evidence and "grassed up" his accomplices. He revealed that nine-year-old Terence Mitchell had climbed onto the roof of the shop and had passed the goods out through a hole in the skylight. With the exception of one boy, the gang, who all lived around Dundas Street, was well known to the police. In fact, five of them had been part of the gang that had stolen the biscuits; the birching they had received for that crime could not have done them any good. For this misdemeanour, the older boys received another twelve strokes and the younger ones again suffered six.

YOUTHS NOT ONLY joined gangs, they were also sometimes the victims of gang violence. On March 16, 1884, sixteen-year-old Francis O'Rourke was walking along Marybone late in the evening when he met a group of eight lads, all aged a year or two older. O'Rourke was asked whether he sold "fusees" or matches. When he answered "no", each gang member took turns to punch him in the face for no reason.

O'Rourke attempted to follow the gang, but they noticed him and turned back to give him another beating. One of the gang then lowered his head and, with the ironical remark, "Isn't it a shame," rushed at his victim and delivered a mighty punch to the chin. O'Rourke was sent flying through the plate-glass window of an egg merchant, where in addition to the injuries caused to the poor lad, the *Echo* reported damage to six shillings' worth of eggs. As a final humiliation, O'Rourke was almost taken into custody, accused of being one of the ruffians, and had to convince the police that he had actually been the victim. The gang ran away.

Youths would often roam the streets looking for trouble. Innocent pedestrians walking alone were particularly vulnerable but groups were also attacked. In November 1886, a party of five fifteen- to seventeen-year-olds went to Lime Street Station to meet a friend. On returning home through Moss Street at 9.45 p.m., they saw a group of fifty to sixty "roughs" marching towards them from the direction of Shaw Street. The gang had some sort of band with them, although they weren't playing music but simply beating a drum in a menacing fashion. They appeared to be some sort of sectarian marching band.

One lad turned to ask his friends what the crowd was when he was unexpectedly punched on the nose and cheek. In the melee, one lad managed to escape up Prescot Street, but the rest of the group were severely beaten with knives, belts and sticks. One was left with a nasty gash over his eye and another with a deep cut on his head. Nobody was arrested for the attack.

There were many local juvenile gangs battling for street supremacy, and on Christmas Eve, 1883, their persistent feuding ended in tragedy.

At 9 p.m. that night, thirteen-year-old Michael Burns and another boy came across a fight between some youths in Commercial Road. The two lads stood watching the disturbance at a safe distance, until a boy called Charles Vaughan ran over to Burns and butted him in the face, knocking him to the ground. The rest of the gang then came over and continued to thrash the lad. He managed to get up and run, but he was soon captured and the vicious beating resumed. Isaac Hatfield whacked Burns on the head with a stick.

*Young Cornerman (1910). A barefooted street-urchin in Eldon Street
displays defiance against poverty.*

"Oh, I'm killed," shouted Burns, "they've struck me on the head
with a poker."

The gang ran away when two men approached. "They've killed
me," screamed Burns. "They've kicked my ribs in." He attempted to
crawl home and was eventually rescued by his mother, who had been
out looking for him. After being put to bed, Burns fell into a deep
sleep, never to awaken.

Four boys were later arrested and charged with his manslaughter.
There were moving scenes at the inquest, as the dead boy's mother
confronted his killers for the first time. She broke into tears and
shouted, "Oh you bad boys, oh you bad villains. You murdered my
Mickey. May God forgive you." The coroner asked the poor woman to
control her feelings, but she continued, "You will excuse me, sir. They
have deprived me of my beloved son, who never went with anybody
but his mother. I will never forgive them. I do not think anybody
would murder an innocent boy."

On February 12, 1884, the four youths, aged between fifteen and nineteen, faced trial at the assizes. It was disclosed that the neighbourhood contained many organised gangs, including the Lemon Street, the Regent Street and the "Pad" lot. The whole episode had started with a title unification fight between the respective champions of the Lemon Street and Regent Street gangs, George Campbell and Thomas Nolan. Charles Vaughan had acted as Nolan's second, charged with the job of picking him up whenever he was knocked down. After brawling for five minutes, Campbell was badly cut over the left eye and decided to call it a day. He shook hands with Nolan and offered to resume hostilities the next morning.

During the fight, Vaughan told a friend to go to a place called "the Pad", a piece of wasteland off Stanley Road, for some more boys, including Hatfield carrying his stick. On their return, Vaughan took off his coat and offered to fight anybody in the crowd. A lad asked, "What is the matter with ye, Charley? Who's been getting at you?" Vaughan replied that he would soon show him what was getting at him and proceeded to headbutt a boy called John Murray. A free-for-all then broke out. Somebody else assaulted Campbell. At this point, Vaughan and the others ran over to attack Burns, who had simply been watching.

The reason the accused were charged with manslaughter, rather than murder, was because it was accepted that they might have thought that Burns was part of another gang ready to attack them.

Four youths were found guilty. Charles Vaughan, as the ringleader, was sentenced to twelve years. William Price, Isaac Hatfield and John McComb each received ten years.

Perhaps the most notorious group of young lads was known as the Blackstone Street Gang. For years they terrorised the neighbourhood at the north end of Great Howard Street. The members were not unknown to the previous gang who had beaten poor Michael Burns to death. In fact, some of them worked together as scalers in the same workshop at the docks. In January 1884, William Orr from the Northern Hospital wrote a letter complaining of an outbreak of violence in the north end of Liverpool.[2] Since the middle of December 1883, there had been no fewer than ten cases involving knives and serious wounding treated at the hospital. Over a period of just three weeks there had been assaults on policemen, unprovoked attacks on sailors and numerous armed robberies and vicious brawls. There hadn't been anything like it for years.

At the beginning of 1884, members of the Blackstone Street Gang were youths on the verge of becoming men. Together they began a new reign of terror on Liverpool's streets. They were capable not only of robbery and random violence, but also of cold-blooded murder.

CHAPTER 11

The Blackstone Street Murder

TEN YEARS AFTER the Tithebarn Street outrage, another crime occurred that shocked the city. Once again, a gang of youths picked on an innocent and defenceless stranger as he walked along the street. Again the man was beaten and murdered without any provocation. In both cases, there was no attempt at robbery, the motive being a simplistic love of brutality. Once again a crowd of people witnessed the attack, but did nothing to help the victim. As had been the case with the Morgan murder, a patrolling policeman had arrived on the scene just that little bit too late to prevent the crime. If the Tithebarn Street murder had been the start of the reign of the Cornermen, then the Blackstone Street murder signified the beginning of the rule of the High Rip gang.

Like the Tithebarn Street attackers, the leader of the gang was another young lad of Irish background. At just over five feet tall and weighing a mere nine stone five pounds, seventeen-year-old Michael McLean, from Steel Street off Boundary Street, was a pint-sized terror. The respectable residents of the Scotland ward were terrified into silence by the depredations of his gang. Before the crime that made him infamous, McLean and his friend, Patrick Duggan, had already been accused of stabbing a policeman in nearby Beacon Street. This had been no mere flesh wound: the knife had been plunged deep into the officer's arm down to the bone, causing permanent injury.

At 10 p.m. on Sunday, January 5, 1884, Exequiel Rodriques Nunez, a thirty-five-year-old Spanish sailor, was returning to his vessel, *Serra*, which lay in the Huskisson Dock. Jose Jiminez, another Spanish sailor whom he had met earlier that evening in the Madrid Café in Pitt Street, accompanied him. Although they had known each other for fifteen years, the two Spaniards had arrived separately in Liverpool and Jiminez's ship, *Magallenes*, was berthed in the Canada Dock. As they went along Regent Road they saw a group of five men, including McLean, Duggan, Alexander Campbell, William Dempsey and Murdoch Ballantyne (sometimes spelt Valentine), standing at the corner of Blackstone Street. The rest of the gang were described as "powerfully-built, rough-visaged youths".

Dempsey, Ballantyne and Campbell had earlier been drinking in the Seven Stars public house in Regent Road. After finishing work on the steamer *Plantin* in the Sandon Graving Dock, McLean met up with Duggan and some other friends and attempted to have a drink in the Northern Lights, but the group was refused service by the landlady. They then went to another pub in Townsend Street before meeting up with the rest of the gang.

They must have been intent on trouble. From various statements rife in the neighbourhood, one of the lads was heard to say "that he didn't care a **** for the police". As the sailors passed, Ballantyne punched Jiminez without any warning. The shocked Spaniard ran away to the safety of his ship rather than retaliate. At the docks, he desperately tried to inform a policeman about the attack, but his command of English was not good enough. He gestured frantically and pointed to his bleeding lip, but to no avail.

Nunez was left to the mercy of the gang but, after a few blows, he also managed to escape. His freedom was short-lived, however. He fell by the dock wall on one side of Regent Road and was kicked and beaten with belts by the gang. Nunez got up again and ran further up the road until he reached a passage leading into Fulton Street, a short distance from the safety of his ship. However, some of the gang had anticipated the route he would take and soon met up with him again as he turned the corner of a building, near to a foundry gate.

"Here he is," shouted Campbell. "Knives, boys, knives!"

At this command, the gang renewed their brutal attack on the sailor. The terrified Nunez got up and ran towards the railway arch in Blackstone Street where he was again captured, kicked and beaten. A few bystanders in the street, including friends and relatives of the attackers, some of them only children, witnessed the dreadful crime.

Duggan was heard to cry out, "Mooney, Mooney, I have done it." Ballantyne's nickname was "Mooney". Duggan and McLean used their

Blackstone Street today. The Spanish sailor was murdered under the railway arch.

knives on Nunez, stabbing him in the lower part of the neck, near to the collarbone; it was a wound that would lead to loss of blood and the Spaniard's eventual death. Duggan went to a passing woman called Mrs Ramsey and asked if he could wipe his bloodied hands on her apron. "No murderer shall wipe his hands on my apron," she replied in disgust.

After the stabbing, McLean turned to Duggan and warned him, "Here's a bobby, let us run." The cool Duggan replied, "No, we will walk," which they did, down Blackstone Street.

Moments later, a policeman was attracted to the crowd of people surrounding what he thought was a drunk lying on the floor. There were no serious marks on the body except the blood, which was flowing from the man's nostrils and a gash on his right cheek. A wheelbarrow was brought to take Nunez to the Collingwood Dock Bridewell. As the group passed along Great Howard Street, which had better lighting, someone noticed that the man had in fact been seriously injured and a telegram was dispatched to the Northern Hospital.

A horse-ambulance arrived quickly to complete the sailor's journey, but he died before he reached the hospital.

It proved almost impossible to ascertain the man's identity. It was suspected that he was a foreign seaman, but that was about it. Somebody came forward and identified the body as that of Michael Mullet, an Irishman who worked as a labourer at the Stanley Dock. Six days passed before the man was correctly identified, after the police had tracked down Jiminez. It took days before the sailor discovered his countryman's fate. Initially, he thought that, like himself, Nunez had escaped the gang's clutches. Jiminez also explained that he had hesitated to come forward because he was afraid of being detained in Liverpool for a considerable time and missing his ship. He was also wary of being wrongly charged with the murder.

After killing Nunez, Dempsey and Campbell went with Ballantyne to his mother's house, where they sent for a half-gallon of ale and sang some songs. There was blood on Dempsey's trousers, which he tried to explain away to Mrs Ballantyne by saying that he had been sparring with Campbell and had accidentally given him a nosebleed. Mrs Ballantyne stated that she had heard there was a man lying under the arch with his throat cut. On hearing this, Dempsey groaned, "I am sick," before going out the back to vomit.

The following day, Dempsey's mother pledged the bloodstained trousers with a pawnbroker called Russell, who was so accustomed to receiving items from the woman that he did not bother to examine them. The police later found the trousers and used them as evidence.

Separated from their colleagues, McLean and Duggan went to a public house with two girls, Mary Reardon and Mary Burke, and then on to an empty house in Fulton Street. Duggan and Burke left at 2 a.m. to go home, leaving McLean alone with sixteen-year-old Reardon, his girlfriend of eighteen months. The pair stayed in the house until the police arrested them the following day. McLean was found standing behind the door of the back bedroom while Reardon was hiding in a cupboard. As he was being held, McLean threw away a knife and a whistle, but two other blades were found in his possession, one of which was stained with blood. The names of the rest of the gang were then given to the police and they were all arrested within days.

The prisoners were tried at St George's Hall on February 19, 1884, before Justice Butt. McLean, a labourer, was seventeen; Duggan, aged eighteen, was a scaler; Dempsey, aged nineteen, was a labourer; Ballantyne, aged twenty, was another labourer; Campbell, also twenty, was a barber.

Holding Cell in St George's Hall. McCrave, Mullen, and later McLean, would sit here awaiting the death sentence.

Originally all five had been charged with murder, but there were difficulties with the case. Because some of the witnesses were relatives of the accused, they kept changing their statements in order to lessen the involvement of each youth. This resulted in a great deal of contradictory evidence. Georgina Ballantyne, the twelve-year-old sister of Murdoch, was one such witness. She claimed that she shouted to her brother not to go under the railway arch, upon which he returned and took no further part in the fatal attack. Margaret Killey, aged eleven, was certain that it was Campbell and Dempsey who had chased the sailor. Under cross-examination, Georgina Ballantyne admitted to having spoken to Margaret Killey on the morning of the trial, telling her that one of the men was Campbell.

Eleven-year-old John Hodge claimed that it was Campbell who had declared, "I've done him." The boy then admitted that it had been so dark on the night that he could not see the faces of the men. He also revealed that he had never seen Campbell before that night. "Hugh Callaghan told me it was Campbell when we were going up before the magistrates," he added. Hodge then stated that he in fact knew Campbell by sight and that he had seen him go around with a concertina.

Catherine Burke, aged fourteen, was the sister of the girl who "kept company" with Duggan. Perhaps understandably, she claimed that Duggan had been standing by her when the fatal attack took place. Peter Burke, aged eleven, revealed that he heard Campbell say, "Give me a knife, my belt's broke," but Duggan replied that he hadn't got one. Peter Burke was certain that he saw no knives used. Mary Burke, the consort of Duggan, was adamant that he had been with her when the man was stabbed. She also denied that McLean had been under the arch. She added that there were several men she did no know under the arch attacking the sailor.

Thirteen-year-old Hugh Callaghan, however, claimed that he had seen McLean and Duggan use their knives on Nunez. Ten-year-old Leonora Johnson confirmed that McLean had had a knife in his hand.

It was revealed at the trial that the victim had been carrying a sheath-knife, hidden between his shirt and jersey, near the shoulder blades. This fact had been kept from the defence, who argued in court that it was a deliberate attempt by the prosecution to suggest that Nunez had offered no provocation. It would, of course, have aided the defence if it could have been shown that Nunez had been the aggressor. Indeed, Dempsey, while admitting that he knocked down the sailor, claimed that one of the Spaniards had first thrown a punch at him.

The evidence against Ballantyne, Dempsey and Campbell as to their actual involvement in the attack proved inconclusive. However, it was conclusively shown that McLean and Duggan were responsible for the sailor's death. Both had been seen kicking Nunez, while McLean had also been seen stabbing him.

In summing up, the judge acquitted the first three prisoners, but used the rule laid down in the Tithebarn Street murder case ten years earlier, that it didn't matter which individual dealt the particular blow that caused the Spaniard's death. If the prisoners acted together, then they were both equally guilty.

Justice Butt. The judge who sentenced Michael McLean to death

The jury members agonised over their decision for fifty minutes. One juror wanted to bring in a verdict of manslaughter, while another asked the judge to clarify some points. The judge explained that if Nunez had indeed brandished his own knife, but that he had otherwise done nothing to justify the gang chasing him to the railway arch and stabbing him, then that would still be murder. However, if there was a simple quarrel, which then resulted in "hot blood", the jury might reduce the verdict to manslaughter.

Eventually, Duggan and McLean were convicted of murder with a strong recommendation for mercy. Upon hearing the verdict, both men vehemently protested their innocence and accused Dempsey of being the murderer. After being told the terrible fate that awaited them, they then walked jauntily from the dock with "a callous smile upon their faces".

After their conviction, efforts were made to gain a reprieve for the men. McLean's application centred on the grounds of his youth and his previous good conduct, despite the fact that he was a well-known terror to the community. An affidavit in support of Duggan was forwarded from Dempsey alleging that Duggan did not use the knife and that witnesses must have mistaken him for Dempsey. Dempsey admitted to stabbing Nunez, but argued that he had only dealt a slight wound and not the actual deathblow.

Both youths were sent to Kirkdale Prison where Duggan was eventually granted his reprieve. McLean was left to await his execution on March 10. The gallows had been erected a week earlier to hang two infamous lady poisoners, Mrs Flanagan and Mrs Higgins. The scaffold was then left standing for the execution of McLean.

The hangman was Bartholomew Binns from Dewsbury in Yorkshire. He arrived at the gaol on the Saturday afternoon drunk, after stopping off for a tipple on leaving the train. After being shown to his accommodation, Binns fell into a deep sleep. When the warders tried to wake him, he became abusive and threatened to hit them. A policeman had to be called to calm him down. It wasn't the best start to an execution.

The morning of the hanging broke with heavy clouds overhead and snow on the ground. The atmosphere was raw and chilling, but it had improved slightly by 7 a.m. McLean rose early and, like the Tithebarn Street murderers, was attended to by Father Bonte. The prisoner received the last rites followed by some breakfast. At 7.45 a.m., he was conducted to the pinioning room, where Binns secured his arms.

At 8 a.m., a door at the foot of steps leading to the scaffold was opened and McLean emerged in the midst of a procession of officials. He was reported to be a handsome, bright and intelligent lad. His youthful lack of facial hair and his chubby features made him almost look girlish. There was also a glow of health on the cheeks of his otherwise-ashen face. Ironically, McLean looked better than he had ever done. Like a turkey fattened up for slaughter, he had gained seven or eights pounds in weight while in gaol, a fact that says less about the generous size of prison portions than it does about the severe malnutrition normally endured by lads of McLean's class in the Liverpool slums.

McLean ran nimbly up the steps without assistance and walked unfalteringly to the spot under the rope. As the straps were being fastened around his knees, he made an effort to speak. In a strong Irish accent, but with a slight tremor in his voice, he addressed the gathered reporters: "Gentlemen, I consider it a disgrace to the police force of Liverpool and to the laws of the country that I am going to suffer death and that another boy is going to suffer imprisonment for life for a crime of which we are both innocent, as God is my judge."

Father Bonte then began reading from the prayers for the dying, but McLean had difficulty following the responses. His lips moved, but his voice was inaudible and he had difficulty in stopping himself from bursting into tears.

By this time, Binns had nervously placed the noose around McLean's neck and fixed the eyelet underneath the right ear. The white cap was placed over his head and the hangman stepped back to operate the lever for the trap door that would send McLean to his doom.

Consciousness ceased as the body dropped, the only movement being a slight jerk of McLean's left foot as the noose tightened. Upon his neck breaking, his head fell to the left. The lad's pulse continued for a further eight minutes, the heartbeat for a few moments longer.

At the inquest, the jury censured the hangman for his lack of scientific procedure. The drop had been incorrectly calculated, leaving

McLean's feet barely eight inches from the floor. It was felt that Binns had estimated the drop by rule of thumb rather than by scientific inquiry. Also, the legs had been pinioned too loosely and the positioning of the eyelet meant that the rope didn't tighten quickly enough. The governor of the gaol commented, "He puts a rope round the man's neck and thinks he hangs him, but it is accidental if he hangs him." Shortly after, questions were raised in the House of Commons about Binns' suitability as an executioner.

Outside the walls of the prison there was the usual gathering of supporters, friends and neighbours. About 500 braved the cold and wet early-morning journey to Kirkdale, the majority of them described as youths of the Cornerman class. McLean's sister and girlfriend were there, but his mother and father were absent. Every now and then a rumour spread that the parents and other relatives were making their way across the little valley between Stanley Road and the gaol. The crowd would make a rush to the edge of the depression, only to resume their former positions when they discovered their mistake.

After Binns left the prison, he drove in a cab to a public house where he had a few drinks. He then drove on to Lime Street, where he had a few more. In jovial mood, he showed his hangman's rope and straps to some interested customers. At the station, he looked so drunk that the ticket inspector hesitated before allowing him on the train.

Days before the execution, William Dempsey, the lad accused by his colleagues of having delivered the fatal wound, sailed from Liverpool to start a new life in California.

THE BLACKSTONE STREET Gang continued to make the news. In November 1884, eighteen-year-old Thomas Gibbons, of Hopwood Street, appeared in court accused of being an accomplice of McLean's during an earlier robbery. It was suggested that they had attacked Elizabeth Hughes, a rent collector. While she was making her rounds in Lincoln Street, Bootle, McLean had thrown cayenne pepper into her eyes and snatched her satchel, which contained over eight pounds.

Gibbons had since gained employment as a fireman on a steamer.

The judge took this into account when handing down a quite lenient sentence. Justice John Day hoped that the lad would return to his work once he had finished his term of one month's imprisonment with hard labour. The judge also acknowledged that McLean had been a bad influence on Gibbons.

Such leniency was perhaps misguided, for on February 10, 1886, Gibbons, still employed as a fireman, appeared in court again, along with eighteen-year-old Michael Trainor, of Luton Street, accused of having robbed a sailor. In the early hours of Sunday, November 15, 1885, John Peterson had been walking home along Derby Road, Bootle, when Gibbons and Trainor asked him for some money. When Peterson stated that he had none, Gibbons head butted him while Trainor kicked the legs from under him. "What have I done to you?" pleaded Peterson. "For God's sake don't kill me; I have nothing in my pockets but pawn tickets." But he was dragged into an entry in Raleigh Street and beaten further. Peterson screamed "Murder!" but Gibbons placed his knees on his chest, almost crushing him, and punched him repeatedly in the face.

Neighbours were attracted by the man's cries and the perpetrators were recognised. One witness heard Gibbons shouting, "We will high rip them." Before they ran away, they attacked a female witness and even attempted to break her door when she ran back into the house. Peterson was left bleeding from the nose, mouth and eyes, sixpence halfpenny the poorer.

When arrested, Gibbons struggled so violently that it took five constables to restrain him. He kept kicking out and shouting over and over, "High Rip, High Rip." On the way to the station, Gibbons threatened that if he had a knife on him he would rip up the witnesses. On being charged with having robbed Peterson, the relentlessly poisonous Gibbons declared, "May the Lord stiffen him." Trainor was arrested later.

At the assizes, the defence claimed that Gibbons and Peterson had been having a fair fight as a result of accidentally knocking into each other in the street. It was claimed that Trainor had simply been trying to separate them. Nobody believed the story. Gibbons received six months with hard labour and forty strokes of the lash, to be given in two separate doses of twenty. He was dragged from the dock shrieking. Trainor was given three months and fifteen strokes of the lash.

Gibbons certainly kept good company. Trainor, like Gibbons's previous accomplice, Michael McLean, was believed to be the leader of a notorious new gang. Somewhere down the line, a group of Cornermen had evolved into something much more terrifying and malevolent – the High Rip gang.

CHAPTER 12

The High Rip Gang

IN 1886, TWELVE years after his death, a curious article appeared in a newspaper claiming that Richard Morgan's attackers had been a gang called the "High Rip", rather than a group of Cornermen.[1] A journalist claimed to be an eyewitness to the Tithebarn Street outrage. He had turned into Tithebarn Street from Hatton Garden when he found himself walking behind the victims. The account appears to be genuine, for it is littered with phrases such as "I shall never forget" and "I can still vividly picture". However, the journalist suggests that, on the fateful night, Alice Morgan was carrying a baby and that her husband was slightly the worse for wear. There is no mention of the presence of Morgan's brother. The street itself was almost deserted. As the couple passed the gang on the corner, a signal was given from a hidden colleague and the ruffians suddenly surrounded Mr and Mrs Morgan. The journalist stated that she had known some of the men.

Instead of asking for sixpence to buy some ale, Campbell, rather than one of his colleagues, wanted to buy tobacco. He urged the couple, "Fork out the price of a bit of bacca." Another man pleaded, "Turning up two winn and a meg won't break yer." Mrs Morgan spoke to one of the men, called Paddy, and bid him begone. As the gang pounced, the journalist, who was by now sixty yards away, claims to have blown a whistle to summon the police. Two officers immediately answered the call from opposite directions. The journalist also ran towards the disturbance and attempted to hit one of the attackers with his stick, but was knocked unconscious. He awoke as Morgan's body was being carted away.

The blow must have affected the man's memory, for all the details given contradict every contemporary newspaper report, the coroner's inquest, committal proceedings and the final trial at the assizes. The man claims to have been a journalist at the time, for he tried to gain entry to the execution, only to turn up too late for admittance. If he was a journalist, his unique eyewitness report featured in none of the newspapers at the time. Nor did this public-spirited citizen give his vital evidence in court. The interesting part of his account is that he says that, as the police approached, the gang not only shouted "Hec! Hec!", but also "High Rip". This last detail would place the name of the gang about eleven years before the term first appeared in the newspapers.

In 1888, a journal published a series of articles on famous executions.[2] In the issue devoted to the Tithebarn Street outrage, the hanging of John McCrave and Michael Mullen is described as "one of the heaviest blows ever levelled at the empire of the 'High Rip' gang". However, both this reference and that of the newspaper are anachronistic. They simply attributed the name of a gang currently in the news to a different one that had existed years before.

At the winter assizes of 1886, during the trial of High Rip victim John McShane, Justice Day revealed that "four years ago I heard there was such a gang", but neither he nor the press seem to have named them at the time. The earliest printed reference to the High Rip appears in the newspapers of February 12, 1885.[3] Edward Boylan and William McConnell, both aged seventeen, had wounded John Grant the previous month. Grant had been beaten with a poker and by the buckle end of a leather belt.

In court, Grant told the jury that his attackers belonged to the "High Rip gang". The following exchange between Grant and McConnell's defence, Mr Lumb, caused much amusement in court:

Lumb:	What gang do you belong to?
Grant:	I am a member of no gang, but I am a member by myself.
	Laughter
Lumb:	Do you consider yourself respectable?
Grant:	No, I am not very respectable.
	Laughter
Lumb:	How many times have you been in prison?
Grant:	Once, for "insulting" a policeman.
	Laughter

Lumb: What did you get?

Grant: I got six pennyworth of imprisonment.

Lumb: What do you mean?

Grant: I mean six months.

           Laughter

Lumb: Had you never been in prison before?

Grant: Well, I have been in prison three or four times for looking at a game of pitch-and-toss, but only once for "insulting" a policeman.

           Laughter

The Judge: I shall call it assault, but the witness uses the word "insult" in another sense. The word "insult" they mean for anything; it is a term of "light respectability".

           Laughter

It was revealed that the High Rip gang was familiar around Back Portland Street, off Vauxhall Road, just north of the city centre. The term was used to distinguish a particular band of ruffians from the rest of the notorious characters of the neighbourhood. One witness went as far as naming Ellen Grant as the "head leader of the gang". However, she doesn't appear to have been the wife or sister of John Grant. A policeman was of the opinion that William McConnell was the ringleader of the "heavy gang" terrorising the area. The judge enquired what the gang did. The policeman replied that members carried knives, swords or any other weapons that they could lay their hands on. The judge then asked where the gang went. The policeman said that they went up and down the streets knocking down anybody that got in their way.

Boylan and McConnell were found guilty of assault and sentenced to six weeks with hard labour.

The second reference to the gang appeared a week later.[4] Under the headline "The High Rip Gang in Blackstone Street", one paper gave an account of Patrick Mannion's attack on Thomas Doyle. Mannion was one of the High Rip gang, members of which were often seen hanging around the area of Blackstone Street, off Great Howard Street, at all hours of the night. When anybody passed them, they were assaulted. Mannion broke into Doyle's house and, without any provocation, hit him on the head with his belt buckle.

The name High Rip must have been new, for in court Mr Raffles, an experienced stipendiary magistrate, asked the arresting officer the meaning of the term. The constable replied that it was what the gang shouted whenever a policeman approached.

Blackstone Street had been, of course, the place where Michael McLean murdered Spanish sailor Exequiel Nunez thirteen months before. The district must have been a hotbed of gang activity. In November 1884, "J.W." wrote a letter to the *Daily Post* complaining of having been molested and kicked in Blackstone Street by two "lewd, rough-looking fellows".[5] The writer urged a greater police presence in the area to prevent further attacks.

Michael McLean had been identified as the first leader of the High Rip twenty months earlier in a newspaper article: "He had a great deal to do with its organisation."[6] However, the newspapers at the time failed to mention the name of the gang. McLean was referred to only as the leader of the Blackstone Street gang. He and his colleagues were seen merely as Cornermen, the successors of McCrave and Mullen. The distinction is worth some consideration.

There was said to be a crucial moral difference between a respectable workman and a Cornerman: "The two may live in the same house and to all appearances may be of the same class – nay, more, the Cornerman may be the better clad and better fed of the two; but, nevertheless, the workman, however poor he may be, is respectable, and, strong in that knowledge, he looks down upon the Cornerman and will hold no communion with him."[7]

Continuing this theme of a hierarchy of respectability, another newspaper also drew a distinction between the honest, unemployed Cornerman and a member of the High Rip. The former it describes as someone who "occasionally indulges in a doleful double-shuffle on the cellar-lid of his favourite [public] house, and even goes so low in the social scale as to leave his 'judy' and her fish-basket to pay the rent of their stuffy room and provide 'vittles' for their ragged offspring."[8] The loafer's condition of employment might be "one day's work, six days' play", but at least robbery was not his sole means of income: nor were Cornermen, on the whole, violent. The same could not be said of the "High Rip Gang", "Bridge Boys", "Canal Bankers" and other "assorted hordes and night-prowling bandits". These were all ruthless, organised criminals.

Others also highlighted the issue of employment in an attempt to draw a distinction between the old Cornermen and the new breed of ruffian known as the High Rip:

> Assaults after dark and outrages of various kinds, gave rise to the belief that the old established Cornermen had suddenly broken through the bounds which had kept them in some measure under control. The "High Rip Gang", however, was not exactly a combination of Cornermen. It was this and something more. It was the union of some of the worst elements of the hobbledehoy, which differs from the professional Cornerman inasmuch as it does at times engage in honest labour, though whether the labour be honest, or that of the treadmill is immaterial to it.[9]

The question of whether members of the High Rip actually worked for a living was much debated. "Who and what are the 'High Rip Gang'?" asked one newspaper:

> With regard to the first question, it may be said that the members of it are young fellows between seventeen and twenty-one or twenty-two – that critical period of life when there is a man's strength without a man's discretion. With regard to what they are, they would, if asked the question by Mr Raffles, say that they "worked at the docks", but the gaoler would find, upon examination, that their palms have a softness only compatible with the absence of labour.[10]

It seems, however, that despite the lads' soft hands, one of the major distinctions between the Cornermen and the High Rip was that the former were largely unemployed and that is why they hung around aimlessly outside pubs, begging for ale money and occasionally engaging in drunken fights with each other and passers-by.

When members of the High Rip appeared in court, they were rarely listed as out of work. They were usually employed in some form of labour at the docks. One was even a barber. However, as proof that the High Rip was a growing menace, a stevedore at the docks noticed the absence of some lads who had been employed by him for some time. Upon querying this, his foreman told him that they had given up work to join the High Rip. Of course, modern conceptions of employment did not apply in Victorian times. The system of work at the docks, known as casual labour, meant that gang members must have alternated continually between employment and unemployment.

The history of the High Rip has become synonymous with Scotland Road. For those not familiar with the geography of Liverpool, the area deserves explanation. "Scotty" Road is perhaps the city's most famous thoroughfare, closely followed by Lime Street for its railway station (and later Mathew Street for its Beatles connection). Scotland Road, all 1,650 yards of it, was not merely the major route out of the town northwards, but an entire district comprising the numerous streets and courts leading off it. Parallel to the west of Scotland Road is Vauxhall Road and the two are linked at intervals along their routes. Great Homer Street runs parallel to the east and is again linked by a series of streets, like capillaries branching off a main artery. It is among this mass of streets, alleyways and tightly packed courts, slums and cellars that much of the Irish population lived. Irish or not, the inhabitants in the 1880s were all desperately poor and that the district bred many hardened youths should come as no surprise.

Only in this wider sense can Scotland Road be classed as being the heart of the High Rip empire. The gang was said to have had a specific and clearly defined area of criminal activity, but the precise location of this differed, depending on which newspaper is to be believed. The local press went to great pains to map out the geography of High Rip misdemeanours. According to one journal, the High Rip was originally established in Toxteth until it was moved on by the police.[11] However, there is no evidence in the newspaper reports of crimes and trials that any of the High Rippers either lived, or were active, in the south end of the city.

The gang was then said to be active in the north, but again received the attention of the authorities. As if by the result of a pincer movement, squeezing the gang closer together, a contingent then settled in Islington, north of Lime Street station, which was a more fertile ground for the gang owing to a scandalous lack of police presence. The High Rip had finally found immunity from the police. The area between Soho Street and Canterbury Street was so entirely taken over by the gang that people who entered the area after dark were called upon to run the gauntlet in a very unpleasant fashion. Congregating at the end of Birchfield Street, the High Rip monopolised the sidewalk and was ready to dispute the passage with any passer-by that they considered easy-pickings.

The north end of the city, particularly the district adjacent to Bootle, was also identified as a High Rip stronghold. Much of the city's crime was reported to be concentrated in that quarter. The evidence was to be seen not only on every public house corner during the daytime, but particularly at night, when the streets were awash with disorder. Bootle itself was known as "Brutal Bootle", where, according to the saying, even "the bugs wear clogs".[12] Owing to its renown as a heavy drinking district, it was suggested that it be renamed "Bottle".

Another newspaper agreed that the worst area was along the line of the north docks. There was a district in the north end, extending into Derby Road, Bootle, which was believed to be dangerous to enter after dark; even the police travelled in pairs.[13] Another publication maintained that "there is as much intimidation and terrorism in the portion of the city lying between Scotland Road and the river as there is in the most disturbed district in Ireland."[14] The warning echoed the words of Methodist minister and novelist Silas K. Hocking who, in *Her*

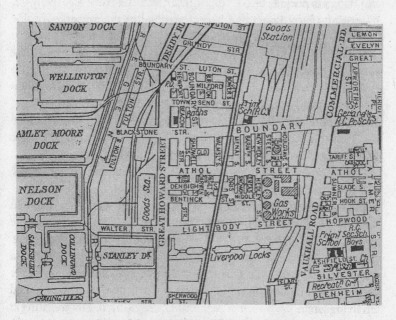

Map of the worst area of High Rip violence.

Benny, his 1879 semi-fictional tale of two Liverpool waifs, wrote, "On the western side of Scotland Road – that is to say, between it and the docks, there is a network of streets, inhabited mostly by the lowest class of the Liverpool poor. And those who have occasion to penetrate their dark and filthy recesses are generally thankful when they find themselves safe out again."[15]

This northern district, sandwiched between the river and Scotland Road, crops up repeatedly in accounts of High Rip activity. Two lengthy thoroughfares, Vauxhall Road and Great Howard Street, intersect the area northwards. The streets connecting these two routes, together with the railway arch in Athol Street, were favourite haunts of the High Rip.

A newspaper correspondent calling himself "Citizen" offered his own views: "The district from Athol Street to Luton Street is infested by these scoundrels. They are to be seen any day loitering about the Sailor's Home, Luton and Milford Streets, or in Athol Street waiting for something to turn up, and if at any time any poor fellow under the influence of drink passes by them they will 'go through him' – slang for emptying his pockets."[16]

Indeed, Luton Street had been identified as the epicentre of the High Rip.[17] The district was known locally as "Sebastopol" after the scene of a notable battle in the Crimean War of 1854. The place became a byword for carnage and bloodshed.

The above-named areas are quite widely spread throughout Liverpool. Islington, for example is to the southeast of Scotland Road, while Luton Street is to the far northwest. This suggests that the High Rip was a number of separate gangs, each based in their own area, rather than one single organisation. Perhaps they all operated under the same common name. It is also possible that the press labelled unrelated criminal gangs as the High Rip merely to sensationalise reports of crime. High Rip gangs might have been like the Cornermen in the sense that they were a number of unconnected groups of youths who banded together outside their own local alehouses and street corners. Cornermen in Toxteth, for example, would have had no relationship with Cornermen in Scotland Road, yet the press classed them all together, as if they were one huge, terrifying gang.

The High Rip, however, was certainly presented as one single, organised gang with a captain or a leader and a hierarchy of members. Information about the leadership is sparse, gained mostly from newspaper opinion and occasional evidence that was given in court, either by policemen or by witnesses.

The first leader of the High Rip was said to be seventeen-year-old Michael McLean, the Blackstone Street murderer. However, it took two years before the press picked up on this.[18] McLean was hanged in February 1884 and it was another twelve months before the press even started reporting the activities of the High Rip. It has already been mentioned that, in a court case in February 1885, a witness accused Ellen Grant of being the leader, while during the same trial a policeman pointed the finger at seventeen-year-old William McConnell. In April 1885, nineteen-year-old George Whitehead was named as the captain of the gang, although he denied it in court. In February 1886, a policeman revealed that eighteen-year-old Michael Trainor was the current leader. By May 1886, Thomas Maher was accused in court of being the captain of the gang, a claim confirmed by the police. It can be seen from the ages of the so-called leaders that these were mere youths and not grown men. The rest of the gang were probably younger still. During a trial in November 1886, a policeman stated that the captain of the High Rip was currently in prison. Unfortunately he did not name him.

Another factor that distinguished the High Rip from the Cornermen was that the crimes of the High Rip were not limited to the drunken and sporadic bouts of violence and opportunist muggings that characterised the street-corner loafers. As will be seen in the next chapter, the High Rip was involved in organised crime, largely involving nefarious "business opportunities" associated with the docks. An important question was: how well organised were the High Rip? Mr Raffles, the stipendiary magistrate who tried many of the gang at the Dale Street Police Court, rejected the idea of any organisation among the ruffians. Some newspapers also queried the constitution of the gang. It was felt there was no proper structure and that the gang simply met on a random and opportunist basis.[19] However, it was also admitted that crimes were planned on street corners, in public houses or derelict properties. This implies some level of organisation, as does the August 1886 march to Walton Gaol, which is described in a later chapter. The siege of the prison by up to

200 High Rippers was no spontaneous action, but a clearly pre-planned protest.

One of the difficulties in reporting the activities of the High Rip was that not much was known about the inner workings of the gang. According to one newspaper, rumour and misinformation were rife: "One authority asserts that the High Rip gang are merely idle loafers; another that they are highway robbers; according to one authority they are quite without organisation, while another will gravely describe how new members are 'sworn in' upon crossed knives in the witching hour of the night."[20]

Gang members were unlikely to give away vital information. The press nevertheless set out to uncover some facts about the High Rip.[21] The question was posed as to why members of the gang were rarely caught and punished by the police. The answer was that victims dared not prosecute for fear of further injury. People also had no faith in the police. There were many cases where shopkeepers who had been robbed by the gang simply refused to complain to the authorities, such was the level of intimidation.

It was also felt that the gang found it easy to escape from the police. When chased, it was not uncommon for the High Ripper to rush into the nearest house, climb on top of the roof and bound from one street to another. Gang members would enter dwellings wherever they found an open door, whether they knew the inhabitants or not, knowing that people would never refuse them entry or inform the police of their whereabouts. The penalty of refusal would entail the resident being "spotted" by the gang and later beaten, kicked or stabbed. Such beatings occurred regularly. The North Dispensary in Vauxhall Road treated about 100 cases of violent wounding a week, about fourteen or fifteen a day. It was acknowledged that many of these injuries were caused by brutal assaults by husbands upon their wives, but this still left a large percentage of attacks by ruffians on helpless victims who dared not prosecute.

The newspaper did not wonder that the ferocity of the High Rip, coupled with the lack of police to deal with them, was a cause of great social concern. Gang members went about in groups of six to twelve, armed with weapons that made the policeman's truncheon virtually useless by comparison. They habitually carried a knife, or "the bleeder" as it was known. The Cornermen's boots had also been replaced by another item of clothing as the High Rip weapon of choice. The formidable new tool in the gangland armoury was the belt, one of which was described as having seven flat brass buckles, all of which had been filed to a cutting edge and arranged to fall to the end of the belt when whirled about. The gaping slash wound from a belt was indistinguishable from a knife cut. The belt had the further advantage of being effective up to a distance of four feet.

Not only were the High Rip better armed than the police, but also they were more cunning. If gang members had little respect for the homes of local inhabitants, they had even less for empty properties. The High Rip would break holes through the walls of unoccupied houses and strip them of grates, doors and sometimes even floorboards. Houses in Stockdale Street, off Marybone, had holes in the walls, which were sometimes covered by wallpaper and used by the gang as a sort of secret door when pursued by the police.

It was debated whether the High Rip was a secret society. One way to have found out would have been for an undercover journalist to join as a new recruit, in the same way that today's investigative journalists work for television documentary *exposés* of the criminal underworld. However, it was feared that the High Rippers were not the sort of people that anybody would desire to infiltrate. The only individuals who could be approached for information about the gang were ex-members who had left to improve themselves morally.

The newspaper was informed by one such person that the gang did indeed have a secret initiation ceremony. This consisted of scratching the wrist with a knife and swearing that "as that blood was drawn, so would he never attack a person without drawing blood; and that he would always be ready to help every member of the gang and avenge any injury done to them." It was left to the readers to decide whether or not such an oath was genuine.

It has already been described how, after the Tithebarn Street murder in 1874, Councillor Chambres went out on an evening mission around Vauxhall Road and Bevington Bush looking for evidence of the Cornermen. During the High Rip scare, the newspapers felt it their similar duty to go in search of the High Rip. The *Daily Post*, in particular, wanted to get closer to the gang and appointed a special "commissioner" to research into them.[22] There was only one way to discover the truth about the High Rip and this involved going into its haunts and studying the gang members' habits at first hand. It would obviously have been too dangerous for a stranger to go alone into "High Rip Land". An escort by a policeman would also have been useless, since the police were the natural enemies of the gang. What's more, the High Rip simply vanished at the sight of a constable.

The newspaper felt that the only escort capable of giving adequate protection was one of the few individuals who provided some of the gang members with employment. There were certain occasional jobs of a lucrative, but not laborious, nature – such as scaling the boilers of steamers – which were sometimes taken by the High Rip, when they did condescend to work. It was felt that the man who provided such work was given enough respect in the community so as to be able to go about his business without being molested.

One *Daily Post* journalist was able to secure the services of such a guide. Aided by two companions, the man was able to take the journalist on a tour of "High Rip Land". However, despite agreeing to accompany the journalist, the guide made it clear that he did not want his name published for fear of reprisals. If they did not kill or maim him, they would certainly have smashed his windows for giving away gang information.

The group began their tour on the main thoroughfare lying in the district bounded by Athol Street and Bankhall Street in the north, Great Howard Street in the west and Vauxhall Road to the east. The headquarters of the gang was in or near Athol Street. In this area, three factors aided their existence: a disgraceful lack of police presence, the menacing darkness of the streets, and the scarcity of dwellings and hence residents. Along Great Howard Street and Vauxhall Road, leading north, rows of warehouses alternated with wasteland that stored timber. The landscape was likened to a backwood forest. Intersecting these two roads were dark streets, at the corners of which the High Rip gathered, lying in wait for unsuspecting passers-by.

On a couple of occasions during the tour, groups of three or four gang members, in "bucco caps", apparently the official headgear of the High Rip, appeared menacingly from behind hoardings or out of dark corners in order to check out the tourists. When they recognised the face of the "escort", they skulked back into the dark.

The escort gave a demonstration of how dangerous such districts were. In the lower part of Athol Street was a public house frequented by the gang. The group made a visit and found about twelve High Rippers in the bar parlour. At the suggestion of one of his escorts, the journalist stood apart from the rest of the group and quietly drank his ale. Each of the gang walked past him giving him a long, hard stare, in the manner of a wolf regarding its intended prey. The gang made their way outside and loitered at the door, dancing what is called "the cellar flap" and occasionally looking in to check whether their man had escaped them.

When the group eventually emerged together from the pub, the gang recognised the companions of the stranger and broke up into twos and threes to let them pass. The newspaper, however, was in no doubt that if the journalist had been unaccompanied then the incident would not have ended so peacefully.

Further proof of the High Rip's level of organisation was also cited. There was said to be an understanding between the members and a series of signs and signals by which they communicated with each other. They had a peculiar whistle of three shrill notes, which they used to summon other High Rips. They also had manual signals; for example, if they wanted to warn a colleague at a distance to keep out of sight, they put up their hands and waved them from their face, palm outwards in a horizontal line. If they wished their companion to come forwards, the signal was to wave their hands towards the ground, palms downwards. These signals could be given without their victims being aware of it. Thus, if somebody worth robbing approached, the members pretended to spar with open hands while at the same time giving a signal to the rest of their gang to prepare for action.

A rigorous form of discipline, enforced with ferocious severity, maintained group unity. Apparently two members of the High Rip were punished for refusing an order to knife a drunken sailor. Their disobedience resulted in them being kicked and stabbed by a posse of their fellow rogues.

Not to be outdone, another journalist, from the *Liverpool Review*, decided to investigate the darker side of Liverpool.[23] In 1886, he went on a late-night trek into the heart of the High Rip hunting ground. His mission was to investigate a Scotland Road gambling den, a place where even policemen were afraid to enter alone. A friend, familiar with some of the ruffians who frequented the place, accompanied the journalist, no doubt also for reasons of protection.

After turning into a side street, the pair knocked on the door of what appeared to be an office, and after correctly answering several questions and bribing the doorman, they were granted admittance. They ascended several flights of creaky stairs and ended up in a games room, where two men were playing billiards while a third lay across a table in a drunken stupor. The rest of the club members comprised an assortment of Cornermen, High Rippers and various other types of ruffian: "A more ill-looking or blackguardly lot never scuttled a ship or cut a throat." Some of the patrons looked young enough to be still at school, but oddly enough appeared even more brutalised than their adult companions. The club was indeed "a nursery for Cornermen".

The visitors journeyed further into the dark interior of the building and finally entered a dingy office labelled "Committee Room", where a card game was in progress. A dispute over winnings was about to come to blows when the establishment's "chucker out" threatened to evict the men. Twenty to thirty spectators watched the game of baccarat while yet another man lay asleep, using his hat for a pillow. Instead of a proper card table, a makeshift tabletop was marked with chalk so that it could be easily erased and returned to innocent furniture in the event of an untimely police raid.

The manager of the club, a frightful-looking man with Fagin features, acted as croupier. The stakes were not very high, mere shillings, but even this seemed a fortune coming from such ragged clientele. The cost of the clothing of the entire group of players was probably worth less than a shilling. A brooding air of menace hung around the room and occasionally the manager had to quell potential trouble with the warning, "Do you know what a risk I'm running and what will happen if the police catch us?" But the police never did arrest them, even though the Dale Street detective office was a mere five-minute walk away.

Illicit gambling in secret back rooms was probably the least of the police's worries, for out on the multitude of streets adjoining Scotland

Road, Vauxhall Road and Great Howard Street, a vicious war was being waged. This time the High Rippers were not playing games to amuse themselves or to win enough coppers to pay for the next round of drinks. This time the stakes were much higher.

CHAPTER 13

Crimes of the High Rip

THE CRIMES OF the High Rip fell neatly into three categories, the wrongdoers' three Rs: random violence, robbery and revenge attacks.

The High Rip was often portrayed as having some level of organisation, which they used to plan criminal activities. However, as shown by the Blackstone Street murder, one of the most terrifying features of the gang was their willingness to engage in random acts of violence. There was often no attempt at theft. It seems that nobody could innocently walk past them without falling prey to some sort of abuse or violence.

Some High Rip attacks were pretty tame. A lone female was a favourite target. Women would be insulted with coarse, lewd comments as they passed or even subjected to a rough jostle on the pavement. If a gentleman passed, he might have his hat crushed. Any retaliation would prompt a beating.

However, assaults against respectable people could be more serious. At the corner of Birchfield Street, Islington, the gang ambushed a gentleman and his lady. The man was punched, but immediately returned a sharp jab, which stunned his attacker. The rest of the gang closed about him, cautiously at first on account of the heavy blow he had just given their colleague. As his lady friend walked on, away from the trouble, the man fought with the entire gang, keeping the first attacker constantly at bay as he worked his way down the street. After giving the ringleader another beating, the man saw an open door and ran in for shelter. During the fracas, the lady had gone off in search of a policeman. Yet even though the house was besieged by a mob of ruffians who were threatening to break down the door to get at their prey, it was a full half hour before an officer could be found to deal with the incident. When the police finally arrived and the siege ended, no attempt was made to follow and arrest the offenders, who seemed to be well known as "them lot".

It would not be the first time that the gang had picked on the wrong person. In 1960, writer Frank Shaw, from Huyton, recalled a story about his father, a professional wrestler who competed under the ring-name of Jack Murphy.[1] One day on his journey to work at a butcher's shop, he had passed through the "Long Jigger", a narrow alley in Cazneau Street, off Scotland Road, where many of the gang members had their haunts. Three members of the High Rip attacked him, but they were no match for the wrestler's strength and skills. The gang admired his bravery so much that they henceforth escorted him to work to make sure he travelled without interference.

Assaults took on a more serious nature when weapons were used. In April 1885, Richard Duggan and Michael Madden were charged with wounding Patrick Howard and Thomas Noon. The men had argued in a public house the previous night. As the victims walked down Scotland Road, Duggan and Madden set upon them using belts and sticks. Howard was also knifed in the head. In court, it was stated that the prisoners were members of the High Rip.

On July 27, 1885, William McIntosh, yet another "rough-looking" member of the High Rip, appeared in court. For journalists, all criminals were either "rough-looking" or "respectable-looking", depending on their class. McIntosh was charged with having stabbed John Smith and having attacked a policeman the previous day. McIntosh and a group of ruffians had been making a row outside a house in Back Portland Street, off Vauxhall Road. Fed up with the noise, the occupier, John Smith, went out to tell them to "clear off". McIntosh announced that he would rather fight Smith instead. He then punched him in the face and stabbed him three times in the leg and twice in the chest.

Members of the High Rip did not limit themselves to terrorising their own neighbourhood; they enjoyed day trips to the seaside, bringing terror with them. On the August Bank Holiday of 1885, the alleged leader of the gang, William McConnell, led a coterie of youths on an orgy of violence in New Brighton. McConnell had been imprisoned for assaulting John Grant earlier in the year, but the jail term had done nothing to curb his aggression.

Athol Street Bridewell. First port of call for many arrested High Rippers.

Their first victim was pork butcher William Bowker, who ran a stall on the New Brighton shore. He had caught McConnell and Samuel Hinds stealing some pig's feet and smacked McConnell in the face, but was then set upon by the rest of the gang. The butcher was hit with a cane and stabbed in the shoulder blade.

Later that evening, the gang went to The Dive public house in New Brighton. A fight broke out between the lads and they all went outside to settle it. John Shute (or Chute), of Limekiln Lane, who worked at the same docks as the gang, happened to be there and ended up being stabbed in the chest and back. It seems that Shute had quarrelled with some of the lads on a previous occasion. His injuries were so severe, it was feared at first that he would not recover from them.

Knives were found on the prisoners when they were arrested, and in October four youths, McConnell, Hinds, James Burns and Thomas Crighton, who all lived off Vauxhall and Scotland Roads, were charged with cutting and wounding John Shute, while McConnell and Hinds faced a similar charge of wounding William Bowker. A witness reported that just before Shute was stabbed, Hinds had been heard to say that he would have the life of the first man who came before him. He had an open knife in his hand at the time.

Hinds was sentenced to five years' imprisonment for the attack on Bowker, but amazingly the other prisoners were found not guilty.

On November 17, 1885, James O'Hare and Henry Moore appeared in court accused of having wounded Thomas Crow, a dock labourer from Chisenhale Street, off Vauxhall Road. Earlier in the month a policeman had been escorting an arrested man to the Chisenhale Bridewell when Moore started to scream "High Rip". Crow told Moore to shut up and go home. Moore responded by kicking Crow on the shin before fleeing. Crow tried to follow him, but O'Hare then tripped him up and stabbed him three times. The magistrate remarked that the youths were connected with a gang, a member of which had been tried the day before and sentenced to be hanged.

Mr Raffles must have been referring to the case of Joseph Flynn, a boiler scaler aged seventeen, who was convicted of murdering twenty-five-year-old Edwin Pearson in Bootle. On Saturday, September 19, 1885, Pearson had been to a dancing class in Balliol Road. After the session finished, at about 11 p.m., Pearson stood talking with some friends at the corner of Brasenose Street and Balliol Road. Pearson heard his name called. He walked over to a gang of youths and Flynn declared, "I am ready to fight any man of my own size." Both Flynn and Pearson took off their coats ready for combat, but were separated by their friends and ended up putting them back on again. Flynn walked away, but then pulled a knife out of his pocket and returned. He went berserk, stabbing three or four of Pearson's group before delivering his victim a fatal blow to the chest. Pearson fell back into the arms of his friends and groaned, "I am done for." He lingered throughout the night, but died the following morning at Bootle Borough Hospital.

Later, Flynn met a boy called Billy Edwards in Derby Road. "Oh Billy, what shall I do?" he asked. "I've stabbed four men and two of them dropped stone dead." He added, "Come with me along Derby Road, or I'll give myself up." Edwards walked with him to the corner of Church Street and then left him to his fate. Flynn was arrested on Sunday at his home in Mann Street.

In court, he admitted that he had only gone along with some friends to see fair play during a fight they were planning. The skirmish, however, did not take place and they had gone to a public house instead. Flynn blamed his actions on drink: "I was mad drunk and I don't know what I was doing." He was found guilty and sentenced to death with a recommendation to mercy, on account of his youth. His appeal was successful and the sentence was commuted to life imprisonment.

However, there is no mention of the High Rip in the trial report published by the press, so it uncertain why, the following day, Mr Raffles thought that the gang had been involved. It could be a case of blaming every knife crime on the High Rip. The term seemed to have become shorthand for describing every stabbing incident.

Another typical street outrage involving knives occurred on September 21, 1886. Three youths were charged with stabbing a drunken man at one o'clock on a Sunday morning. The victim's wife had been escorting him home through an unnamed rough district when the gang set upon him. It was felt that in any other part of Liverpool the man would have been safe on his journey, but in a district infested with the High Rip, the victim stood no chance.

The High Rip, however, was more interested in stealing money than in beating up strangers for no reason. The gang's modus operandi involved intimidating dock labourers. They were so well organised that they had perfect information about their intended victims. They were able to tell a man how many days he had worked and the amount of wages that he had earned: at that point, they would demand a slice. Some dockers even gave up their employment and moved to another district to escape the attentions of the High Rip.

Those foolish enough to linger about the streets after being paid would be hit behind the ear. The gang would then crowd around the fallen victim in order to screen the body from passers-by. If he had fallen face down, he would be rolled over and the gang would then "go through him" like a plague of locusts.

When the High Rip went thieving, not even the police could stand in their way. On August 21, 1885, Thomas Kelly assaulted a constable who had been trying to prevent a lad from stealing in Blandford Street, Islington. The incident erupted when James Hesketh was arrested for stealing a pair of boots. Kelly, said to be a member of the High Rip, intervened and tried to rescue the footwear. A crowd soon gathered, many of them youths. Kelly shouted, "Belts off, boys!" The policeman was then viciously attacked by a whirlwind of slashing buckles, suffering a fractured skull and a burst eyeball. A brave bystander picked up the policeman's whistle and blew it to summon assistance. There would undoubtedly have been a murder had an officer not rescued his colleague quickly.

A few days later, a detective arrested Kelly in a cocoa room in Byrom Street, off Scotland Road. He gave his name as John Hughes, but afterwards admitted his true identity. He declared, "All I did was push the boy away and steal the boots. I did not touch the policeman at all."

In December 1885, an anonymous resident from the north end of Scotland Road wrote to the newspaper complaining about the behaviour of a local gang.[2] The name High Rip is not mentioned, but the crimes committed by the lads fit the bill perfectly. According to the letter, members of the gang randomly assaulted passers-by and ran down the street robbing goods hanging outside the shops, deftly passing the spoils from one to another to confuse witnesses. The author claimed that they were so feared that they were able to deposit their plunder in two out of every three houses in the district. They began their "working day" at 11 p.m. when drunken and defenceless men were coming home from the pubs. The police were aware of the gang, but seemed so afraid of them that they didn't interfere. The writer spoke to an old woman who had been the recent victim of the gang. The lady was asked if she knew her attackers. She pointed to one of them and said, "That's Tom ******, the leader of the band; but if I gave them in charge I could not live in the place." The lady was afraid of reprisals, but bravely offered the names and addresses of the gang for the attention of the Head of Police, if only her identity could be kept secret.

On the December 30, 1885, Michael Scully and Mary Blenington, together with Anna and Margaret Fitzpatrick, appeared at the City Police Court. They had been charged with breaking into the house and shop of John Shea of Headley Street, near Vauxhall Road, the previous week. The gang had broken six panes of glass and stolen property worth eight pounds. On entering the house, Scully boldly introduced himself to the occupants as "one of the High Rip Gang". The youth's defence argued that the label High Rip was being used repeatedly in court "in every case in which it was desired to excite feeling against the accused". The defence also stated that certain items of furniture had been thrown out of the window at the accused. Mrs Shea denied that anything had been thrown through the window or that her husband had ever fought with the gang. Witnesses were called who testified that a man called O'Brien had been the one who

Dale Street Police Court. Second port of call for many arrested High Rippers.

had smashed the windows. However, the magistrate found the gang guilty and ordered them to pay ten shillings each for the damage with an additional fine of one shilling.

ON AUGUST 8, 1886, Thomas Donnelly was one of a number of High Rip members who beat up William Hignett in Scotland Road. The gang had ordered Hignett, of Harrison Street, to pay for some spruce beer. When he refused, he was knocked down and brutally kicked about the body and head.

In another of his letters to the press, the "Citizen" reported a similar High Rip case.[3] In the late months of 1886, a man had been walking under a bridge in Lightbody Street, off Vauxhall Road. At about 6 p.m., a gang confronted him and asked him to "stand half a gallon of ale". When he refused, the man was knocked down and kicked insensible. His money, knife and keys were stolen.

The Citizen also reported that, on February 14, the gang had surrounded a sailor at his home in Luton Street. The man, who was with his wife, had been paid earlier that day. In broad daylight, at around midday, they took him into the bottom room and held him while they robbed every penny and then kicked and abused him for daring to call out, "Police." The writer revealed that there had, in fact, been a policeman in the area, but that the High Rip had been able to keep a watch on him so that he did not interfere.

Another reported case involved a man who had been unemployed for three months. On regaining employment, he had only done three days' work when the gang attacked him in Howe Street, off Derby Road in the north end. Because he dared to put up some resistance, the man was kicked unconscious in front of his young son.

In a 1960 newspaper feature on the High Rip, eighty-six-year-old Elizabeth O'Brien offered childhood reminiscences of the gang. Born in 1874, she lived in Hornby Street, off Scotland Road, and was a young girl of twelve during the High Rip's heyday. Mrs O'Brien recalled her grandfather coming home from work with his money-belt slashed; the gang had taken all the cash. He didn't dare go to the police for fear of reprisals.

It wasn't just adults who were robbed; children were equally at risk. In 1886, a schoolmaster wrote to the newspaper to complain that a mother had recently brought her thirteen-year-old son to him.[4] The boy had been beaten up and robbed, apparently by two members of the High Rip. Upon examining the lad, it was discovered that his body was covered in bruises from the blows of a buckled belt. The mother told the teacher that she knew the names and addresses of those who had beaten her son but, on being advised to go to the police, confessed that she had dared not. She would be too afraid to walk the streets or open her door. She knew of the fate of others who had gone against the High Rip. The schoolmaster called for tougher police measures to combat the gangs in Liverpool.

His letter inspired an editorial that compared the High Rip to the Dacoits of Burma. The Dacoits were wild bands of robbers. It was felt that Liverpool had become as bad as Mandalay.[5]

In 1886, a poultry dealer from St John's Market set up an additional stall in the new Exchange Station in Tithebarn Street. The station was in the process of being rebuilt. In late October, with no watchman present, the High Rip was able to break in and steal from the shop; they took a large quantity of poultry and game. A witness remonstrated with the gang, but they threatened "to do for him" if he opened his mouth. Shortly afterwards, Scotland Road was awash with turkeys selling for a shilling and chickens for thruppence. Several other robberies had taken place in the vicinity during the previous few weeks, although the culprits remained at large.

There were numerous High Rip outrages, including the attack on another sailor in Regent Road, which ran alongside the docks. After gagging the man, the gang cut out his pockets with a knife and left him both penniless and helpless. In Boundary Street, off Vauxhall Road, they also split open someone's skull with a scaling hammer because he had refused to hand over tobacco.

As proof of their audacity, gang members were reported to have engaged in particularly novel crimes. A master scaler would hire members of the gang to scale the boilers of steamers. As the High Rips were generally small in stature, he used to take on a number of them. However, one day, one of his best workers with the scaling hammer was out at a wedding party. The master scaler went searching for him and found the party in full swing in the cellar. He called for the lad he wanted and waited patiently in the street for him to appear. While he was standing there, some passing High Rips who did not know him slipped off the coal grid, seized him by the legs and dragged him down the hole as far as his armpits. They then robbed his money, watch and chain. However, when the gang discovered that the man had come for one of their colleagues, his property was returned with apologies. The father of the ringleader of the thieves then knocked out his son and gave him a severe thrashing with both his fists and feet.

In another example of High Rip ingenuity, an engineer was about to scale a boiler. As he quietly approached the entrance, he heard some lads inside boasting of their exploits. They told of how they had got a "cop" (a victim) down into a cellar in "Teapot Street" (Raglan Street, Derby Road). After tripping him up they claimed to have fastened a rope to his feet and passed it through a pulley, which had been rigged up to the ceiling. The man was then hauled up by his heels and shaken until all of his money had fallen out. He was then kicked into the street before the gang ran off. The lads were very much amused at their own wicked resourcefulness.

One of the most horrific High Rip crimes involved a vicious assault on a young child when, during a couple of hours on February 4, 1887, the gang went on the rampage through the streets of Liverpool.

John Baker, Francis McTavey, Bernard McCall and George Baker were all labourers aged nineteen or twenty and lived in a lodging house in Silvester Street, connecting Vauxhall Road and Scotland Road. At about teatime, the four men were standing at the corner of Westmoreland Street, near to where they lived, when James Marsden and a friend walked past. The gang took up the entire pavement and the two men cautiously stepped into the road to avoid them. Without any provocation, Baker launched a vicious attack on Marsden, striking him on the head with his knife. The blade cut through the victim's hat and inflicted a serious wound.

The gang then moved on to Lewis Harrison's pawnbrokers in Scotland Road, where they attempted to steal a coat and some other articles. As the owner tried to prevent them, McTavey drew his knife and tried to stab him. When McTavey realised that Mr Harrison was going to put up a fight, he decided to run for it. By this time, a crowd

Silvester Street (1897). Home of the four gang members who went on the rampage in Scotland Road, and of High Rip "captain" Thomas Maher (see Chapter 14).

had gathered outside the shop and, in order to make his escape, McTavey slashed and stabbed indiscriminately as he cleared a passage to freedom.

Not to be outdone, the gang then returned to the shop and attacked the owner again. This time, however, Harrison managed to keep McTavey at bay with a long wooden pole. Meanwhile, the rest of the gang cut down various items of clothing before running away.

They next struck at Rimmer's pawnshop in Latimer Street. Rimmer's assistant had half his waistcoat, containing a pocket with four shillings, torn off. One of the gang shouted, "Out with your knives, lads," but luckily for the shop assistant they used the blades only to cut down more clothing from the display outside the shop.

Remaining in Latimer Street, the gang then paid a visit to a confectionary shop. The owner's daughter, a Mrs Morris, was standing at the door with an infant in her arms. George Baker smacked the child in the face, leaving the woman screaming that her baby had been killed. McTavey, brandishing a knife, then kicked Mrs Morris. The woman's two brothers, upon hearing the commotion, rushed to the rescue, but were also beaten by the gang. One brother suffered a cut to the head and the other a severe wound to his back. The four ruffians then smashed the shop windows.

Drunk on violence, the gang moved on to Mr Smith's butcher's shop further up the street. McTavey or Baker grabbed hold of Smith, who was then stabbed in the back.

The gang next appeared in Scotland Road at Newport's pawnshop, where a boy and a shop assistant called Pitt were both attacked. Pitt bravely tackled the gang with a wooden board, but was struck on the knee by John Baker's slingshot. The gang then tried, unsuccessfully, to cut down more items of clothing that were hanging outside the shop.

The gang ran off down Dalrymple Street, where they knocked down two women and hit another child. The orgy of random violence and robbery ceased when they made their way back to Scotland Road where, for a finale, they attacked an assistant at yet another shop.

The police acted on information and managed to arrest all of the gang. George Baker was found with a bloodstained knife in his pocket, while the slingshot was found in the possession of John Baker. McTavey still had Harrison's shirts. Three months later, the four rough-looking men appeared in court accused of eight counts of maliciously wounding with intent to do grievous bodily harm and robbery with violence. They were described in court as "imperfectly educated" labourers.

The jury found them guilty of the robbery against Harrison and the judge decided that it would not be necessary to continue with the other charges against the prisoners. By way of defence, Mr Segar, acting for McTavey, argued that no violence had actually been used in the Harrison case, a position that neatly sidestepped the issue of the gang's savagery during the rest of the rampage.

Justice Day stated that he had initially thought that only a long sentence of imprisonment would be appropriate. However, taking into consideration the youth of the prisoners, he would instead pass a sentence that would prove less burdensome to society, which would only have to pay for their upkeep in gaol. John Baker received eighteen months, George Baker, sixteen months, McTavey, fifteen months and McCall, twenty-one months, all with hard labour. The best was saved till last. Each of them would also suffer three separate floggings during their stay in gaol, receiving twenty lashes on each occasion. The severe methods of the beady-eyed, bespectacled, bewhiskered Justice Day will be seen to play a central role in the fate of the High Rip (see Chapter 17).

The *Echo* was scathing in its criticism of the gang's savagery.[6] It said that in Malay, for example, a native, after getting high on opium, would sometimes run amok, charging down the street and stabbing anyone in his path – but that was in Eastern Asia, not Liverpool! The newspaper felt that the crime justified the running of the feature on "Savage Liverpool".

The High Rip was not only responsible for random violence and robberies. By August 1886, they were reported to have been behind a number of audacious revenge attacks on people who had dared to give evidence against fellow gang members.

Harold Buck, a young labourer of Bower Street, off Luton Street, was lying in bed on the night of August 1, 1886, when he heard the sound of gunfire in the street. He went out to investigate and saw John McShane, aged thirty-two, standing about fourteen yards away with a pistol in his hand. McShane aimed the six-chambered revolver and fired indiscriminately at the crowd of people gathered. Unfortunately, the bullet hit Buck, wounding him in the foot.

In court, Buck stated that he had not even spoken to the gunman, nor had McShane uttered anything to him before he fired. In his defence, McShane submitted a written statement that was read out by the clerk. He revealed that, on a couple of previous occasions, several of the High Rip gang had visited his house, smashed the windows and tried to force the door. They also called him a "police spy". A gang member called Michael Trainor warned McShane that "he had done three months and a flogging for one fellow and he would do five years for him." This was the youth who had earlier been gaoled with Thomas Gibbons for the attack on a sailor. McShane threatened to call the police, but the gang boasted that they did not care for the police and that, in fact, the police were afraid of them.

A police constable furnished the judge with some information about Trainor. He was a very bad character who, when previously tried for wounding, was believed to have been the captain of the High Rip.

McShane revealed that the gang had repeatedly attacked his house and threatened him because he was a caretaker for the Lancashire and Yorkshire Railway Company and because he had refused to allow the ruffians to meet in one of the company's empty houses, for which he held the key. On one occasion, they had knocked at his door and, when he opened it, bricks had been thrown at him. McShane claimed that he had needed a police escort on more than one occasion.

The prosecutor asked Police Constable 507 if the High Rip gang had been in the street that night.

Police Constable:	I don't know about the High Rip Gang.
Prosecutor:	But you know the High Rip Gang?
Police Constable:	Yes.
Prosecutor:	Were any of the members known to you there?
Police Constable:	No, not to my knowledge.
Justice Day:	Do you mean to say there is such a gang about Liverpool now?
Prosecutor:	It is a matter of common knowledge, my lord.
Justice Day:	It is very discreditable to the police if there is such a gang now. Four years ago I heard there was such a gang, and I was unwilling to believe that the police of Liverpool would allow such a gang to control the streets.

Witnesses confirmed that McShane's windows had been broken on previous occasions. Justice Day, in amazement, asked Mrs Nolan, one such witness, "What part of the town is it where these rowdies and ruffians control the police?" The witness, smiling, replied, "Sebastopol, my lord."

McShane was found guilty of unlawful wounding, but the judge postponed sentencing upon his entering into recognizance to be of good behaviour.

The next day, August 2, Patrick Corcoran saw a twenty-nine-year-old sweep called Patrick Webb and another man beating up two boys in Banastre Street, off Vauxhall Road. Corcoran went to intervene, but was also attacked by Webb. Seeing a disturbance, Martin Welsh and Charles Jansen then tried to help Corcoran. Webb stabbed Jansen and ran away. Welsh immediately pursued him, but Webb turned around and knifed him as well. Following his arrest, Webb argued that he had attacked the men in self-defence.

In his defence, the prisoner put a written statement into court explaining that the High Rip gang had previously attacked him. On the day before the assault, Webb had given evidence for the prosecution in a wounding case. Later in the day, while out walking with a friend, one of the gang had cried out, "Here's the two who gave evidence against our two lads this morning. Let's pay them out." The gang then ran at Webb and his friend yelling repeatedly, "High Rip, High Rip." One of them also shouted, "Give it them for being witness against Murray." Webb admitted that he had threatened to use his knife on the gang, but added that he was reluctant to do so, as he had a wife and children. He screamed, "The first man that comes near me, he or I will fall." The High Rip menacingly joked that they would make him eat the knife.

During the trial, the judge asked Webb if he had any witnesses to call. "No, my lord," he replied. "Their lives have been threatened if they give evidence in my favour." Despite Webb's plea of self-defence, he was sentenced to seven years' imprisonment.

CHAPTER 14

Gang War

EVERY GANG HAS its enemy or archrival, and the High Rip was no exception. Its major foe was the Logwood Gang, originally formed as a "mutual protection society or vigilance committee" of working men brought together by their collective fear of the High Rip. The name derives from the logwood sticks that the members carried as cudgels.

It is not known precisely when the Logwood formed, but they eventually patrolled their area in large numbers and were vigilantes as lawless in their way as those they sought to combat. When they caught a small group of High Rippers, they were said to force them down on their knees to make a vow to work. The image is almost comic. The big question was: what would happen if a gang member refused to comply? The unnamed leader of the Logwood, when asked by a journalist, replied that "he couldn't quite say, but something would be done".[1] Although the newspapers disapproved of this American type of lynch law, they nevertheless felt thankful that at least there was one organisation actively trying to put an end to the High Rip; it was a thinly veiled criticism of police inaction.

A newspaper correspondent, calling himself "One Who Knows", explained the origins of the gang.[2] He revealed that concerned citizens had formed the Logwood in order to protect both themselves and their parents from the High Rip, who had assaulted and robbed them on a number of occasions. He admitted that the High Rip had been "too cute" for the Logwood by giving information to the police, leading to the Logwoods being bound over to keep the peace. With the Logwood weakened, the High Rip was able to carry on committing crimes unhindered. "One Who Knows" proudly asserted that not one of the Logwoods had ever been committed for felony. They were all respectable and hardworking young men who, when they came home from work in the evening, stood around Great Crosshall Street, at the lower end of Vauxhall Road. The High Rip, on the other hand, was to be found further north on the street corners from the top and bottom of Sawney Pope Street in a line from Marybone and Scotland Road, as far as Athol Street.

How respectable the Logwood gang was is debatable. Perhaps inevitably, it eventually developed into a mob that itself thrived on violence and robbery. In December 1886, Catherine Grealey of Back Blake Street was attacked in her own home. Mary Melia, aged seventeen and Joseph Williams, aged nineteen, smashed their way through the front door with an iron bar, with Melia shouting, "Here's the Logwood gang." Thomas Johnston, aged twenty-three, and others joined the pair in ransacking the house. Grealey's coat and some ginger beer and food were stolen. What they didn't take, the gang smashed to pieces in front of the terrified woman.

The only reason Grealey could give for being targeted was that, earlier in the year, she had given evidence in court against the sister of one of her attackers. At Liverpool Police Court in Dale Street, Melia and Williams were convicted and given three months, while Johnston received one month: all of the sentences came with hard labour.

THE MOST BRAZEN attempt at revenge by the High Rip was the march to Walton Gaol on Saturday, August 28, 1886. Earlier in the year, following what appears to have been a pitched battle between the High Rip and the Logwood in a Scotland Road public house, a man had been stabbed to death. Two youths aged nineteen were eventually convicted and sentenced to fifteen years. A man called Mathers, who had formerly been a member of the High Rip, gave evidence at the petty sessions court against one of the murderers. Mathers received six weeks' imprisonment for his own part in the affray.

That, at least, was one story circulated by the press. However, the tale was told differently in the account given at the assizes in May 1886. That is if the two events are the same; there don't seem to be any other reports of a murder in a Scotland Road public house. Thomas

Entrance to Walton Gaol. Scene of the High Rip revenge attack.

Donlan, a married man aged thirty-six, was charged with murdering Patrick Heston, aged twenty-three. Two months earlier, Heston, from Bent Street off Scotland Road, had been to a foot race at Walton with a gang of friends. Afterwards they ended up in an alehouse in Scotland Road. Donlan and two colleagues entered later. When Heston began to sing "A Lad from Ireland", Donlan told him to shut up. An argument followed. One version has it that Donlan shouted, "I'll fight you", though witnesses for the defence later claimed that it was the other group who wanted to start trouble. Patrick Rogan, one of Heston's gang, stepped up and was willing to fight, but Donlan felt that he was too tall for him to take on.

At this point, Thomas Maher (not Mathers), who was not part of any group, approached Donlan and said that if Rogan had been too big then he certainly wasn't. Maher, from Silvester Street, then attacked Donlan, punching him and knocking him under a table. At the first sign of a brawl, everybody in the bar jumped up and a general scuffle followed. James Gallagher, another friend of Heston, tried to hit Donlan on the head with a barstool.

During the altercation, Heston jumped in and attempted to separate the men. Upon seeing something glistening in Donlan's hand,
somebody shouted, "Watch out for the chivvy," but it was too late.
Heston had been stabbed twice, once in the heart, and died instantly.
In the struggle to disarm Donlan, Gallagher was also knifed.

Donlan's defence tried to argue that his client didn't have a
weapon. Just before they entered the bar, Thomas Gregory was
supposed to have asked his friend Donlan to lend him a knife to cut up
tobacco and was told that he didn't have one. There was said to be
more blood on Maher's clothing than on Donlan's, the implication
being that Maher had been the owner of the blade. According to
Donlan, two men held him while four others hit, kicked and head-
butted him. He also claimed that the gang had robbed him. Finally,
Donlan accused Maher of being the captain of the High Rip, a claim
that was confirmed by the police. The gang was said to loiter outside
public houses, interfering with working men.

As the affair had been the result of "hot blood" the charge was
reduced to manslaughter and Donlan was sentenced to six months'
imprisonment. The press did not note the length of Maher's sentence,
although he did go to prison for his part in the affray.

Whatever the origins of the quarrel, at 5 a.m. on the day of Mathers'
(or Maher's) release from prison, a mob of between 150 and 200 High
Rippers gathered in Marybone. They then marched through Scotland
Road to the gaol with the intention of kicking Mathers to death for
what today would be termed "grassing up" a colleague. The siege of
the gaol had been organised at two wakes that had been held in
Marybone the previous week. Since most of the gang had been regular
"gaol birds" themselves, they knew that the prison released its inmates
at 8 a.m.

Fortunately, the police got wind of the plan. Using such modern
technology as the telegraph and telegram, the Walton and Bootle
police were waiting at the gaol before the crowd had even left Scotland
Road. Nevertheless, as Mathers stepped out of the gate, the mob tried
to grab him. They almost succeeded, but PC Wynn and two other
policemen managed to drag Mathers back into the prison, from where
he was later smuggled out down Walton Stiles, accompanied by three
constables. The High Rippers screamed abuse and swore terrible
oaths that they would have their revenge. Many shouted that they

would "do for" Mathers yet. No arrests were made, however; the police presence had merely been there to protect the man.

On Tuesday, August 31, three of the Logwood gang, John Jeffers, Michael Davy and Edward Selborne (or Sebborn), appeared in court charged with tumultuously and riotously assembling in Marybone on the morning of the Walton siege. Detective Grubb, prosecuting, stated that the prisoners had chased some people down the street and that they had thrown stones at them.

Members of the High Rip – despite their own contempt for snitches – appeared in court as witnesses for the prosecution. They gave an alternative version of events. Some testified that it had been members of the Logwood gang who had been on their way to Walton Gaol to meet a released prisoner with whom they had a grudge. Perhaps Donlan, the man convicted of manslaughter, was a member of the Logwood, in which case they might have been after Thomas Maher for giving evidence against him. This, however, is conjecture.

As the Logwood made their way through Marybone, itself a High Rip district, they attacked the High Rippers with sticks and stones. It is not explained what the High Rippers themselves were up to out on the street so early in the morning. Although the High Rip witnesses identified the three prisoners as being part of the crowd, none of them would accuse the men of being responsible for any personal violence. Because the witnesses remained tight-lipped on this score, the magistrate had no alternative but to bind the three men over to keep the peace. He warned that if he had had clearer evidence before him, he would have sent the case to the Sessions Court.

"One Who Knows" offered yet another explanation of the reasons behind the march to the gaol. He denied that the High Rip had intended to kick to death a colleague who had turned traitor. Instead, he claimed that they had gone to kill a member of the Logwood gang and to enrol two or three comrades who they thought would not join them against their rivals. The Logwood also went to the gaol after the High Rips in order to protect their colleague. They also managed to rescue and bring home one of the High Rips who had left home months earlier. The lad confessed that he had only joined the High Rips for his "scoff and dos" (food and lodgings).

The true motivation for the siege of Walton Gaol is now lost in the mists of time. All that is certain is that some sort of protest march took place and that gang rivalries and bitter animosity between the High Rip and the Logwood lay behind it.

The correspondence from "One Who Knows" provoked a reply from another letter writer identified only by the initials W.H.[3] The writer asserted that gangs such as the High Rip and Logwood could be hired for a small fee to do any dirty business. As evidence, W.H. cited an incident in Hamilton Road, Everton, just two weeks earlier. A youth had been eating his evening meal when a knock came at his door. His sister answered and a mysterious male asked for her brother by his first name. The young man rose to speak to the stranger and was told that a young woman wished to see him at the end of the road. He grabbed his hat and made his way with the man.

However, as they passed an entry, a signal was given and three ruffians appeared and joined the other man in giving the lad a severe beating with buckled belts. The young man's mother and sister heard his cries and ran to help him, but they were also assaulted. The police were nowhere to be seen and the four ruffians escaped. The writer of the letter does not explain why these men might have been hired to beat up the young man or even how he knew that they were members of the High Rip. It is not clear either whether the assault was a revenge attack for something the man had done against the gang. The letter was nevertheless headed, "The High Rip Gang".

JOHN JEFFERS WAS one of the three members of the Logwood gang who had been bound over to keep the peace on the morning of the march to Walton Gaol. He had also dared to stand up in court against a High Ripper called Patrick Doyle the previous August, and for this the gang marked him out for revenge.

In late September, the High Rip visited Jeffers at work and threatened to cut him up. On October 2, as he left a shop in Scotland Road, the gang, determined upon revenge, finally set upon him, led by two nineteen-year-olds, Peter Tedford and Edward Higham. Tedford stabbed Jeffers in the arm, while Higham cut him in the thigh. Another unnamed man beat him about the head. A witness who went to Jeffers' aid was also jabbed in the hand. When arrested, Higham promised that he would make Jeffers suffer "if he got time".

In court, both Tedford and Higham stated that the case against them was a conspiracy by the Logwood. In fact, one of the witnesses in the courtroom was pointed out to be the leader of the mob who had marched out to Walton Gaol after the High Rip. During cross-examination, Higham urged Jeffers to clarify some details about the attack. He asked, "Hadn't I got my working clothes on?" Jeffers replied, much to the amusement of the court, "You? You never did any work in your life." The youths were found guilty and received fifteen years' imprisonment.

In defence of the severity of the penalty, the formidable Justice Day warned of the need to quash any attempts to thwart justice through attacks on witnesses. "There had been no calendar in Liverpool in which there had been so many cases of outrages, wounding with the knife, wounding with firearms, deliberately and without passion, with motives of revenge, and for the purpose of defeating justice," he said.

ON NOVEMBER 10, 1886, in a scene straight from Graham Greene's novel *Brighton Rock*, a gang of youths, armed with knives, bludgeons and a cutlass, were seen menacing people at Aintree racecourse. It was the beginning of a sequence of events judged to be "one of the most audacious and wanton crimes attempted in the district since the Tithebarn Street tragedy".[4]

At about 2 p.m., two of the group, George Edwards, aged eighteen, and George Whitehead, aged twenty, both from the Scotland Road area, attacked Edward Selborne, a twenty-year-old iron-dresser from nearby Circus Street. Selborne was another of the Logwood gang who had been bound over to keep the peace after the march to Walton Gaol.

As they approached their victim, Edwards turned to Whitehead declaring, "We have only one life to lose – let us stand to it."

"We came out here to die, and we might as well die," agreed his friend.

With that, Whitehead let out a shout of, "You bastard; I have it in for you, and I will kill you," and stabbed Selborne in the shoulder.

Despite his wound, Selborne bravely tried to chase Whitehead, but Edwards also stabbed him. Selborne collapsed on the floor, begging for mercy, but Edwards screamed, "You pig, you'll get no mercy from me." On seeing a knife being used, some gallant members of the public laid into Edwards with their sticks, connecting with a good few blows to his head.

About twenty police constables responded to the incident by forming a large circle before steadily closing in on the crime scene. A stampede followed as ruffians dispersed in all directions dropping sticks, bludgeons and the cutlass in an attempt to mingle innocently with the crowd. Afterwards, as a result of the discarded weapons, the racecourse resembled a battlefield. The police must have anticipated trouble, as they had turned out in increased numbers and their tactical response appeared to have been well rehearsed.

Selborne's attackers ran off to a tent, but were soon captured and appear to have taken something of a beating – when he later appeared in court, Edwards's head was a mass of bloody pulp, consisting of putrid wounds from old injuries covered by fresh cuts from his recent battering. Selborne, meanwhile, was carried to the bridewell at the back of the grandstand, where a passing doctor gave emergency first aid.

While held in custody, Whitehead explained to the injured Selborne, "This is all through going against Hoare." About a month previously, Selborne had given evidence against Owen Hoare, a companion of the men. Hoare had been accused of attempting to stab a man, but the case had collapsed after the frightened victim refused to give evidence.

At the police station, Selborne told Whitehead, "You cannot deny that you stabbed me."

"Yes, I did, but what did you do?" said Whitehead. "Hadn't you a bit of logwood wrapped in brown paper up your sleeve?"

"God forgive you," uttered Selborne.

He was rushed to Bootle Borough Hospital where he was treated for serious wounds to both the chest and the shoulder. A journalist interviewed him in his hospital bed, although the nurse attending to him requested that the conversation be brief. Selborne, looking very pale and evidently in great pain, revealed the circumstances of his stabbing. He concluded that his attackers belonged to the High Rip gang: "I know it. I fell to the ground and don't know any more."

At the assizes in February 1887, before Justice Hawkins, Edwards was acquitted while Whitehead was found guilty and received five years' imprisonment.

Whitehead was not the only member of his family with a penchant for violence. His younger brother served time for killing a young boy. On New Year's morning 1885, eleven-year-old John Stanfield, from Ascot Street near Scotland Road, was sent out to call his sister. The boy had a speech impediment and could not speak properly. Other children called him the "German" because of his strange pronunciation. Fourteen-year-old David Whitehead went up to Stanfield and said, "Oh, so the 'German' has got a new pair of trousers and jacket on." The boy replied, "I'm not a German; I'm English." Whitehead picked up a stone and threatened Stanfield: "I'll cut the German heart out of you." Seconds later the missile bounced off the back of the younger boy's skull. Stanfield ran home clutching his bloodied head, screaming, "I'm killed." His mother examined the lump, but didn't think that the injury was serious. The boy continued to play out, but the following day he became ill and died. Whitehead was found guilty of manslaughter and sentenced to fourteen days' hard labour.

Perhaps David Whitehead was merely following in the footsteps of his older brother, who was constantly in trouble with the law. Like his friend Edwards, George Whitehead had appeared in court a total of eight times for a variety of offences, including felony, wounding and assaults on the police. On April 25, 1885, Whitehead was charged with having wounded Hugh Cunningham in Titchfield Street, near Vauxhall Road, the week before. At the previous assizes, Cunningham had given evidence against two members of the High Rip who had consequently been gaoled. Whitehead was paying him back. Cunningham had been attacked with a belt and, as he tried to defend himself, was stabbed three times in the head. In court, Whitehead was described as "the captain of the High Rip". The defendant admitted that he had formerly associated with the gang, but that he had had nothing to do with them for some time. He received five months with hard labour.

Ironically, at the end of the trial, Mr Raffles, the magistrate, expressed the opinion "that by this time the gang was almost broken up". In fact, as far as the press was concerned, it was only just beginning. While condemning the actions of the High Rip, newspapers also thrived on sensational stories about the gang. For the next eighteen months, the Liverpool public would be fed a constant diet of horrific tales of High Rip atrocities.

Yet, despite plentiful evidence of physical violence and brutality on Liverpool's streets, for some people the gang was merely a figment of journalists' imaginations.

CHAPTER 15

Denying the High Rip

IN THE AUTUMN of 1888, London was in the grip of a fear as a mysterious character known as Jack the Ripper stalked the dark streets of the East End, butchering five women before vanishing off the face of the earth. Two years earlier, Liverpool had suffered its own autumnal reign of terror as a local band of rippers took over the streets, knifing and robbing anybody in their path. Between October and November 1886, the High Rip gang was at its most infamous. They then disappeared, not quite as suddenly and dramatically as Jack the Ripper, but there was certainly a massive reduction in their criminal activities, or at least the press reporting of those activities.

The analogy between the name of the High Rip gang and Jack the Ripper is interesting. Those Ripperologists who point to a Liverpudlian murderer, for example cotton merchant James Maybrick, often cite the similarity in names as proof that the Ripper had a "Scouse" connection. Indeed, on October 3, 1888, a letter claiming to be from the murderer was sent to a London news agency signed, "George of the High Rip Gang".

During the Ripper's reign of terror, indeed before the last victim, Mary Jane Kelly, had even been murdered, an anonymous author published a forty-eight-page pamphlet giving a semi-fictional account of the crimes that had been committed so far.[1] An invented detective called Dick Ryder stalks the East End of London looking for clues. He even infiltrates the High Rip gang, hoping to find the murderer. However, after meeting these cockney High Rips and their captain, Red Rip, the detective discovers that they are innocent.

Jack the Ripper certainly existed: we just don't know his true identity. However, the same could not be said of the High Rip gang. We have the names and addresses of many of its alleged members; we just don't know whether the gang existed as a single, organised entity or if the name was used as a catch-all media term for a number of unconnected groups or individuals.

Despite constant newspaper references to the High Rip in 1885 and 1886, not everybody believed in the gang's existence. There were many of the opinion that the much-publicised reign of terror had simply been the product of hype, an attempt to sell more newspapers.

A debate ensued in the pages of the local dailies. A newspaper had described the squalor and filth at the north end of Great Howard Street, a district supposedly inhabited by the High Rip. It was alleged that drunken workmen were often beaten up and robbed when they passed through the area.[2] Later in the month, a correspondent called J.G. responded to the report by calling it "absurd fiction".[3] He claimed that the article did not contain a word of truth. Dismissing the threat of danger on entering Fulton Street, the supposed stronghold of High Rippism near to the docks, the writer pointed out that there were only seven houses in the street and that these were the homes of respectable people with regular employment in the shipping industry. The newspaper's reference to Paget Street was also said to be misleading. The correspondent admitted that there was a great deal of squalor in such areas, but argued that poverty itself was never a crime.

As for workers being robbed of their wages on a Saturday night, the writer felt that such men would have to be blind drunk and lying unconscious in the road before any robbery could take place. Furthermore, a helpless drunk would be equally at risk even in a more middle-class district, such as Abercrombie Square. The letter writer did not deny that the district had a small rough element, but he argued that it was no worse than other places in the country, which were as densely populated.

The editor of the newspaper replied in a footnote that the author of the original article had not been implying that the High Rip lived in Fulton Street and Paget Street, but that the gang loitered on the street corners and harassed the respectable inhabitants of those communities.

The serial letter writer "One Who Knows" felt the need to refute J.G.'s argument that the district was as safe as Abercrombie Square.[4] He pointed out the perils that workmen faced after they had been paid their wages. For example, as he made his way home near Commercial Road, twelve of the High Rip attacked a boilerman called Burns, punching and kicking him. Not only did the poor man receive a black eye, but a piece of flesh was kicked out of the cheek beneath the other eye. The man's wages and other valuables, including his tobacco, were taken.

In answer to J.G.'s dismissal of the High Rip as "absurd fiction", the writer compiled a catalogue of evidence of the gang's presence. He listed the names of McLean, Duggan and Campbell together with the Blackstone Street murder and the Athol Street pepper robbery. He cited the figure of 100 wounded people treated each week at the Northern Dispensary. "One Who Knows" felt that there had been no exaggeration of High Rip activity and went on to refer to the view of Dr Wilde, of the Northern Dispensary, that the epidemic of ruffianism was, if anything, under-reported.

The writer did not doubt that many decent people lived in the area, but he went on to demonstrate how such respectability was often the target for the High Rippers. A few days earlier, a family living in Blackie's buildings had been eating a wedding breakfast when the door burst open and seven or eight of the High Rip entered, with the same number keeping watch outside. The uninvited guests greedily devoured and drank everything on the table before leaving "without giving the happy couple their blessing".

Another writer to the *Liverpool Echo*, calling himself "Rent Collector", also acknowledged the existence of the gang.[5] He congratulated the paper on highlighting the problems of the High Rip and criticised previous correspondents who had denied their existence. As somebody who entered the rough districts on a regular basis, the "Rent Collector" knew the activities of the High Rip all too well and felt that the problem was so obvious that it was unnecessary to add to what had already been written. The writer blamed the police for not doing enough to tackle the problem.

In an attempt to get to the bottom of the affair, a lengthy article questioning the existence of the gang was published.[6] Under the headline "Does 'High Rip' Exist?" a journalist interviewed one of the heads of the police department:

"I want you to tell me all about this High Rip gang."
    "Oh," was the reply, with a smile. "You must go to the *Daily Post* for information on that subject."

"*But surely you must have full acquaintance with the organisation.*"

"You call it an organisation, but I can assure you we have no knowledge of such. We are aware, of course, that from time to time persons are brought up in the court for assaults and robberies. They are dealt with by Mr Raffles in the ordinary way, because the cases are ordinary cases, and when they are disposed of and the reports in the evening papers come out we learn that we have been dealing with members of the 'High Rip Gang'."

"*But you cannot pretend to ignorance of the alleged existence of such a body.*"

"Of course not; and I have made a point of endeavouring to some extent to get to the bottom of the matter. Prosecutors have come into the office and I have questioned them about the 'High Rips', but the amount of actual information they give amounts to nothing. Had the 'High Rips' any real organisation we should be sure to know of it, for you can't suppose that people of the class of these 'High Rips' are likely to keep their affairs darker than a Fenian or other secret society succeeds in doing; and we generally have an idea of what these last gentleman are about."

"*Nevertheless, these 'High Rips' have created quite a scare.*"

"Thanks to you gentlemen of the press. If such a result has happened, it is you who have produced it."

"*How do you make that out?*"

"Because of the sensational reports that appear in the papers, particularly the evening papers. Cases of a very ordinary nature are magnified and sensationalised almost out of recognition. I suppose the editors of the *Echo* and *Express* must have some big line to put in their bills, to sell their paper, and 'another atrocious outrage by the High Rip Gang' makes a very good headline for the purpose. This practice has a double result. It not only alarms the public and gives them an exaggerated notion of the depredations of the gang, but it incites the 'High Rip' themselves to violence. The evening papers have a very large sale about Scotland Road, and what you would call, I suppose, the 'infected district', and when the young ruffians of the neighbourhood see their doings blazoned forth in such a style it actually, I believe, puts fresh ideas of violence into their heads."

"*Then the* Echo *and* Express *are the 'penny dreadfuls' of the slums?*"

"Exactly ... and serve a similar purpose."

"Still, if an evil exists, exposure is necessary, even though some collateral harm be done in the course of that exposure."

"That may be true enough in the abstract. But does any district evil exist in this case? What are these 'High Rips' after all? They are mere lads, many of them 'scalers' or following similar occupations. When trade is bad they lose their employment and have little to do but hang about street corners and public houses. You know what lads are, especially those of the rough class, and how skylarking and horse play lead to quarrels and violence. Many of those who suffer from the 'High Rips' really bring their trouble on themselves. Instead of quietly passing a knot of the 'Rips' and going about his business, a man will make some remark to them. Then, of course, there is a retort, and from words they get to blows in a very few moments."

"But do you mean to say that one man would knowingly give offence to half a dozen?"

"Yes; there are lots of men who believe themselves 'able' for a score, and plunge into a row for the sheer love of the thing. Of course, they get the worst of it."

"Then your conclusion is that the notion of an organised body of ruffians prowling about in search of plunder and for the committal of outrage is baseless?"

"Yes. You must remember that in large cities like Liverpool there is always a certain number of persons hanging about ready for any deeds of ruffianism – the criminal classes, in fact, or perhaps I should say the classes which develop into criminals. When labour is scarce offences increase. It's the old case of 'Satan finding mischief still?' We may be bad enough in Liverpool, but we're no worse than the average, remembering our peculiarly large population of the poorer class. The 'High Rip Gang' I believe to be practically a myth. Perhaps when we get our increased number of police enrolled we can spare a few of them to look after the young blackguards who seem to have given the *Daily Post* so much concern, and its special commissioner may then take an evening walk into his 'High Rip land' without feeling like 'an unarmed hunter in a tiger haunted jungle'. Ha, ha! Good morning. I hope my views upon the matter may tend to relieve public anxiety."

Denial of the High Rip seems to have been the official police line. In a report written in 1887, a policeman was asked if he believed in the existence of the gang. The officer denied that there was any organisation of the sort:

> There are always a large body of men in this neighbourhood, who have
> no regular work, who in fact, seem to do no work, and how then, do
> they exist? I have to work for my living, and you for yours, but these
> men don't. Is it any wonder then, that they are up to mischief? They
> lounge about in little crowds at the corner of streets, and are only too
> glad of an opportunity of laying their hands on anyone who may afford
> the chance of plunder. They are mostly growing boys, from thirteen
> and fourteen years of age upwards. Of course, the danger is not the
> fear of two or three of them, but of the crowds of them who hang about
> the district.[7]

The policeman was not denying that ruffians exist or that street crimes are committed: he merely denied that the youths were banded together under the general name of the High Rip.

In his autobiography, published years after the event, Sir William Nott-Bower, the Head Constable of Liverpool during these troubled times, also dismissed the High Rip as a fictional invention:

> It was suggested that the large number of crimes of violence in the
> Scotland Division was due to the work of an organised gang, banded
> together for purposes of plunder and violence, and executing
> vengeance on all who ventured to give evidence against them, or inter-
> fere with their nefarious work. And, not content with inventing the
> "organisation", a most euphonious name for it was also invented, and
> it was stated that this organisation was known as the "High Rip
> Gang"... It was impossible, for such a gang could not have existed
> without the police ever *hearing* of it.[8]

As the man ultimately responsible for crushing the High Rip, it is not surprising that he should have denied its very existence. That's one way to solve the problem. In his annual report, the Head Constable further refuted the gang's existence, save "in the imagination of newspaper correspondents".[9] He also denied that the residents of the north end of the city were being put at risk by a combination of increased gang attacks and the incompetence of the police. In his defence, Nott-Bower quoted crime statistics, which, in the opinion of the *Echo*, "simply prove the inefficiency of the police to cope with the conspiracy."

When the High Rip went on the rampage around Scotland Road, in February 1887, hitting young children and stealing clothes from outside shops, a newspaper noted that, although the Head Constable did not like to use the term "High Rip", because he didn't believe that the gang existed, the inhabitants of the affected district nevertheless referred to the four lads by that very name. For the newspaper this was proof enough the gang did indeed exist.[10]

Robert Watt, who worked as an agent for Carver & Co., a firm of general carriers and railway agents with a head office in Dale Street, wrote a letter to the *Daily Post* correcting some errors about the High Rip that had been written in a previous article:

> That some idle youths do call themselves by this name may be true, but they are an insignificant lot such as our police can easily deal with and quite unworthy of the notice taken in yours of 20th. I think your representative has much overstated the case, for my stables are off Vauxhall Road near to Athol Street, and on the spot he calls the "Happy Hunting Ground of the Gang", yet I have gone to and from them at all hours of the day and night for these twenty years and have not been interfered with nor have I had complaint from any of my men... Boilers, Scalers and Classical Sweeps have a dirty job and I fear their black appearance sometimes gets them a black name, and while some may be vicious and belong to this gang, they are in general not worse than other youths with the same upbringing.[11]

The letter was not published, perhaps because it didn't fit in with the agenda of the newspaper, which at the time was actively promoting horror stories about the High Rip. Watt then wrote to the editor, informing him that he was sending his letter to the Watch Committee instead. This was perhaps the most important of the corporation's sub-committees, acting as the supervisory body of the police and responsible for the appointment, promotion and sacking of all ranks of officers. The Head Constable worked under the Watch Committee's guidance, and in return for doing a good job, the committee supported him. Nott-Bower quoted the letter in order to demonstrate how the press was misrepresenting the whole issue of the High Rip by suppressing views with which it did not agree.

Others, however, were critical of the way that the police constantly denied the existence of the High Rip, despite the obvious evidence of some form of organised ruffianism on Liverpool's streets. If the High Rip didn't exist, it seemed odd that members of the gang appeared in court on a regular basis. It was felt that at least Justice Day, being a judge with considerable experience of dealing with the gang, was more in touch with what was going on. With a neat play on words, it was explained: "[He] doesn't intend to use rose-coloured spectacles provided by the police authorities. He prefers his own daylight."[12]

However, even Justice Day wasn't convinced of the existence of the High Rip. He wished it to be understood that he in no way endorsed evidence of the gang. At the close of the 1886 winter sessions, he made the following point: "There may be found in Liverpool, as in every large town, a very large number of ruffians who do indulge in vice and ruffianism... I have never seen and cannot believe that there is anything in Liverpool of the nature of an organisation of ruffians banded together against the law. All I say is that there may be, but I have seen no evidence of it."[13]

The press responded to these comments in different ways. The *Daily Post*, which to some extent relied on the existence of the High Rip for its sensational stories, dismissed Day's comments as "idle talk".[14] The *Echo*, however, played around with Day's words and came to the conclusion that the judge certainly acknowledged that there were gangs of ruffians; he just didn't know them by the name of High Rippers. As the newspaper put it, "A rose by any other name would smell as sweet."[15] Therefore, once Day had gaoled the ruffians, the High Rip would cease to exist.

The *Liverpool Review*, on the other hand, ended up taking the opposite line. The journal was very much an establishment publication and, despite some initial harsh criticisms of the police, by March 1887 it had come down firmly on the side of the constabulary: "So far, we have been in sympathy with the police authorities, who we considered were doing their best under difficult circumstances."[16] The journal's final verdict on the gang was that the threat of violence was overestimated: "We have always regarded the stories of High Rip outrages as somewhat mythical, at any rate to the extent that we believed them to be worked up to a point of serious exaggeration for sensational poster purposes."

Any discussion of the existence of the High Rip must take into account the political situation at the time. The major contributors to the debate about the gang were the *Daily Post* and the *Echo*. Both newspapers not only gave plenty of coverage to the activities of the gang, but also made regular attacks on the Watch Committee. The timing of the High Rip scare is important.

On August 28, 1886, the *Daily Post* reported that the Watch Committee had decided to increase the number of police in the city. Sixty-five extra constables were proposed, bringing the ratio of police to one officer for every 560 inhabitants. This controversial decision meant an increase to the ratepayer. The newspaper was a strong critic of extra police numbers and concluded "there is nothing in the social or moral condition of Liverpool to compare unfavourably with other centres of population". In other words, there was nothing exceptionally bad about Liverpool to warrant the employment of extra policemen.

However, just over a week later, the *Daily Post*, under the damning headline "Savage Liverpool", complained about the explosion of brutality in the city. It claimed that although the police were doing their best, there simply weren't enough of them! It was not as if such ruffianism was a new phenomenon: it had been growing for years under the eyes of the authorities: "For some two or three years this gang of thieves have made themselves notorious by the frequence [sic] and violence of their depredations." If this was so, why didn't the newspaper draw attention to the High Rip in 1883 or in 1884?

On September 20, the *Daily Post* ran another highly critical editorial, again entitled "Savage Liverpool", but this time putting the blame squarely on the Watch Committee and the Head Constable. The newspaper criticised the Watch Committee's habit of keeping silent on the problem of gangs and of dismissing the numerous reports of the High Rip as exaggerated. The newspaper felt that the very existence of the High Rip was proof of the police's failure to act. The Head Constable was warned that the public was not interested in how good his constables were at drill or how well the police band played: they simply wanted officers to keep law and order. "Let the streets be made safe for honest citizens to go and return from their work. Let it be made plain that violence is a mistake, and that outrage will be met by swift punishment," concluded the editorial.

The temptation for the newspapers was to attribute any crime of violence to the High Rip, therefore giving a sense of organisation to what could well have been random and unrelated criminal acts. In turn, by proving the existence of a highly coordinated criminal gang brazenly working the streets of Liverpool, the press was able to attack the inefficiency, extravagance and complacency of the police. The Head Constable wanted more money for extra officers, but he seemed to be doing absolutely nothing about the High Rip!

The letters published in the press demonstrate how the High Rip reign of terror stirred up the public's imagination. In this way, the newspapers no doubt succeeded in increasing their sales while at the same time embarrassing both the Watch Committee and Head Constable. When there is political power at stake, it is the press, as much as politicians, that determine the issues that become news-worthy and, more crucially, when they become newsworthy.

Then, as now, law and order were big election issues, as crime historian Rob Sindall points out in his book on street violence:

> The High Rip episode lasted from late August 1886 until mid-November and reached its climax in October. The dates are important, for, with the benefit of hindsight, the cynical observer may be forgiven for feeling that while [headlines such as] "Savage Liverpool", "The High Rip: Is it a Secret Society?", and "Does the High Rip Exist?" are all important questions of the day, the main issue was the holding of municipal elections on November 1, 1886.[17]

It turned out that the election result vindicated the Watch Committee. The Conservatives went on to increase their hold on the council over the Liberals from 42–22 to 47–17. Nott-Bower was also exonerated. He had argued that the publicity about the High Rip had created a state of public alarm, which turned out to be quite unjusti-fied. Indeed, the Head Constable was able to present figures in his annual report for 1886 to show that the number of indictable assaults for the period had, in fact, fallen.

So, did the High Rip actually exist in the sense of a large, organised or semi-organised gang? With regard to the newspapers' reporting of the phenomenon, there was undoubtedly some exaggeration. On the other hand, there was also some suppression of the facts. The press had vested interests in either denying or publicising the gang's existence. The police themselves had good reason to play down the gang's offences, for the presence of the High Rip on Liverpool's streets was an embarrassment to them.

Also, rather than being part of a proper gang, some delinquents could well have joined together on a temporary basis to commit one-off crimes. Some newspapers would nevertheless have referred to them as being fully paid-up members of the High Rip. Some criminals could also have claimed to be members of the gang simply to gain respect and notoriety. Shouting "Here's the Logwood" or "Here's the High Rip" would certainly have struck fear into victims. Perhaps it could be argued that the public itself became conditioned to blame every crime and misdemeanour on the gang. At the Liverpool International Exhibition of 1886 there were some disturbances and isolated incidents of rowdy behaviour; initially the High Rip was blamed, but the culprits turned out to be medical students! In the public's imagination, the High Rip certainly did exist, for the gang has become part of Liverpool folklore.

However, despite the odd reference to the gang, from 1887 onwards the term High Rip seemed to fall out of favour with journalists and, as the year progressed, the gang itself seemed to disintegrate and become extinct. Acts of murder, extortion and violent robbery went on as before and continued to make headlines, but the perpetrators were only rarely identified under the old name.

In March 1887, three rough-looking men called Edward Jackson, Frederick Jones and James Smith (alias Arthur Morley) were charged with having attacked Jonas Radnor in London Road. At midnight, three plain-clothed detectives observed one of the men creep up on his victim from behind and wrestle him to the floor before robbing him of nine shillings. One of the gang then pressed Radnor's hat over his face, as if to smother him. When arrested, Jackson was found with a packet of pepper in his pocket. In addition to its use as a food seasoning, pepper was used to blind people during robberies. Had such a crime been committed a few months earlier, the gang would almost certainly have been called the High Rip. The *Echo* simply saw the attackers as old-fashioned garrotters and failed to make any fuss about them.

Another example of how press treatment of the High Rip became less intense involved Owen Hoare. It will be remembered that in November 1886, two men stabbed Edward Selborne at Aintree Races, a revenge attack by the High Rip because the previous month the victim had given evidence against their Hoare.

In March 1887, Hoare was in the news again, this time charged with cutting and wounding nineteen-year-old Richard Cooper, from Sparling Street, off Park Lane. Cooper had been innocently standing at the Waterloo Pierhead watching a ship depart when Hoare came up to him.

"This is the famous Cooper isn't it?" said Hoare. "I'll cut your throat for you."

"What for?" asked Cooper.

In place of an answer he was stabbed in the cheek. The victim called a policeman who ran after Hoare and arrested him.

At the Liverpool Police Court, Mr Raffles claimed that "the use of the knife among lads was a new development, and was far worse than the assaults of the High Rip gang". In his twenty-seven years on the bench, the magistrate had never experienced so much use of the knife by young lads. Nowhere in the newspaper reports is it mentioned that Hoare was supposed to have been a member of the High Rip, while the comments of Mr Raffles suggest that the heyday of the gang was already over, only to be replaced by a fresh, violent craze. This is despite the fact that the High Rip, as its name suggests, was notorious for using knives.

The name of the High Rip nevertheless lived on as a general term for ruffians. In June 1888, a police constable called Luny was attacked at the corner of Clare Street and Springfield Street, off Islington. A gang of lads had just left a public house and were fighting among themselves over the possession of a watch they had stolen. As the officer went to investigate, he was kicked and punched by the entire gang. The policeman managed to hold on to Michael Gindley, but had to blow his whistle for assistance for a full fifteen minutes before any of his colleagues turned up. After his beating, the officer was too ill to even give evidence in court. One newspaper called the gang "high rippers", but the term seems to have been used loosely, in lower case letters, to refer to a bunch of ruffians rather than to the actual High Rip gang.[18]

In July 1888, a gang including James Mulholland, Richard O'Neill, James Moore and Edward Bray, all aged seventeen, were charged with robbery with violence from Margaret Armstrong in Bootle. The woman was returning home at midnight through a court between Seaforth Street and Bostock Street when a gang of about sixteen lads attacked her. She was dragged into an empty house, kicked and knocked unconscious. When she regained consciousness, she discovered that several items had been stolen. The youths had taken money hidden in her cleavage, ripped a ring from her finger and made an attempt to "violate her". Her shawl was later found in Bray's backyard. When arrested, he warned the officer, "If I get taken for this, you will have to take a hundred more as was with me." The gang was found guilty and the four members were each sentenced to fourteen years' imprisonment. The headline in the *Liverpool Weekly Mercury* announced that the gang was the High Rip, but no evidence for this was given in reports in other newspapers.[19]

That December, Inspector Nesbit, in charge of the fire police at Athol Street, off Scotland Road, was returning to the station after an incident at the North Docks. At midnight, as he passed along the deserted warehouses in Boundary Street, six lads jumped out of a dark corner, tripped him up and kicked him unconscious. When he came round, Nesbit could only summon enough strength to crawl on all fours to a warehouse step, where he rested for half an hour. He eventually made it back to the station, which was only a few hundred yards away, where he was found to have injuries to his face, arms and legs. He was confined to bed for days afterwards. A newspaper again referred to the gang as "High Rippers", in capital letters, but it is still uncertain as to whether or not the term was used loosely to describe a band of ruffians.[20]

Nevertheless, the High Rip was still in the news as late as 1897. Richard Owens, a twenty-year-old labourer from Liverpool, was found guilty of wounding Peter Montgomery. The victim was Owens' foreman at the Pumpfields depot of the National Telephone Company, off Vauxhall Road. After being informed by Montgomery that his employment was being terminated, Owens struck him about six times on the head with a piece of iron or stone. *The Times* stated that Owens was a member of the High Rip. He was sentenced to seven years.[21]

However, the account of the crime in a more local newspaper, the *Echo*, makes no mention of the High Rip. Owens is simply called a "ruffian", and "probably one of the leaders of a gang that infested the neighbourhood of Pumpfields". The term High Rip is used loosely by *The Times* in a similar way that people today use the general label "hooligan" to refer to any young violent criminal, rather than the particular gangs of youths known as the Hooligans who had terrorised London in the 1890s. Indeed, the term "high rips" started to be used by the press for any violent gangs. Today, they would be called muggers.

CHAPTER 16

The Social Causes of Gang Violence

REPORTED CASES OF stabbings and grievous bodily harm averaged about 250 a year in Liverpool during the 1880s. Annual cases of common assault amounted to about 2,000. However, a great deal of crime must also have gone unrecorded. It has been estimated that an annual total of 9,000 cases of violence went unreported in the north end of Liverpool alone.[1]

In his autobiography, published in 1926, the Head Constable of Liverpool, Sir William Nott-Bower, gave an account of the social problems behind the rates of violent crime in the city:

> Liverpool is a seaport, where a vast amount of shipping is being constantly loaded and unloaded, involving a great amount of intermittent and precarious work and wages; the latter sometimes being so large as to be a temptation to drink and excess, sometimes so small as to cause dire poverty and discontent. Large numbers of the "failures" from other places flock to the town in the hope of finding work at the docks, and do not find it. These people are all crowded together in the lowest quarter of the town, veritable slums. They lived mostly in the "Scotland Division", and were largely an Irish population, with the reckless, violent disposition of that people, and with the unfortunate taste of preferring whisky, which makes them dangerous, to beer, which would make them sleepy. There were many absolute ruffians among them, brought up in poverty, without education or religious influence, wearied with the struggle of life, with a hatred of society,

and none of the surroundings which might wean them from drink and vice and violence.[2]

The Head Constable was not alone in his view about the disastrous social effects of immigration. Years earlier, it was argued that Liverpool's status as a magnet for visitors from around the globe had been a contributory factor in the Tithebarn Street murder.[3] The town was said to act as something of a sieve "retaining the dregs and impurities of the ever-changing population and letting the clear grit pass through to havens beyond". Those "dregs" included a large Irish population. The reference almost certainly refers to the influx of Irish immigrants into Liverpool during the famine years. The result was that the town became a "harbour and refuge of the most desperate ruffians unhung".

Between 1846 and 1853, roughly one-and-a-half million Irish arrived in Liverpool. Although many went on to sail for America, about 60,000 remained: the "failures" or "dregs", as some people viewed them, crammed into the Vauxhall, Exchange and Scotland Wards. By 1871, the population of the borough of Liverpool was 493,405; the number of Irish-born amounted to 76,761, or 15.6 per cent of the population. Liverpool had the largest concentration of Irish-born people in England. As social historian Frank Neal points out, "When one takes into account the number of English-born children of Irish parents brought up in the Irish areas of Liverpool, then the numbers of 'Liverpool Irish' far exceeded the number of Irish born."[4] In 1870, Father James Nugent estimated the Catholic (Irish) population of Liverpool to be at least 150,000.[5]

A number of the Irish in Liverpool were certainly involved in crime. In 1910, the Nationalist Councillor for the Vauxhall Ward, Thomas Burke, observed, "This immense mass of Catholics around the Tithebarn Street and Vauxhall Road area entailed serious consequences social and economic to the town which have not wholly disappeared to this hour, and brought about the erection of further chapels and schools, but for which the citizens of Liverpool have been brought face to face with insoluble problems of crime and lawlessness."[6]

Living so near to the docks must have afforded the impoverished Irish irresistible opportunities for theft. Also, heavy drinking often led to assaults, disorderly behaviour and vagrancy. The Tithebarn Street murderers were all Catholics of Irish background. The press immediately seized on the Irish nature of the perpetrators: "Outrage by Irish Roughs in Liverpool: A Man Kicked to Death", ran a headline shortly after the murder. On the same day, another newspaper noted: "As is generally the case in these brutal cases in Liverpool, the assailants are Irish... [People] will begin to think that we are living in the midst of a reign of terror and that Irish rowdyism is supreme."[7]

Ironically, two days later, in an article entitled "British Brutality", the *Catholic Times* argued that for too long English journalists had relied on shock-horror stories from Ireland that libelled the entire Irish race. Certain headlines were common: "Another Irish Outrage", "Another Irish Murder", "Another Agrarian Crime in Ireland". As the *Catholic Times* pointed out, "For the most part, the so-called 'Irish outrages' are but mild specimens of crime daily indulged in by Englishmen." The paper added that "wife beatings and kickings to death have become an epidemic in Lancashire, and British domestic cruelty is acquiring a fame that will render it historical." Yet it was still the Irish, albeit the Liverpool Irish, who were being blamed for many cases of northern brutality.

For years, Irish navvies had a fearsome reputation in Liverpool. During the mid-1840s, about 4,000 Irish workers were employed to build the Merseyside docks and railways. "Every week," according to social historian Kellow Chesney, "from Saturday night till Tuesday, uproar and confusion reigned in the northern quarter of Liverpool where most of them lodged – some in dwellings they had colonised without the proprietor's permission."[8]

The Commissioner of Liverpool Police revealed to the 1846 Select Committee on Railway Labourers that it was extremely difficult for even two or three policeman to arrest a single Irishman in his own neighbourhood. The situation wasn't helped by the fact that the labourers took their short, sharp-edged spades home with them. The commissioner recalled one case where a gang of Irishmen had been fighting among themselves in a court. A policeman went to investigate the disturbance and the gang immediately turned from fighting each other to attack the constable. They wrestled him to the floor and were in the act of butchering him with their spades when

A group of navvies enjoy a break from work.

another policeman arrived, bravely grabbed a spare spade and stood his ground at the narrow entrance to the court. He warned the gang that he would knock them to pieces if they continued their assault. Fortunately, the severely injured policeman was dragged away to safety.

Years later, an indignant journal article appeared, which responded to Justice Day's comments about the number of imported Irish ruffians who were committing crimes in England.[9] It was argued that if Irishmen were being convicted, it merely showed how depraved they had become through contact with English criminals. Nevertheless, the Irish were generally viewed with suspicion by the authorities and were often the subject of police attention. The prisons at Kirkdale and Walton were both filled with a disproportionate amount of Irish Catholics.

It must be stated that the Irish experienced great prejudice and discrimination. They also suffered unemployment and poverty and inhabited the worst housing.

After the Tithebarn Street murder, a letter to a national newspaper, from R.W. Pitcher of Kirkdale, made a valid point about the effects of overcrowding: "In your remarks on the brutal temper prevalent in Liverpool among the labouring population, you seem not to take into account the deplorably crowded state such people are compelled to live in, surrounded with almost unparalleled temptations and facilities for debauchery – circumstances calculated to make them savages."[10] The writer revealed that the lower-class courts lacked any sort of police presence. Officers rarely ventured into such districts either to deter or to arrest the criminals and, therefore, hardly any acts of violence and robbery came to the attention of the authorities.

It was a sentiment shared by another newspaper correspondent who called himself "Humanity".[11] The writer commented on Justice Mellor's condemnation of Liverpool as a seat of "drunkenness, ignorance and vice" and pointed out the squalor, filth and depravity of the neighbourhood of Hare Place, at the lower end of Scotland Road. The newspaper, in an earlier article, had called the passage "filthy enough to account for an epidemic of all the round of contagious diseases". "Humanity" added that this was true of countless courts around the town.

Indeed, he went on to say, "In this densely populated district, people live with putrescent muck-heaps that would rejoice the heart of the most manure-loving farmer, almost literally under their noses." The writer asked: who could blame people for turning to drink, if they were compelled to live in such conditions? Indeed, how could people living among such violence and crime manage to avoid turning to both in order to survive? "Humanity" criticised a building programme that neglected the need for breathing space for its inhabitants and blamed the town council for allowing respectable streets and courts to have become dens of infamy. He concluded with a call for more municipal expenditure to right past wrongs: "Theirs the power and theirs the duty."

An editorial in *The Times* warned that the population of these wretched regions was continually increasing as more and more new arrivals were crammed into the cellars and courts. The solution had more to do with town planning than policing. The newspaper recommended that "these squalid dens should be pulled down and proper buildings erected in their place".[12]

Yet better architecture did not instantly produce better citizens.

Nineteen months after its call for improved housing, *The Times* was forced to point out the irony of Liverpool's juvenile gangs using the brand-new model lodging-houses as bases from which to launch their burgling sprees. The newspaper felt that it was a "strange satire upon the benevolent purposes of their founders".[13]

Nevertheless, better social conditions were still seen as the solution to criminality:

> Let anyone walk in the bright sunlight, into the dark, dismal streets and courts lying between Scotland Road and Vauxhall Road; let him witness the narrow lives of the inhabitants of that district, their sole relief to the constant offence against sound and sight and scent to which they are ever exposed being the coarse animal pleasure offered by the gin palace; let him picture a lad born in the midst of this wild welter of misery, knowing nothing of nature except under her most perverted and degraded forms, seeing nothing of the glories of the country, never having seen, in all probability, a flower growing in the garden, or having heard the song of a bird upon a tree; always at odds with the representatives of law and order, and with all this, having to fight against hunger and the ill-usage of those who should protect him – imagine all these conditions, reader, and you have the explanation of the existence of the "High Rip Gang".[14]

The message was clear: atrocious social conditions bred violent criminals.

In Victorian times, there was a great desire among the middle classes to uncover the dark side of life, to see how the other half lived. People wanted to know not only about the primitive savages in distant lands, but the destitute beings of their own country, even their own city. Both journalist Henry Mayhew and social reformer Charles Booth, for example, tirelessly tramped the streets of London in order to write multi-volume works which painstakingly documented and analysed the lives of the poverty-stricken underclass.[15]

In a similar spirit, although on a vastly reduced scale, between November 5 and 10, 1883, the *Daily Post* ran a series of articles entitled "Squalid Liverpool". Over a number of days, a journalist went into the very worst areas and reported at first hand the dreadful social conditions across the city. He revealed atrocious housing in a passage off Great Howard Street, where crumbling brickwork was so eaten by putrid green slime that it was easy to push a stick right through the wall of a house. A report was given of a "den" in Toxteth, where a baby had somehow clung to life amid the absolute squalor. The mother was out with her basket earning a pittance. She was not due back until evening, when hopefully she would bring some food. The father was "dead with fever". A little girl, sitting wedged in a chair with no seat in it, nursed the infant, whose faint cry sounded more like the mewing of a kitten. The only food in the house was an old crust and some grease smeared onto a broken plate, the leftovers of a meagre meal. Necessity being the mother of invention, the little girl tenderly fed the baby the bread wiped in the dirty grease.

The journalist also told amusing stories of the Scotland Road "disabled" conmen, some balancing on one leg while begging, or sweetly singing in their blindness. As soon as they had enough money for a drink, they would miraculously sprout a limb and regain their sight as they dashed into the nearest alehouse. Because the middle classes rarely, if ever, entered such areas, it was considered important to make them aware of what was going on in their own city.

Three years later, in 1886, in an attempt to understand how the poverty experienced by the High Rip might have given rise to their criminality, the *Daily Post* went back to the slums to describe two typical homes of gang members.[16] The first, in Paget Street, contained a bacon box for a table, a heap of shavings for a bed, an old tin can for crockery and a small box for a chair. Another chair consisted of two holes cut into the floor through which the legs of the person sitting "can be dropped quite comfortable". The other home was in Fulton Street. The back room boasted an inch-deep carpet of excreta from a couple of chickens kept there. The newspaper wondered why the sanitary inspector permitted such atrocious conditions. However, it was admitted that no man in uniform, with the sole exception of the postman, dared show his face in the street. "It is from squalid and pestiferous surroundings such as these that Savage Liverpool is recruited," concluded the newspaper.

However, the notion that unfavourable social circumstances could lead people to commit crime was sometimes taken to comical extremes. A ninety-two-year-old man from the Wirral appeared before Clarke Aspinall, who as well as being coroner served as a magistrate for the Hundred of Wirral, on a charge of being drunk and incapable. The magistrate asked him when he thought he would be old enough to start behaving himself. The old wag pleaded, "I am an orphan, sir." He was discharged.[17]

It wasn't just the head of police and newspaper editors who were starting to appreciate that poverty, bad housing and lack of education could help both influence and determine people's behaviour. In his final address to the jury at the winter assizes of 1886, Justice Day outlined the conditions he considered contributed to the state of chronic ruffianism in Liverpool.[18]

The town, he explained, was a port where a great amount of shipping was loaded and unloaded. The population was huge and always attracting more outsiders, all desperately looking for work. Employment was precarious: casual labour involved periods of comfortable wage earning alternating with periods of atrocious poverty. Competition for jobs, together with competition in the wages market, often led to terrible poverty as workers were forced to accept lower pay.

Justice Day went on to admit that many poor people were honest and respectable, but pointed out that there would always be a criminal element. Such people had experienced neither education nor the moral influence of religion. They became "wearied with the struggle of life". Poor people lived in an environment in which they were constantly exposed to vice. Such people naturally herded together to form groups. They also assisted each other in their enterprises, constantly looking out for each other. The criminal element naturally took revenge upon people who they considered to have wronged their friends. Such people included witnesses who had been willing to stand up in court and testify against the accused. This last point perhaps explained the glut of High Rip revenge cases faced by the judge in the autumn of 1886.

Other enemies of the criminal were the police and judges. When Michael McLean and his gang appeared at the Police Court charged with the murder of the Spanish sailor, an anonymous threatening letter was sent to magistrate Thomas Stamford Raffles. Raffles claimed that what really annoyed him was that the postage hadn't been paid! An earlier death-threat letter sent to the same stipendiary magistrate illustrates the strength of the unity of Liverpool's criminal fraternity.

At the Police Court in January 1878, John Welch and Frederick Jones were both charged having burgled Robert Parry's butcher's shop in Islington in 1877. The rest of the gang escaped. The men were sent to the sessions for trial. Mr Raffles then received the following note:

Dear Sir,

I was with Jack Welch and Fred Jones when that bastard Watchman told that Bobby that they were in Ole Parries Mate Shop. I gave the lot of them Bobbies the slip and I got away with a Showlder of Mutton and a lot of cash which I mane to stick to unless Poor Jack Welch splits on me. Well, Raffles I've Bane before you 3 Times alridy but you may be surprised when you larn that I mane to murder you for sending them poor fellars to the Sissions for such trifle I know you and I will surely shoot you whin I mate you coming out of the Coort to morrow on my Oath I will kill you and old [detective inspector] Karlisle too when I mate him. Well my letthur is draw-ing to a close and SO is your LIFE.

Signed Daniel Jones
            Poor Jack Welch and poor old Jones
            But where I live I will not tell you.
            Ah Ah.

At the end of the letter was a sketch of a coffin containing a man, with the inscription "Raffles" on top.[19] It wouldn't have taken a detective long to come to the conclusion that the writer of the letter was related to, perhaps even the brother of, Fred Jones. The man's address was no doubt in the court records system.

Yet despite Justice Day's liberal understanding of why people committed crime, the judge refused to allow sociological reasoning to soften his legal judgement when passing sentence on violent offenders. When it came to administering violence, he was a match for any Cornerman or High Ripper from the Scotland Road cellars and courts.

CHAPTER 17

Judgement Day

A Word to the "Rough"

You ruffian, you scoundrel, you brutal Yahoo!
There's a good time, to be sure, coming for you.
You dull, drunken savage, malignantly mad!
You dastard, you blackguard, you criminal cad!

You'll be taught to take care how your fury you wreak,
How you fell the defenceless and trample the weak.
How in face, mouth and eyes folk with clenched fist you slog;
Knock down, stamp on, and smash them with iron-bound clog.

You shall know, you foul sot, you shall feel in your skin,
What it is to gouge eyes out, and ribs to kick in;
Or, in bestial affray with some wretched compeer,
To bite your antagonist's nose or his ear.

See you this knotted scourge of nine thongs? Tis the cat!
You have feelings which may be appealed to with that.
On garrotters, your like, with effect it was tried.
And your hearts too, no doubt will be reached through your hide.[1]

IT WAS ALL very well looking for the causes of crime: what the public wanted to know was how to stop it. Then, as now, the big question of the day was: what was to be done about criminal behaviour? The "hang 'em and flog 'em brigade" is certainly nothing new. Following the Tithebarn Street murder, the main topic of conversation on the floor of the Liverpool Exchange was that "nothing could be too strong to be done to stop such acts and to repress such creatures that 'catting' is too good for them, and hanging not too bad."[2]

The "cat" or cat-o'-nine-tails, a whip containing nine nasty leather thongs, was society's favourite solution to crime. "What is wanted is known as the 'cat'," declared one journal.[3] At a Town Council meeting on August 5, 1874, councillor P.H. Rathbone stated, "The real remedy is the cat',"[4] A newspaper correspondent calling himself J.S. offered a punishment that was both cheaper and more effective than prison: "The remedy is simple and ready – 'Cut the brutes with the cat'. The bigger the bully the bigger the coward, and cowards always reverence a good castigation... Let the cat play on his spine and on his ribs with his nine claws to the tune of thirty to fifty good scratches."[5]

Initially, *The Times* also favoured flogging. It felt that if the so-called garrotting outbreak had been cured by the "cat" then so would the violence of the Cornermen. Garrotting was a form of street robbery achieved by creeping up on the victim from behind and choking him. A typical garrotting gang worked in threes, consisting of two lookouts, known as a "front stall" and a "back stall", and the aptly named "nasty man", who did the strangling. It wasn't exactly a new crime, but a flurry of cases in London in the winter of 1862, initiated by an assault on a Member of Parliament, had led to media frenzy, which, in turn, had led to changes in the law. The Security Against Violence Act was passed as a direct result of newspaper pressure for the government to do something. Flogging, which had been abolished in 1861, was rapidly reintroduced in 1863 for robbery with violence.

A common feature of all moral panics is the urge to change the law and to introduce tougher measures to combat the evil that confronts society. Even before the Tithebarn Street murder, violence was very much on the parliamentary agenda. In July 1874, measures had been discussed about the possibility of introducing new legislation to combat domestic violence. In October, following the Liverpool murder and its accompanying press uproar, the Home Secretary, Richard Assheton Cross, sent a circular regarding all forms of violence to every judge and magistrate. The aim of this fact-finding letter was to help establish the best measures for tackling violent crime.

A Remedy for Ruffians. Another attempt at promoting the "cat" as
suitable punishment for street violence.

Most replies to the Home Secretary were enthusiastically in favour
of flogging. A Bill to bring back the "cat" was introduced, but later
dropped. By the spring of 1875, the newspapers had gone quiet on the
issue. Ironically, it was *The Times* that, after stirring up so much of the
trouble, warned against legislating in haste. It was felt that there was a

danger of brutalising ourselves in the attempt to combat the savagery of others.

It was also argued that if flogging was to be used as punishment, juries would be discouraged from convicting.[6] Lord Aberdare, the ex-Home Secretary, pointed out that whipping had previously failed as a means of controlling crime and that garrotting, if it had been stopped, had been curbed by prevention through better policing, rather than by the threat of the punishment that awaited the criminal after the event.

One journal[7] advocated giving the members of gangs a taste of their own medicine. What follows is a heart-warming tale of street justice.

One night a young man and his girlfriend were strolling down Church Street, in the town centre, when three drunken roughs approached arm-in-arm. The method was common among ruffians and was a version of a practice known as "holding the street", whereby innocent people were knocked out of the way. They had already hustled several pedestrians off the pavement and looked set to knock the young lovers into the gutter.

The man took his fiancée and placed her in a doorway for safety. As there was no policeman about, he neatly turned up his cuffs, buttoned his coat, selected the biggest ruffian and knocked him to the ground. The other two roughs swore some oaths and attempted to gain revenge, but were also punched to the ground in quick succession. The man, cool as cucumber, then drew down his cuffs, unbuttoned his coat and once again gave his arm to his lady. The couple continued their stroll down Church Street as if nothing had happened.

The journal acknowledged that not everybody had the necessary courage or boxing skills to deal with such incidents, nor did it advocate citizens taking the law into their own hands, but the writer nevertheless delighted in telling the tale.

For others,[8] the solution to street crime lay not in any particular punishment, but in the very *certainty* of punishment for wrongdoing. It was felt that the leniency of the magistrates was to blame. If the victim of a vicious assault managed to live, the attack wasn't deemed serious enough for harsh punishment. Brutal violence was met with either fines that were all to easily paid or short terms of imprisonment, which were greeted with sneers by the prisoner. Even some attempted murders carried sentences of as little as six months.

The whole issue of the value of prison was raised. Today's tabloids often highlight the view that prisons are little more than holiday camps and that they, therefore, provide little deterrent to crime. In a similar vein, a journal correspondent thought that locking people away was ineffectual. Prison held no terror for the worst offenders: "It was a punishment they too often care little about."[9] It must be remembered that the persistent offender McCrave earned his nickname, "Holy Fly", precisely because he was continually flying in and out of prison. Gaol was seen merely as an occupational hazard for career criminals. The regime at Kirkdale may have been tough, but so was life on the streets. In 1849, stipendiary magistrate Edward Rushton pointed out that the gaol of the borough of Liverpool offered the wretched Irish criminals better food, shelter, clothing and more cleanliness than they could get elsewhere.

In his memoirs, Sir William Nott-Bower, the Head Constable of Liverpool, quotes remarks made by Mr Justice McCardie on the futility of a revolving-door policy of short sentences. He felt that, while it was right for first offenders to be treated leniently, for hardened criminals, it merely resulted in them going to prison, coming out with the intention of committing more crime, living on the proceeds and then going back to gaol. In other words, they found it worthwhile to live two lives – one in prison and the other out of prison.

If ever there was an example to illustrate the argument that prison does not work, then it is the case of Bridget McMullen, described as "an elderly woman of miserable appearance", although she was only forty-three years old. In April 1886, she was charged with being drunk and disorderly in the very corridor leading to the courtroom. Locked up, she then proceeded to break ten panes of glass in her cell. She received fourteen days' imprisonment. It was her 113th conviction and her 160th spell in custody. By August 1888, she had clocked up her 202nd court appearance after being found drunk and riotous in Paradise Street. She was gaoled for seven days. It was her 147th conviction. McMullen is probably the same Liverpool-Irish flower seller who, in 1897, held the national record for convictions. The widow had been prosecuted 356 times for drunkenness, assaults, criminal damage and begging.[10]

It was felt that a long spell of imprisonment, rather than corporal punishment, was the best solution to crime. For the habitual criminal,

Thomas Stamford Raffles. The Stipendiary Magistrate who tried most of Liverpool's gang members.

it was argued that only a life sentence, without any hope of release, could prevent him from re-offending. "There is no apparent reason why he should not be treated as other wild animals are and permanently locked up for his own good and that of the public," said one newspaper.[11]

Father Nugent, as chaplain of Walton Gaol, was also against short sentences, not because he wanted to punish offenders for longer periods, but so that he could be granted more time to achieve reformation of the prisoner's character. A long sentence gave convicts a chance to reflect on their crimes and withdrew them from the temptations of their usual lawless surroundings. Prison also gave them a chance to gain some sort of education and religious instruction.

Not only was prison a poor deterrent, there were also, for the middle-class readers of journals, economic factors to be taken into consideration. One correspondent complained about the burden on the "innocent taxpayer" who had to pay to keep criminals imprisoned for years. He felt that offenders should repay their debt by some form of labour.[12] It was a sentiment extended by another newspaper correspondent: "Are the ratepayers to be forever called upon to support women and children, in or out of the workhouse, because their husbands and fathers are sent to prison to be kept also, because they have been kicking their wives or someone else?"[13]

The tread-wheel, or treadmill as it was better known, was introduced into prison both as a means of punishment and to make prisoners earn their keep. Kirkdale Gaol was a pioneer in its use. Inmates would climb, in complete silence, a never-ending sequence of steps, like a giant hamster wheel, earning the contraption the nickname the "cockchafer" or "shinscraper". The energy generated from the wheel was used, for example, to grind flour or power a circular saw, which cut up firewood to heat the prison. In some gaols, the wheel was used to drive looms.

The hard-labour regime at Norwich Gaol in the 1870s required prisoners to step on the treadmill between 9 a.m. and 12 a.m. They then had dinner and returned to the wheel for another three hours between 1 p.m. and 4 p.m. The prisoners earned five minutes' rest after every fifteen minutes. When they had finished on the treadmill, they would return to their cells to pick okum, which involved untwisting and teasing out old tarred rope. At 8 p.m., the prisoners retired exhausted to bed for a welcome respite from the drudgery and monotony.

In 1888, a gang of pickpockets was caught acting suspiciously in Church Street, one of Liverpool's major shopping districts. When searched, Albert Meredith had a small notebook in his pocket in which he had either composed or copied in pencil a little poem on the perils of the treadmill:

> Just six months ago
> I was hungry for a meal,
> When I stepped into a cookshop
> To see what I could steal.
> I slipped behind the counter
> As silent as could be!
> I eat my fill, secured the till,
> When a policeman said to me
> "Do not forget me! Do not forget me!
> You should not take the till!
> When again you feel inclined to steal,
> Remember your turn – your turn on the mill."[14]

The verse was clearly ineffective as a deterrent. The gang each received one month's hard labour.

For the repeat offender, for whom prison, hard labour or the "cat" did not work, one journal correspondent, writing after the Tithebarn Street murder, offered a novel solution that included an added economic bonus. Hardened criminals were to be broken into obedience, just as a wild horse is tamed:

> He should be treated as other animals are treated to make them fit for the ordinary work they are wanted to do. It may be that a few lives would be shortened by this mode, but it cannot be said that they are valuable ones, or that the community will be a loser by their extinction; while the effect would be that those who survived the ordeal (and a medical man would probably be able to say what percentage that would be) would have little inclination to get among their old associates, would be more likely to seek quiet and honest ways of getting a living and would no longer be the instrument of increasing the dangerous class.[15]

The Victorians feared a sense of disorder and of impulses raging out of control. They wanted self-governing and responsible individuals who were fit for society. The writer therefore proposed some form of social engineering – perhaps a medical experiment? – that would transform criminals into law-abiding, almost meek, citizens, who could be easily controlled and who could become financially self-sufficient.

Hanging was always a last resort. The death penalty was seen not just as a means of ridding the streets of its violent criminals, but also as a deterrent to others. One newspaper felt that the hanging of Michael Mullen and John McCrave was not merely a just punishment for their crime but a warning to others that the values of civilisation would triumph over evil.[16]

However, the inadequacy of capital punishment was revealed in a letter to a newspaper written by J.W.S. from Mere Lane, Everton. He questioned the deterrent effect of hanging by listing a number of recent victims of the gallows, all of whom had not been prevented from committing murder by the example of other hanged criminals. He pointed out that, not long before the execution of the Tithebarn Street murderers, a man had been hanged for stabbing someone in the street and yet, on the very morning of his execution, three other stabbings had taken place "under the very gaze of the scaffold".

Instead of hanging, the writer went on to extol the benefits of making a public example of the criminal, but combined this with the old favourite – corporal punishment: "I hold that with such an instrument as the 'cat' we have a better means of appealing to the brutal instincts of the 'rough'. I think that instead of leaving him dangling at the end of a rope, if he were dragged out periodically before the mob, in order that they might hear his cries and see him writhing in agony at each stroke of the lash, we would have fewer criminals of this class."[17]

Yet it was the public's sadistic enjoyment of the spectacle of brutality that had been one of the most shocking aspects of the Tithebarn Street murder, as shown by the deplorable behaviour of the spectators.

With the advent of the High Rip ten years later, the public's desire for flogging showed no sign of abating. The serial newspaper correspondent calling himself "Citizen" explained why a good beating was more effective than other punishments. If the cowards had one dose of the lash, they would not come back for a second. He also argued that gang members commit crimes because they know that if they are caught they will merely be charged with riotous conduct and allowed to pay a fine or receive a spell of imprisonment of between seven and fourteen days. Such a short spell inside, he claimed, was a "pastime for some of the lazy scoundrels, who would not work if it was put before them".[18]

In another letter, the same writer pointed out the inadequacy of merely fining gang members, since their friends all sat in the court ready and willing to pay the fine for them. The public-spirited "Citizen" even volunteered to administer any beatings: "I should have much pleasure in administering the dose to each and every one that would be so sentenced; this would I do willingly, pay my own expenses and find the regulation 'cat' which, I think, is a treat in store for the High Rippers or any other gangs that come to me for treatment."[19]

Such enthusiastic supporters of flogging eventually found their champion. The scourge of the High Rip was a judge with the grand name of Mr Justice John Charles Frederick Sigismund de Haren Day. The judge presided over many Liverpool Assizes between 1883 and 1893. Head Constable Nott-Bower became friends with Justice Day and, during dinner together, the Head Constable offered to take him on a tour of the rough districts of Liverpool. On Saturday, November

12, 1886, accompanied by Day's son, two detectives and Justice Grantham, the men timed their visit for when the public houses let out. They then spent up to three hours entering houses and introducing themselves to the inhabitants.

The group walked along Old Hall Street to Great Howard Street through to the neighbourhoods including Milford Street, Luton Street, Boundary Street, Blackstone Street and through to Athol Street, where they entered a lodging house and the bridewell. The group was generally mistaken for a squad of detectives and the first thing asked of them as they entered houses was "who are you looking for?" or "there is no one here, but you can look around if you like". The group took up the offer and saw many overcrowded rooms with people drinking, people drunk and people sleeping it off. They continued through Scotland Road, visiting the "long jigger" off Cazneau Street and a lodging house in Bent Street known as the "Red Lion". They stopped at another lodging house in Ben Jonson Street, called the "Loose Box". The tour continued through almost every rough district, and finally finished at 1.50 a.m.

The judges admitted that the experience had been a revelation to them and that it would prove useful when considering how to deal with the criminals appearing before them in the dock. "They were greatly struck with the extreme poverty of the district, the squalor of the surroundings, the drunkenness and debauchery only too visible, and the apparently wild and lawless character of the inhabitants," observed Nott-Bower.[20] However, Justice Day's own conclusion was that he did not see a great amount of disorder on Liverpool's streets, or anything that was likely to alarm respectable people. He certainly saw no evidence of the existence of the High Rip.

It could be argued that, having witnessed the appalling social conditions of the people living in Scotland Ward, Justice Day would have taken an enlightened and sympathetic view of criminal behaviour. However, any suggestion that the experience could have led to a softening touch when it came to sentencing could not have been more wrong. Justice Day, a devout Roman Catholic, remained a hard-line judge and someone who was unsympathetic to liberal views about the treatment of criminals.

At the Liverpool Assizes in February 1886, Day told the grand jury, "Long sentences are a misfortune to prisoners and to society, which has to maintain the criminals. I am an advocate of stringent corporal punishment to those who are guilty of crimes of violence." As local historian Richard Whittington-Egan put it, "His pity – he was not a cruel, sadistic, or unmerciful man – was always directed towards the victim. He regarded it as his duty to avenge the weak and innocent."[21]

Justice Day had a son who became a Jesuit priest at St Francis Xavier's in Liverpool. Local writer Frank Shaw, from Huyton, remembered him well. He always spoke of his father as "the gentlest of men", although he had a bitter hatred for hooligans.

At the November 1886 assizes, Justice Day was confronted with a particularly heavy calendar of offences, featuring a great many cases of wounding and robbery with violence. The High Rip was then at its peak. Day's response was that the law should be strongly enforced. Around twenty violent offenders were dealt with during the sessions. As each verdict of "guilty" was announced the judge ordered that each prisoner should be put back to await sentence on the very last day of the assizes.

Finally, the prisoners appeared in the dock to learn their fate. Justice Day's son outlined his father's method of passing sentence:

"I shall not sentence you to a long period of imprisonment." The wretch would grin at the prospect of lenient treatment. "I consider yours a case in which the rate-payers' money would be expended to no good purpose; so I shall not send you to penal servitude." Were the prisoner ignorant of this judge's methods, he would by now be jubilant. "But I shall sentence you to twelve months' hard labour, with twenty-five strokes of the cat when you go in, and another twenty-five when you come out." At this the criminal would collapse; and the judge would add: "Show your back to your dissolute friends when you come out."[22]

The spreading of the flogging over two sessions was done for practical reasons. According to Day's son, "At first the mistake was made of inflicting a short term of imprisonment with the maximum allowance of the cat: then, in one or two cases, the doctor intervened and declared the culprit medically unfit for so many lashes."[23] The way to get round this was to administer two shorter doses of the "cat". This not only allowed for physical recovery, but also enabled a lengthy period of mental torture as the criminal anticipated his forthcoming flogging.

A contemporary account of a flogging gives a taste of the savage violence inflicted on Victorian prisoners. In 1876, William Woodward, aged twenty-one, was found guilty of taking part in a cowardly gang attack on Richard Clare and two other men in Wavertree. On February 5, the group had been drinking in the Coffee House Hotel and were making their way home down Broad Green Road. Clare was knocked unconscious and had his purse, containing ten pounds, stolen. During the beating, his set of artificial teeth had been knocked out of his mouth. He had been so badly injured that he was forced to take two weeks off work. Woodward was found guilty and sentenced to seven years' imprisonment with twenty-four lashes. His two companions received twelve months with hard labour on a lesser charge.

Woodward was reported to be a good-looking man were it not for his low forehead, which ruined the overall impression of the rest of his face. He had a dark complexion with very smooth skin, although that was about to change. The prisoner, stripped to the waist, adopted a cheerful demeanour as he walked from his cell. He was then strapped to the triangle, which had been set up in the central corridor of the gaol. In the gallery above some prisoners convicted of similar violent assaults were placed so that they could witness the flogging. The governor and surgeon, together with a few journalists, were also present.

A prison official administered the whipping using the "cat". During the first few strokes, Woodward bravely tried not to flinch. The only sign of suffering was that his body heaved convulsively in the effort to breathe. After a few more strokes, the man's self-control had broken down and he received most of his remaining punishment wincing and howling like a dog.

The chief warder counted the strokes, which were given at intervals of about five seconds. The blows were dealt systematically all over the exposed flesh. The first lash fell heavily on his right shoulder and the second a little below it. The third was placed on his left shoulder and the fourth carefully aimed just underneath. At the fourth stroke Woodward uttered his first cry of pain, which was repeated at the fifth, sixth and seventh blows. As the eighth lash cut into his flesh, he roared in agony and apprehension, since he now began to turn his head to see when his torturer was about to deliver the next stripe.

Upon another stroke, Woodward struggled and tried to free himself from the frame. After the next blow his limbs seemed to give way as if he had been shot. He hung from his wrists and panted as if suffering a fit. This pitiful behaviour continued until the sixteenth lash when Woodward dropped his head on his shoulder and briefly sobbed like a child. The seventeenth cut jolted him back to a more familiar shriek of agony. His purple back was by now deeply scored around the shoulders and blood trickled down in rivulets. The weals at either shoulder were united in the centre by fainter lines where the lash had not fallen as heavily. At the eighteenth stroke, Woodward was beaten into passivity, no longer even able to utter a cry. The nineteenth cut produced a slight groan, followed by a whine in response to the twentieth. The last four strokes produced groans deeper in intensity although audibly fainter until at last a sigh of relief greeted the final stroke.

Woodward's face was deathly pale, but he was not altogether exhausted and, with a cloth thrown over his shoulders, he managed to stagger back to his cell. On his way, he looked up at the gallery and shouted to some prisoners, including one who had particularly seemed to have enjoyed the entertainment, "Let this be a warning to you, chaps."

Justice Day's son proudly pointed out that statisticians calculated that, in fourteen years, the judge inflicted 3,766 lashes on 137 criminals, an average of 28 strokes per man. During his ten years at Liverpool Assizes, Justice Day ordered a total of 1,961 lashes of the "cat" or strokes of the birch. It is no wonder that his severe policy earned him the nickname "Judgement Day". His son added that "all Liverpool people who have ever talked to me about it admit gratefully that John Day did much toward stamping out crime; but members of philanthropic societies, and some others, denounced the 'flogging judge' as a well-meaning brute."[24]

One of those critics was Joseph Collinson, who produced a book arguing the case against flogging for the Humanitarian League. Collinson pointed out, "At Liverpool, where flogging was largely resorted to, the crimes of violence did not decrease, but actually increased, in despite of terrible long sentences of imprisonment and double and treble doses of the lash."[25] He added that before Justice Day began his flogging regime at Liverpool, there was an annual total of fifty-six cases of robbery with violence: at the end of Day's reign of terror, there were seventy-nine cases![26]

Justice Day. The scourge of the High Rippers

Collinson dismisses the argument that the High Rip was wiped out as a result of Day's flogging policy. He admits that simple street ruffianism – although not robbery with violence – was reduced, but argues that this was achieved without the use of the lash. In fact mere ruffianism – which he felt members of the High Rip were mostly guilty of – was not even a floggable offence. High Court Judges had the power to flog men only under The Security from Violence Act 1863. This Act covered the offence of robbery *with* violence, but not of violence alone.

Collinson also points out that spreading the floggings over two or more instalments, with the final dose given after the prisoner had served twelve months, was also illegal. He quotes Home Office regulations that state: "In no case shall such whippings take place after the expiration of six months from the passing of the sentence."

Nott-Bower nevertheless observed that "the sentences had a stunning effect in Scotland Division, and gave many 'cause to think' before incurring the risk of like punishment."[27] Day's severe method of discipline showed one way to deal with the High Rip. Nott-Bower writes with disapproval of an alternative judicial approach. It seems that, "While Mr Justice Day was administering a law of terror, the then recorder of Liverpool [Mr Hopwood, Q.C.] was administering a law of leniency. Mr Hopwood was probably the most pronounced advocate of light sentences (no matter how serious the crime, or how habitual the criminal) that has ever been known."[28]

Nott-Bower gives an example of the discrepancies in sentencing during the period when Justice Day was waging his own war on violence. In one case, in Park Street, Bootle, on May 20, 1888, Arthur Burns struck James Sidwell on the head with the buckle end of his belt, which resulted in a compound skull fracture. Later in the day, in the same street, Burns went on to attack James Cooper in the same manner. It seems that there had been a series of gang disturbances in the area, which had lasted the entire day. Burns was tried before Mr Temple Q.C, and was twice found guilty of common assault. For each offence he was sentenced to twelve months' imprisonment with hard labour, with the two sentences to run concurrently. Sidwell thanked the judge. Even this sentence was considerably less than he would have received from Justice Day.

In contrast, in a separate case, although related to the same series of disturbances, some people were passing through a notorious street and were attacked by the High Rip. John Duggan stabbed Janet Bell in the head. The attacker had the good fortune to be tried by Mr Hopwood who sentenced him to be bound over to keep the peace! After a good telling off and a warning as to his stupidity, Duggan was immediately freed. The sentence caused uproar in the press, provoking comments such as "undoing of the wholesome work of the Judges of Assize", "folly and inconsistency", "mockery of justice".

Nott-Bower records the High Rippers' opinion of this inconsistent sentencing with a little rhyme that was popular at the time:

> Oh, Mr Hopwood, what shall I do?
> They've sent me to the Assizes,
> And I wanted to go to you,
> For though I may only get the sentence of a "Day",
> Oh, Mr Hopwood, the cat may spoil my stay.[29]

Criminals certainly knew where they stood with Justice Day. A Liverpool detective recounted the time when he had arrested a man who was caught bang to rights. The prisoner asked which judge would try him. He was told, "Mr Justice Day." The man replied in a dejected tone, "Oh, then it's a five years job."[30]

Yet perhaps the judge did have a heart after all. He didn't always flog convicted prisoners, much to the disgust of some members of the public. A newspaper correspondent calling himself "Liverpudlian" asked why Day didn't sentence High Rippers Peter Tedford and Edward Higham to a flogging rather than gaoling them for a mere fifteen years? The writer argued that such evil men were not bothered by prison.[31]

The writer was probably correct. For some ruffians, a spell in gaol, however lengthy, meant nothing. Sixteen-year-old Patrick Loftus is a good example of a wicked lad who had seemingly lived beyond the influence of the criminal justice system. In February 1886, he was charged with wounding a thirteen-year-old girl. She had been walking down Raleigh Street, Bootle, when Loftus, who was standing at the doorway of an empty house, called her over. He gave her some money and asked her to bring him some beer. When the girl returned, he grabbed hold of her, threw her to the floor and assaulted her. The girl screamed, but Loftus warned her that if she continued he would throw her out of the window. The girl became silent, but then threatened that she would tell her mother about what had happened. Loftus grabbed her by an arm and a leg and proceeded to throw her out of the window. The girl dropped fourteen feet and received a serious wound as she cracked her skull on the cellar steps.

When Loftus appeared at the assizes he was already in custody for having hit a policeman on the head with a hatchet. In court, a constable informed the judge that Loftus had terrorised the neighbourhood for four years, picking up four convictions for assault. The judge warned the lad that if he were an adult he would send him to prison for the rest of his natural life. On account of his youth, he instead sentenced him to seven years. From the dock, Loftus turned to a crowd of his supporters and shouted cockily, "Cheer up, boys, it's nowt."

If prison and physical punishment were useless deterrents to some hardened criminals, then society had another remedy for crime. Before the gangs ever saw the inside of a cell or felt the sting of the lash upon their backs, they faced a formidable force of organised police officers determined to keep the streets clear of ruffians and villains.

CHAPTER 18

The Police

IN HIS FINAL address to the jury at the winter assizes of 1886, Justice John Day was gushing in his praise of the Liverpool police force. He thought it impossible that a gang such as the High Rip could exist in a town with a police force that was "so powerful, so admirably organised, so effectively handled and constituted of men so able, so intelligent and so courageous".[1]

However, not everybody shared this laudatory view, particularly after the death of Richard Morgan, which had taken place twelve years earlier. At the time, Major Greig had been the Head Constable of Liverpool, a post he held from 1852 to 1881. He was an ex-military man who was instrumental in the development of the Detective Department, the very body of men who had helped bring Morgan's killers to justice.

Nevertheless, the lack of police presence on the streets during Morgan's murder caused a political and media storm. Liverpool Town Council and its Watch Committee immediately came under fire from the press. The *Weekly Albion* complained: "The carnival was undisturbed by a single policeman! Was ever a scandal in police history heard to surpass this?"[2] The *Liverpool Town Crier* joined in: "We are inclined to think the police are more inactive than inefficient.'[3] According to *The Times*, such inefficiency could lead only to the management of the police being transferred to some other body that was more capable of delivering results.[4] J.B. Aspinall, Q.C. to Liverpool Borough Sessions, warned that central government could take powers away from the Watch Committee if it was not up to the job.

Major Greig. Head Constable of Liverpool at the time of the Tithebarn Street outrage.

It is a recurring theme of both local and national politics that those in opposition take every opportunity to attack the ruling party over its record on crime. It has already been suggested that, during the High Rip scare, certain newspapers attempted to make political capital out of the police authority's failure to deal with the gangs. To this day, it is still common practice for newspapers that support the opposition party to join in attacks on the governing party's inability to maintain law and order; there are plenty of political points to be scored by highlighting and publicising the other party's failures. It was against this background of outrage, anger and political animosity between the ruling Tories and the Whigs [later Liberals], that the press and politicians waged their own battle for the support of public opinion in Liverpool in 1874.

The Tithebarn Street case was brought up at the Town Council meeting on August 5. James Picton, the leader of the Whig-radical minority, raised a vital point. He thought it strange that no police constable had been in the vicinity during the entire attack. He asked Mr Alderman Livingston, the vice-chairman of the Watch Committee, to institute an inquiry into the matter and, if people could not be protected on Liverpool's streets, he suggested that they would have to arm themselves with guns. Mr Livingston promised that the matter would be strictly investigated.

On August 11, a report was presented by the Watch Committee about the "alleged absence of the police in Tithebarn Street, during the time that Richard Morgan got kicked to death". Here it was established that "the spot where the murder was committed was visited by the inspector, the acting inspector and six police constables" between 9.15pm and 9.45pm. Indeed, at the coroner's inquest, PC Adam Green stated that he passed the place where the murder had been committed about ten minutes before the incident took place. His beat was down Vauxhall Road to Highfield Street, up through St Paul's Square and down by Smithfield Street and Lower Milk Street to Tithebarn Street. If he kept moving, he said that he would have been in Tithebarn Street for five minutes every half hour. He would only have been absolutely out of Tithebarn Street for about twenty minutes in every half hour.

On the evening of the murder, there had been a pile of damaged cotton in Vauxhall Road, which PC Green had been told to keep an eye on. There was also an officer whose beat was from Highfield Street to Exchange Station. In fact, the police served the area very well. A common modern-day criticism of the police is that the policy of patrolling in motor vehicles has robbed communities of such close contact with a "bobby on the beat". Yet it is seen that even in such a well-policed district, violent crime could still explode in the intervals between foot patrols.

Despite such a strong defence, the press raised a big question mark over the police's efficiency. Liverpool was the most heavily policed town in the country. Although London had thirty times the mileage of Liverpool's streets, it had only ten times the number of police. The worrying implication was that Liverpool at that time must have been an atrociously bad place.

For some, the debate was not simply about the matter of police strength, but of management and priorities. It was felt that the police allowed rioting and disorder in certain districts. This didn't make it easy for those decent people who had to pass through these neighbourhoods. Therefore, it was proposed that the police should disperse any groups of ruffians who hung around street corners.[5]

It was also felt that the authorities were in denial of the problem of street violence. A newspaper correspondent argued: "The worst thing Alderman Livingston and Major Greig can do is to deny the existence of the chronic ruffianism which has been allowed to grow up in certain districts of Liverpool."[6]

Yet a report compiled by Major Greig, for the chairman of the Watch Committee on January 4, 1875, presented a very different account of the circumstances of the murder. The report argued that Tithebarn Street was normally "an orderly place, as compared with Marybone, Standish Street and adjacent streets, nothing having occurred there either before or since". Major Greig stated that, with the exception of Marybone and Scotland Place, there had been no reports of ruffianism. The police also anticipated potential trouble spots, during religious festivals such as St Patrick's Day, for example.

The Head Constable went on to say that he regretted the loss of police time taken up with court appearances, but added that the number of cases prosecuted testified to the very efficiency of the police. Finally, Major Greig pointed out that, although the mere assembling on street corners was not a punishable offence – except on the grounds of obstruction – the police had full instructions to prevent people from gathering in groups, even in small numbers. Indeed, in a few cases, they had been forced to move people on.

In another letter to the *Daily Post*, signed rather enigmatically, "A Member of the Fourth Estate", it was pointed out that the difficulties with the Cornermen had arisen years earlier and that it had taken the form of bullying decent people for beer money on pay days.[7] A chief superintendent, aided by some beat constables and officers in plain clothes, had successfully quashed the problem. The men sought out the offenders in Thomas Street, Whitechapel, and had a quiet word with them, warning them of their future conduct. No arrests were made, but thanks to this pro-active approach the nuisance was stopped. The writer felt that the problem had only resurfaced because experienced officers had been removed from the beat and that men "without special knowledge and qualifications" had replaced them. What was needed, therefore, was the return of officers who would not be intimidated by the Cornermen and who would be willing to use a bit of force if necessary.

Unhindered by potential accusations of police brutality, there was a call for a tougher form of policing.[8] It was felt that while police excesses were deplorable, there was no danger of being too hard on the big strong ruffians of Liverpool's streets. If anything, the danger was all the other way. It was felt, therefore, that the police needed the full support of management in tackling gang members.

The police were seen not only as keepers of law and order, but also as the agents of intelligence. The issue of police numbers was almost a red herring. As regards street violence, it was not merely a question of having more police on the beat, something that had been suggested at the Town Council meeting, but of putting pressure on the ruffians to keep them moving and never allowing them to settle for long enough to cause mischief. Known gang members were to be kept under surveillance: "They must be made to feel that society has its eyes upon them, and that its eyes are wide open."[9] One hundred and thirty years later, society would indeed have its eyes on such criminals, in the form of CCTV cameras in every city centre. The Big Brother society is now very much a reality, and the identification and pursuit of known criminals, through targeting, is also something that is now common police practice.

For some, however, the long arm of the law did not reach far enough. It was felt that the police were failing to patrol the smaller streets and courts of the lower classes and that they concentrated solely on the major thoroughfares, over which they had adequate control.[10] Perhaps these people forgot the fact that Tithebarn Street itself *was* a leading thoroughfare.

Another of the major problems discussed was a perceived police policy of non-interference. While for some people, the police were always absent when they were needed most, for others, even when constables were present they did nothing. It was felt that criminals had no respect for ordinary citizens and that they had a fear only for the police. Yet officers, for their part, often refused to interfere in incidents of street crime. Therefore, ruffians treated respectable workers as easy prey, because if a labourer had been the victim of an assault, the police tended to regard the affair as just a general brawl in which one side was likely to be as much to blame as the other.

Officers were often accused of turning a blind eye. Just after the Tithebarn Street murder, "A Gentlewoman" from New Brighton related her own experience of police apathy. A few nights previously, she had been leaving Exchange Station in Tithebarn Street when she witnessed a man being knocked down and brutally kicked in the face. She had looked for a policeman and, after taking some time to find one, was astonished when he informed her that he was sorry she had put herself out looking for him. He told her that the police never interfered in the Tithebarn Street rows and that if ever she saw a fight again in the same street, she should not bother troubling herself, as they always left them to battle it out. The lady asked whether it was any wonder that the shocking murder of Richard Morgan had taken place if this was the attitude of the police?[11]

The issue of police non-interference prompted several other letters to the newspapers. E. Lucas of Leeds Street wrote that he had not been surprised that somebody had been kicked to death. He too had been knocked down in Vauxhall Road, at the corner of a street, and yet the policemen had appeared to be very friendly with his attackers. Mr Lucas raised two important questions: where were the police when the attack took place?; and why were the gangs allowed to assemble in the first place? The writer went on to question the function of the police. If officers did not see it as their duty to act against the gangs, then he urged people to apply to parliament for a Coercion Bill to remove the roughs from the street corners forcibly, such as had occurred in Ireland.[12]

The letter prompted a reply from the enigmatic "XX":

Sir – Will you kindly permit me space for a few words on the scum of society, which infests our streets? I have occasion to pass down Athol Street twice a day. I generally notice a most despicable collection of roughs and blackguards of the Corrigan and McCrave type at almost every public-house corner from Latimer Street downwards, all evidently denizens of the back slums of this street. No one can deny that these back streets – Latimer Street in particular and its branch streets – is a black spot on the map of Liverpool. It has more than its quota of roughs, vagabonds and drunken women, and their language is really disgusting to the passers-by. On a Saturday and Monday, the street corners are in a state of habitual disturbance, and the police, with their characteristic snail-pace, do not seem to interfere until some unfortunate fellow has had more than his share in these cowardly knock 'em down and brutal kicking cases of late so common, and in many instances fatal. It is clear that the authorities should at once grapple this evil with a stern hand, and the police should be armed with power to seize all these well-known detestable and idle characters to blot out this taint, to eradicate the great evil, and to root out the pestilence which exists in this and other streets.[13]

There is some exaggeration as to the number of fatalities involved in these kicking cases, since Morgan's death seems to be the first and only one up to this point, but the chaotic nature of such rough districts is nevertheless made plain.

In reply, the equally mysterious "Q" claimed that both Ascot Street and North Latimer Street, off Scotland Road, were hotbeds of vice and drunkenness.[14] These streets had been identified as the noisiest in town, with the exception of Ben Jonson Street. On the previous Monday, it had been painful to witness the disgusting scenes and commotion in Ascot Street as men and women armed with pokers engaged for hours in a brawl. It had been utterly impossible to pass safely through the dense and infuriated rabble. All this had taken place within sight of the police station, but the gentlemen in blue had made themselves conspicuous by their absence. The writer urged that steps should be taken to control such disgusting sights and that the notorious members of the "Holy Fly" fraternity, who lounged menacingly about the public-house doors, should be hastily rooted out.

It is difficult to decide who comes out worse for criticism, the ruffians or the police. Indeed, most members of the public, or rather those middle-class people who took the trouble to write to the newspapers, placed great emphasis on ridding the streets of ruffians by preventing them from congregating or otherwise dispersing them. The current criminal justice jargon is to "reclaim the streets". Yet what the police did in moving people along was merely to change the location of the undesirable behaviour rather than to put a stop to the behaviour itself. The question of where the gangs were to go, and what they were to do when they got there, was never addressed.

As an antidote to the public's anger, and in a generous spirit of what today would be labelled "do-goodism", a religious journal offered a sense of Christian hope that would make the need for police intervention redundant: "By our compassion and our guidance some of [the Cornermen] may 'move on' into paths of industry, sobriety, purity, happiness and godliness."[15]

As we have seen, by the spring of 1875, there were signs that the Cornermen phenomenon was running out of steam. The moral fear around the country that had been caused by the murder of Richard Morgan was short-lived and failed to develop into a full-blown panic, just as had been the case with the garrotting outbreak in London. Perhaps this was because the crime had occurred outside the capital, or because the perpetrators had only been youths. Perhaps it was because the Cornermen had only attacked members of their own class, albeit respectable members like Morgan.

In a report written for the Watch Committee on January 4, 1875, Major Greig himself concluded: "Much as the Tithebarn Street occurrence is to be deplored, still the case is an isolated one there, and a serious case may take place in a noisy and bristling thoroughfare."[16] Others were dismissive of the press exaggeration of the danger posed by street-corner gangs. It was pointed out that Cornermen rarely used extreme violence. The press was blamed for making the public feel that it was at the mercy of every man standing on a street corner. In fact pedestrians were more at risk from bad language and spitting than they were from fatal violence.[17]

The Cornermen, of course, remained outside the public houses and it was the press itself that moved on. Headlines such as "Liverpool Roughs: Another Cornerman", from the *Daily Post* on January 16, 1875, began to dwindle after the execution of McCrave and Mullen. "And there it all stopped," remarks crime historian Rob Sindall. "Cornermen suddenly became unnewsworthy. The Watch Committee and Major Greig attended to their duties as before and Liverpool continued to grow both in prosperity and squalor."[18]

However, ten years later, when the High Rip gang emerged onto the scene in an orgy of violence, robbery, intimidation and extortion, the press had a field day once again and criticised the failings of Liverpool's policing. It was felt that the police were completely useless in tackling the threat of the High Rip. The force was accused of being merely an ornamental body that was neither suited nor intended for active service on the streets of Liverpool. Officers were admittedly well drilled and organised, but they lacked the practical skills to combat street disorder. The fact that the city centre was unsafe even in the middle of the day was proof of the constabulary's failing.

Parallels were drawn between the Tithebarn Street murder of 1874 and the fresh upsurge of violence ten years later. It was felt that, after Richard Morgan's death, the police had done a good job of clearing up the streets. However, over a period of time, "with the cessation of fear came a cessation of vigilance on the part of our guardians".[19] In the meantime, a new generation of ruffians had grown up and they had taken advantage of the police authority's complacency.

Captain Nott-Bower was the Head Constable during this difficult period. He succeeded Major Greig in 1881 and held the post until 1902. He had previously served in Dublin and was perhaps seen as the ideal candidate to deal with Liverpool's Irish problem.

The press piled on the criticism: they had heard reports that the High Rip had reduced Islington to such a condition of disorder that ladies were shunning the affected area altogether. It was pointed out that this area housed the business premises of old and respected tradesmen and that it also contained the residential property of upper Islington. It was further noted that Islington was still one of the most convenient thoroughfares for reaching the city from the east. Inhabitants were urged to put pressure on the Watch Committee to strive to secure the services of a new mounted force of police.[20]

The police were said to have given up on some areas. It was stated that tradesmen who had lived in Islington for many years felt that it had become a no-go area into which policemen seldom entered. When people had occasion to seek for their services, they would have to trek to London Road or Richmond Row and, upon discovering an officer, they would have to beg him to overcome his natural aversion to doing his duty in the district.

The trepidation of the police when faced with gang violence is illustrated by the following account of a street robbery that took place in June 1880. Frederick Milton had been walking along Mansfield Street late in the evening. Five menacing-looking youths were standing on the corner of Wakefield Street, near Islington. As Milton passed, one of them said: "There goes the fellow that's got the

Sir William Nott-Bower. Head Constable of Liverpool at the time of the High Rip.

money, let's follow him." Before he had reached the end of the street, Milton had been jumped from behind and pinned to the wall by his throat. As the gang searched him, another lad shouted: "Punch him, punch him, he's got more than that." The gang wrenched at his watch chain, gave him a few more smacks and then ran away. The poor man went off in search of a policeman but, when he eventually found one, the young officer told him that he was too afraid to go into the street alone and that he would therefore have to wait for some assistance to arrive. At the trial, the magistrate was sympathetic with the young officer, saying: "I don't wonder at it. The street is a disgrace to the town."

There were many faults with the system of beat policing. Officers who patrolled High Rip areas took their lives into their hands. Even so, they did not dare enter the very worst areas and only kept to the main thoroughfares. If they did go into the side streets, they were likely to be stabbed or hit with a brick. The High Rip boasted that some police officers had to be taken off the beat because of threats to their lives.

In February 1887, a gang of about fifteen roughs congregated in Athol Street, off Scotland Road. A group of nine or ten policemen tried to move them on, but the gang drew knives and defied them. A scuffle followed and one prisoner was taken. The "Citizen", in another of his letters, complained that he hadn't seen any reports of the incident in the newspapers. It was as though such occurrences had become so common that they were no longer even considered newsworthy. The "Citizen" also called the gang the "gentle High Rip", not because of their gentility, but because of the "gentle" approach that the police seemed to have adopted towards them.[21]

However, not all policemen were in awe of the High Rip. In 1960, a Mrs O'Brien recalled that a policeman with large fists, known as "Pins", had been the scourge of the High Rippers. Pins had no fear of the gang as he walked his beat along Scotland Road. He would tackle the ruffians single-handedly and earned the respect of the High Rip as a result. "Pins is coming!" was the terrified alarm given at his approach.[22]

However, the High Rip always seemed to be one step ahead of the police. The gang knew at what times the officers signed on and off duty. They knew when and where they had to meet their inspectors. They calculated how long each beat would take and where an officer would be at any given moment. The High Rip was therefore able to plan their crimes with both great precision and success.

A solution was proposed that a strong patrol of police, armed with the long sticks that were normally carried by sergeants, should pass through the districts at irregular times in the hope of catching the gang off-guard.[23] Similar advice was offered to Head Constable Nott-Bower on the best way of rounding up the High Rippers: "Tell off thirty or forty men in plain clothes, give them something to protect themselves with and let them parade in sixes or sevens on Great Howard Street, Vauxhall Road, Scotland Road and Great Homer Street and lock up all gangs that tend to break the public peace. Let them also clear them away from the corners of streets and pay occasional visits to the public houses and beer houses in the streets off the above-named roads."[24]

One newspaper correspondent, who requested that his name not be published for fear of being consigned to the undertaker, gave his own views on how the High Rip could be tackled. He felt that the police would remain powerless for as long as the public continued to turn a blind eye to crime. The High Rip would always be on the lookout for the police, or "slops" as they called them, when they had a job on hand. The gang also had scouts who raised the cry of "Hec Hec" when the "educated savages", as he called them, were in danger of being "copt" or caught. The gang would then scarper, even though there were plenty of people around to witness their crimes. The writer doubted whether anything like this happened in any other English town and called for Liverpudlians to unite as one man against the High Rip.[25]

Somebody called "M" suggested that if "the authorities are unable to cope with this band of marauders, it is surely time that a meeting of citizens should be called to consider what shall be done".[26] The letter hints at vigilante justice. On 19 November 1886, a correspondent to the *Echo* went one further. He proposed that the famous general and Victoria Cross recipient Sir Redvers Buller be recalled from his military duties in Ireland to deal with the High Rippers in Vauxhall Road. Such was the strength of local opposition to the gang.

There was a strong desire to reclaim the streets. The police were criticised for failing to enforce the existing law relating to street obstruction: "The evil-looking scoundrels, young and old, who hang about public-house corners in Scotland Road, and such thoroughfares should be systematically and relentlessly driven away, and locked up if they refuse to move."[27]

The press, of course, had been here before with the problem of the Cornermen. Respectable people wanted the streets to be cleared of ruffians, but for many of these loafers there was nowhere else to go. The damp and fetid slums they lived in were hardly inviting places to spend an evening.

Not all people hanging around public houses and street corners had criminal intentions. Nor is it is true that the police ignored the gangs. On March 13, 1884, a group of nineteen lads appeared at the City Police Court charged with loitering in the footways and causing obstruction. The accused lived in various streets around Scotland Road, including Sawney Pope Street, Dryden Street and Bostock Street. The charges came after the police had repeatedly cautioned the youths, many of whom had previously been fined for similar offences. The lads were found guilty and were fined once again, this time between two shillings and sixpence and twenty shillings. A couple of them protested that they lived in the courts and that they had only gone to the top of the street to take "a bit of fresh air after tea".

In another case, two youths had been summoned for loitering in Breckfield Road North, but they argued that they lived only yards from where the police had picked them up. The chairman acknowledged that it was difficult for respectable people to walk along the streets, but he also made the point that the police should be careful in the discrimination of cases when they brought up "worthless people". He pointed out that the officer should have made inquiries to check that the lads lived in the street. The police constable replied that one of them had given him a false address. As there was no evidence of any wrongdoing, the two lads were dismissed.

It was also felt that the police had got their priorities wrong. They would rather persecute basket women and street traders who were merely trying to earn a meagre living than tackle the more important menace of the Cornermen and High Rippers. It is still a common criticism of the police today that they do not do enough to tackle the major problems – such as violent crime – but that they focus instead on the smaller problems.

Another issue was that some people had no respect for the police because they had lost faith in them. In October 1886, a disturbance had taken place in a public house at the corner of Cavendish Street and Marybone. The High Rip had staged a revenge attack on the landlord, a man called McLaughlin. A plate-glass door window had been smashed and the landlord had been left whistling for help from an upstairs window for a full ten minutes before the police had arrived. In the meantime, the mob below threw stones at the man's head.

The following day, a journalist called at the Central Police Station for information, but was brusquely turned away. He then visited the public house, which was surrounded by police officers standing among the broken glass. It was obvious that there had been an incident and yet the police attitude was very terse and discourteous, with officers refusing to provide any details. The journalist was left with the opinion, apparently one that was shared by many others, that the police treated respectable citizens as their natural enemy rather than as the people they were paid to protect.

Indeed, the newspapers included regular reports of police brutality against individuals. For example, in September 1883, James Mackenzie, from Blake Street near Brownlow Hill, had fallen asleep on some steps. Two policemen woke him up. As he got up, a constable knocked the cap off his head. As Mackenzie stooped to pick it up, the officer delivered a tremendous rugby kick to his stomach, causing massive internal injuries. The victim managed to give an account of the attack before he died the next day.

HOWEVER, THE ROLE of the police in keeping the streets of Victorian Liverpool safe must not be underestimated. Officers may have occasionally overstepped the mark, sometimes outrageously, but they were on the front line of the fight against organised crime. Reports such as the one above were matched by equally brutal assaults on the police by criminals resisting arrest or simply for the fun of it. The dangers of Liverpool's streets can be illustrated by relating three incidents that were dealt with by the Police Court over a period of just eight days in February 1882.

In the first case, five men set upon two policemen in Christian Street, off Islington, after a constable had broken up a fight. Annoyed at having their entertainment disrupted, the men shouted: "Let's kill the bastard." The ruffians then thrashed the policeman with their belts, while one of them threw a brick at him. A colleague came to his rescue, but the pair had no chance and the beating continued.

Another group of five powerful-looking men attacked two policemen walking along Scotland Road. As they reached Silvester Street, the officers heard a commotion and females screaming. Two women lay on the ground surrounded by a crowd. The police were trying to take the two people into custody when Patrick Fennan shouted, "Don't go with the pigs." He then fractured a policeman's nose by hitting him with an object he was holding. Fortunately, some plain-clothed officers were on hand to help restore order, but they were also pelted with stones. As the officers took their charges into custody, John Jennings took off his belt and swiped two policemen in the face with the buckle end. Francis Kennedy then threw two bricks at a policeman, while Silvester Cussion forcibly tried to rescue his friends from arrest. Just outside the Athol Street bridewell, Peter Murphy launched a running kick at an officer, nearly taking the legs from under him.

In the third case, three days later, John Keating took offence at being asked to "move on" along Boundary Street. He pulled out a knife and jabbed the policeman in the chest. Luckily, the officer's heavy topcoat prevented the blade from penetrating his skin. A second stab sliced off part of his coat sleeve.

Some ruffians took their assaults on the police very seriously. In another case, in Marsh Lane, Bootle, in May 1883, Timothy Cain – no doubt influenced by recent political events in Ireland – resisted arrest by shouting to a crowd of friends, "Assassination, Assassination!" The officers were forced to draw their truncheons to beat off the angry mob.

There wasn't even safety in numbers for the police. It must have been a lot worse for individual officers who had to patrol without back-up. Walking along strictly pre-planned beats, armed with only a truncheon and a whistle, police officers were expected to deal with any situation that confronted them. It was not until 1891 that the Watch Committee was persuaded to invest in three patrol wagons. These horse-drawn prototypes of the modern police van could both carry violent prisoners away from the scene and quickly bring rein-forcements of officers to help provide support in cases of the worse street disturbances. However, during the reign of the Cornermen and High Rip, the individual officer, walking his solitary evening beat through dark, hostile streets, was a brave, but vulnerable, figure.

A last word about the police must echo the words of Justice Day, by paying tribute to the courage and tenacity of some of the officers. Nowhere was this bravery more evident than in the following example of an arrest made by two policemen in 1876.

The large piece of wasteland between Kensington and Boaler Street was studded with water-filled pits, which the local population used as public baths. To the disgust of the residents of the area, men and boys regularly stripped naked to go swimming there. The problem was that, as they passed the pools, respectable women and their children were subjected to gross displays of indecency.

On a sunny Sunday afternoon in August, two policemen tried to arrest one of the adult bathers, Bryan Lynch, a married man of Martin Street. As they were taking him to the police station, a gang, howling abuse and throwing stones, pursued the officers. The commotion attracted more ruffians from the area around Division Street and Martin Street. Within a matter of minutes, a mob was raining rocks on the police, with some of the missiles finding their target with deadly accuracy. The officers refused to let go of the prisoner and took refuge in a drill shed in Coleridge Street. At the time, the building was being used as a Sunday school and the children had to be safely evacuated during a temporary ceasefire.

One of the policemen had already escaped to seek reinforcements. As his colleague stepped out of the shed, the mob was suddenly reminded of why it was gathered there and the stones began to fly through the air once again. The building was subjected to a barrage of missiles for twenty minutes. Windows and lights in the shed were smashed to pieces. One newspaper was astounded that such a savage attack could be directed at a Sunday school, especially, it reported without a hint of irony, one within a stone's throw of a police station.[28]

A cry of "police" resulted in a brief cessation in hostilities, but more stones soon followed when the mob realised that it had been a false alarm. One courageous man, armed with a whip, ran at the crowd, but the stone-throwers simply turned their attentions to him and he had to retreat under a hail of bricks. The newspaper congratulated the public-spirited citizen for having created a temporary diversion, however brief.

An inspector and an officer eventually arrived on the scene and the attack stopped. Lynch was interviewed and set free after apologising for his behaviour. To make sure that he had given a correct address, the inspector and a policeman escorted him to his house. The crowd cheered as Lynch was led home in a triumphal procession. However, the cheers were mixed by loud and deep groans for the police. Bricks were thrown once again, but Lynch held up his hands to quell any possible riot. However, once Lynch had been released, the stones again started to fly in earnest. Only the officers' helmets saved them from serious head injuries. The inspector made several forays into the crowd, but the dispersed men returned to renew their volleys of bricks. The police finally retreated, physically wounded but with their pride intact, for not once did they shirk from their duty. Such was the bravery of Liverpool's constabulary.

Liverpool's police could take whatever comfort they could from the fact that they were not alone in the fight against gangs of rebellious youths. The problem of gang disorder was countrywide and not just specific to Liverpool. It is to some of these other gangs that we must now turn for a different perspective on the problem of street violence.

CHAPTER 19

Scuttlers, Hooligans and a Sense of Style

WHILE THE CORNERMEN and High Rip were terrorising Liverpool's streets, the rest of the country had their own violent gangs to contend with. Two of the most infamous late nineteenth-century gangs were the Scuttlers of Manchester and the Hooligans of London. The Peaky Blinders of Birmingham also deserve a mention, but they are less well documented.

These gangs were all fashion conscious to a much greater degree than their Liverpool counterparts. A distinguishing feature of most teenage gangs is that they wear a uniform, which acts as a means of identification that both binds members together as a group and sets them apart from rivals. Style is also a useful means of displaying defiance to the authorities. It might simply mean wearing a cap set at a particular jaunty angle, or adorning a belt with some distinctive markers. Clothing could also double up as a weapon, particularly studded belts and iron-plated boots or clogs.

Caps could also be lethal. The Peaky Blinders were active in Aston and Birmingham from 1882 to the early 1900s. Their name derives from their distinctive headgear. The official version of the origin of the name is that the gang wore caps with the peak pulled down; done not only for fashion purposes, but also to avoid recognition by witnesses. In this way, they pre-dated today's baseball cap and hoodie-wearing generation by over a hundred years. However, legend also has it that members sewed razor blades into the peaks of their caps and a swipe of the hat could blind a victim. The gang was also known as "sloggers", no doubt after the slugging form of fighting they often engaged in. Peaky Blinders also wore bell-bottomed trousers, a neck scarf and that weapon for all emergencies, the leather belt.

Liverpool's "Slouch Hat Brigade", a name invented by a newspaper, had their own particular slant on headgear, and once again, this had more to do with the practical reason of hiding their faces than to do with any fashion statement. On a Friday mid-evening in November 1886, a gentleman was walking through the Whitechapel district of Liverpool. A youth approached him and asked him for some money. He was wearing a hat with one side of the brim bent downwards over one eye. The gentleman kindly obliged with some coppers. However, shortly after, another lad with the same distinctive headgear made a similar request for spare change. The gentleman again found some coins to give. Sensing an easy touch, a third figure with a slouch hat then appeared and asked for some more money.

The gentleman had by now realised that his charity was being abused and refused any further donations. The lad in the hat warned him that if he didn't give something he'd knock his eye out. As he spoke, a gang of about five or six fellow ruffians dressed in identical headgear surrounded the gentleman and pinned him against a shutter. Somebody shouted: "Look out for the knife." Luckily for the gentleman it was a friend who proceeded to punch the nearest hat-wearing head and then blow a policeman's whistle to summon assistance. The slouch hats fled.

In contrast, Liverpool's Cornermen do not seem to have shared other gangs' obsession with style. In the 1980s, the "Scouse scally" and football supporter may have led the country in fashion, but a hundred years earlier the dreadful poverty and squalor of Liverpool's slums meant that style was not that important. Finding money for the next meal or next quart of ale was probably of more immediate concern. Richard Morgan's attackers were no trendsetters. Peter Campbell wore dirty trousers and a shabby coat that was too short. Mullen and McCrave also appeared in court in filthy clothing. Compared to other gangs in the country, the Cornermen did not seem to have any sense of style. The gang's uniform merely amounted to tattered clothes and a pair of boots. As one contemporary writer noted: "Generally the Cornerman's appearance is very repulsive. The grand idea of the human creature – 'God created man in his own image' – is utterly lost."[1]

The best description of a High Rip uniform is given in a letter to a newspaper in 1885.[2] The anonymous writer, calling himself "A Resident of the District" for fear of comebacks, describes a gang terrorising the northern area of Scotland Road, including Epsom Street and Doncaster Street. The lads wear a "blue jacket, greasy pants, and a tight cap, with a large muffler – in fact a real fighting man's regalia". The clothing seems pretty unremarkable and there is no mention of the footwear, so it is difficult to see why such a uniform is particularly related to violence. However, since it was the uniform of a gang – a gang that caused so much trouble – the clothing must have inspired terror in the neighbourhood, in a similar way that the sight of a hooded top does today.

The only item of clothing that seems to distinguish the High Rip was a "bucco cap". Cornermen also wore such hats. Peter Campbell was wearing one when he went on the run. In fact, hats were such a treasured possession that some people went to extraordinary lengths to obtain them. Robberies and fights were often started deliberately by the act of knocking off or crushing a stranger's hat or cap. "Bonneting", as it was called, would spark retaliation, which in turn would lead to a robbery or a fight that sometimes escalated to fatal violence. A policeman killed James Mackenzie after knocking off his hat. The Irishmen murdered Robert Bradshaw after he had tried to retrieve his stolen cap.

In January 1878, Peter Rowan had been sitting comfortably at home in Prince William Street, Toxteth, when Frederick Spike entered the house and snatched the cap off his head. The youth fled outside and joined another boy. An angry Rowan ran out after the thief, but the pair then threw him down the front steps. As Rowan lay helpless on the floor, Spike took off his belt and struck him on the head with the buckle end. He died of his injuries a few days later.

As Richard Morgan lay dead in the road, John McCrave's first instinct as he ran away from the approaching policeman and a certain murder conviction had been to grasp the man's sealskin cap and to stuff it into his coat. In the very midst of his savagery and with his own execution looming over him, the lad at least aspired to a sense of style. McCrave, of course, exchanged the hat for the executioner's white cap a few months later.

A last word about the Liverpool ruffian's desperate desire to lay his hands on any clothes that were available is neatly illustrated by the story of the soldier and the street rogues. In November 1894, Richard Spring, aged eighteen, and William Staging, aged twenty-three, asked Private Thomas Wood for some money to buy beer. Like Richard Morgan, the soldier flatly refused and was consequently knocked to the floor and kicked. However, the man got up and offered to thrash his attackers. As a disciplined military man, instilled with honourable notions of a fair fight, he carefully took off his topcoat, body coat, shirt and belt and squared up for a proper contest. The men then ran off with his clothes.

PERHAPS THE FIRST fashion-conscious youths were the Scuttlers. The term can be traced back to the 1870s, although the gangs were more common in the 1880s and 1890s. In the rough districts of Manchester and Salford, rival gangs of lads and young females, aged between fourteen and eighteen, would engage in neighbourhood-based fights or "scuttles". The name probably derives from the manner in which the gangs scurried and scampered along the streets in search of bother; the name also carries the destructive connotation of scuttling a ship. It has been suggested that the first "scuttles" involved teenagers who had been re-enacting mock skirmishes from the Franco-Prussian War of 1870–71. The excitement and danger of mass violence seemed to spread across Manchester, leading to the formation of a series of ruthless gangs.

In 1905, youth worker Charles Russell published a book called *Manchester Boys*, which included a chapter on the Scuttlers. He described the fashion sense of a typical gang member: "A loose white scarf would adorn his throat; his hair was plastered down upon his forehead; he wore a peaked cap rather over one eye; his trousers were of fustian, and cut – like a sailor's – with 'bell bottoms'."[3]

The trousers measured fourteen inches around the knee but flared out to twenty-one inches at the ankle. The cap was usually tilted to display what was known as a "donkey fringe". Brass-tipped pointed clogs, hidden under the flared ends of the trousers, were also essential, particularly for kicking opponents. As with the High Rip, the belt was another vital accessory, which served both to keep the trousers up and to hold the enemy at bay. The belts of the Scuttlers often had ornamental patterns of metal pins worked into them. Alex Devine, another pioneer of the lads' club movement, described such artwork:

"These designs include figures of serpents, a heart pierced with an arrow [this appears to be a favourite design], the Prince of Wales' feathers, clogs, animals, stars, etc., and often either the name of the wearer of the belt or that of some woman."[4] However, such arty craftwork should not blind us to the real purpose of these fancy strips of leather, which was basically to crack people over the head.

Local gangs included the "Bungall Boys" from Salford, "Buffalo Bill's Gang" from Pendleton and the "Bengall Tiger" and "Forty Row" from Ancoats. Unlike the Cornermen and High Rip, the gangs were not concerned with robbery. Honour, territorial pride and defending one's area from an attack by rivals appear to have been the prime motivations for Scuttler violence. In this sense, they resemble latter-day football hooligans, who defend their "end" or section of the ground.

Gangs in Liverpool did not engage in community rivalry to the same extent. There was the odd sectarian street feud, such as that between the Addison and Hodson Street neighbours or Catholic Kew Street versus Orange-supporting Bostock Street, but nothing along the lines of, for example, Toxteth youths fighting gangs from the Vauxhall area. Cornermen would fight with anybody who passed: it didn't matter where they came from and it was normally individuals rather than rival gangs who were the main targets of their violence.

The captain or leader of the Scuttlers was somebody who had proved his worth as the champion fighter among the group. Charles Russell felt that Scuttlers had some moral principles, in that they didn't beat up lone individuals from rival gangs. If they did manage to corner a single member from another neighbourhood they would line up to fight him one by one. On the other hand, it might have been quicker and easier to be beaten up by the whole gang at once rather than have to face a constant stream of fresh opponents, one after the other.

However, such words can be taken with a pinch of salt, as there were plenty of cases where gangs abandoned the notion of a fair fight and proceeded to beat up individuals – and not just single members of rival groups, but solitary strangers who had unwittingly entered a particular district. One such innocent lad was passing through Miles Platting when he was ambushed and stabbed in the calf by a group of outraged Scuttlers.

Entry into another gang's territory was viewed as a major act of provocation. Strangers would be challenged and interrogated if found out of their areas. In November 1878, John James Hughes and Jeremiah O'Brien were convicted of stabbing Thomas Dwyer in Ancoats. Dwyer had been walking along the road minding his own business when a gang stopped him and asked him where he was going. Because Dywer refused to answer, Hughes then stabbed him twice in the back and O'Brien jabbed him in the shoulder. The lad lost a lot of blood and had to be rushed to the Ancoats Dispensary. The doctor remarked that during the last month he had treated five stabbing cases, all of them arising from the scuttling craze. The boys were sentenced to two months' imprisonment with hard labour.

In February 1887, seventeen-year-old Charles Burns was murdered after a chance meeting in another Ancoats street with a group of Scuttlers. Burns, a member of a rival gang, ran into a house hoping to find sanctuary, but the other lads followed him. John Brady, aged eighteen, then stabbed him seven times in the stomach. He died on the spot.

In February 1897, two lads from Manchester, named Tynan and Fleming, were attacked after they walked two girls home to Salford. As they entered a district called Greengate, a cry went up: "This lot is out of Manchester." A gang wielding belts and knives surrounded the youths. A Salford lad called Hopwood warned, "If you come this way, we will rip your bleeding hearts out." Tynan was then stabbed in the lung, a wound that nearly killed him.

Attacks on individuals, however, were an incidental form of aggression. Gang fights were the preoccupation of the Scuttlers. Bloody vendettas went on for months, with tit-for-tat raids into rival neighbourhoods. In the 1890s, the feud between the Hope Street and Ordsall Lane gangs lasted for about eighteen months and involved numerous stabbings as the opposing factions battled to regain honour with vicious acts of revenge and counter-revenge.

For the Scuttlers, territory was everything. The alehouse, sometimes known as the "blood-tub", was the centre of local supremacy. The Prince of Wales public house in Salford was the target of a particularly audacious Scuttler ambush. Inside, members of the Hope Street gang had been having a quiet drink, seemingly safe in the heart of their own stronghold. The peace, as well as the windows, came to a shattering end. The startled lads rushed outside, only to be confronted by their archrivals, the Ordsall Lane gang, led by Peter Moffat. In the resulting bloodbath, Moffat was stabbed seven times and was lucky to escape with his life. Eighteen battle-scarred gang members were later arrested.

Gangs would sometimes pre-arrange fights with other districts to take place in local parks. One such skirmish, in Newton Heath in 1890, involved up to 600 combatants. The pitched battle between the "Clock Alley" lads and the "Greengate Gang" was also particularly vicious.

Gangs normally had up to thirty members, armed with sticks, stones and knives. However, ingenuity was the name of the game. Weapons confiscated from Scuttlers by Manchester Police included cutlasses, pokers, leather straps with iron bolts attached and the tops of stone mineral bottles tied at the end of a piece of string, which were ideal for whirling about the head. Jerome Caminada, the former Chief Detective Inspector of Manchester Police, confessed that of all the ruffians that he had met in his long career, the Scuttlers were by far the worst, since they used knives to maintain gangland superiority. Most Scuttlers used the blades to maim rather than to murder. They usually stabbed opponents in the body, although there were still a handful of fatalities during the thirty years between 1870 and 1900.[5]

Rivalries existed not just between different gangs but also between prominent individual members of gangs. Thomas Callaghan, the "king" of the London Road Scuttlers, had a nasty confrontation with John Joseph Hillyar, alias Red Elliott, the self-styled "King of Scuttlers": he actually wore a jersey bearing the legend. In May 1891, outside the Casino Music Hall, Callaghan cracked Hillyar on the head with an iron bar, hospitalising him for two weeks.

In November 1893, Hillyar singled out Peter McLaughlin by stabbing him in the back. In court, Hillyar admitted the wounding, but attempted to justify it by stating, "McLaughlin thinks he is the champion scuttler in Salford, and he has got to see there is some one who can ... take him down." Hillyar was sentenced to six months for the attack. Following his release from prison, other Scuttlers, either for revenge or desperate to make their own reputations, targeted Hillyar and meted out similar violence.

William Willan was another infamous Scuttler. In May 1892, Willan, Edward Fleming and Charles Davidson, all aged sixteen, were charged with murdering Peter Kennedy. The accused and the deceased belonged to rival Scuttler gangs. In court, a lad named Hand provided the evidence that Willan had threatened to "dose" Kennedy with a knife. When Willan and his Lime Street Gang saw Kennedy approaching with his own group in Ancoats Street, a fight broke out and the victim was stabbed in the chest. Willan was found guilty of the murder and sentenced to death, with a recommendation of mercy from the jury. On hearing the verdict, he screamed, "Oh, master, don't, have mercy on me, I'm only sixteen. I'm dying."

Willan's girlfriend, Hannah Robin, was perhaps the most infamous of a fearsome band of female Scuttlers. Following her arrest for a disturbance, she was found to be wearing not only a thick leather Scuttlers' belt but also to have had a tattoo on her right arm with the words, "In loving remembrance of William Willan." The tribute proved premature, since her boyfriend was reprieved.

Female Scuttlers even had their own uniform, comprising blouses – sometimes adorned with coloured braid – and straight skirts with a stripe down them. Some wore their fringes long in a similar style to the lads. In this way, Manchester's young women seemed to play a greater part in the gangland scene than was the case with the Liverpool women, although it has been claimed that there were female members of the High Rip.

"There were women in the High Rippers, too," recalled the elderly Elizabeth O'Brien in a *Liverpool Echo* interview in 1960. "They identified themselves by a flower or by a plume in their hair, and most of them were more vicious and wicked than their menfolk." Of course, one witness in court even identified Ellen Grant as the "head leader of the gang". However, the newspapers do not report any violence by female High Rippers. The mistresses of gang members were known as "Donahs". Although they did not accompany men in their criminal pursuits, they nevertheless proved useful to the gang, sometimes acting as decoys, scouts or as sources of false alibis. The Blackstone Street murderer, Michael McLean, hid from the police with his girlfriend, while the consort of Patrick Duggan gave him a useful alibi in court.

As the name suggests, the Cornermen were exclusively comprised of males, although there were "corner women, too, hanging about the gin shop for the same purpose; though in justice to the sex, it should be observed that the corner women are relatively few. The drinking women, as a rule, enter the public [house], have their drink, come out wiping their mouths with their aprons, and depart somewhat hastily, being apparently ashamed to stand and be seen by all that pass along the street."[6]

The avid spectators of the Tithebarn Street kicking would undoubtedly have featured a large number of women among their number. It was a female who shouted "give him it" while Morgan was being booted across the street. It was also a group of women who prevented Samuel Morgan from pursuing John McCrave. It will also be recalled that Mary McCrave could kick as well as any man.

In the main, however, Liverpool women, unlike their Manchester counterparts, do not seem to have joined the gangs as active participants in any violence. Liverpool certainly had its violent women, but they tended to engage in one-to-one brawls, armed with the housewife's weapon of choice, the poker.

Liverpool newspapers were littered with reports of female poker assaults. The following, from August 1876, is typical. Mary McIver was remanded for seven days after wounding Mary Fitzgerald in Prince Edwin Street, off Great Homer Street. The victim, who appeared in the witness box with her face covered in sticking plaster, revealed that she had argued with McIver, who had then clouted her across the nose with a poker.

In contrast, young women Scuttlers were often to be seen in the thick of battle alongside the men. Crime historian Andrew Davies[7] has identified numerous incidents of female involvement in scuttles. In Bradford, in 1877, rival Scuttlers, amounting to 200-300 young men and women, fought a pitched battle armed with sticks and bricks. In 1885, Ann Flannaghan appeared in court alongside two male Scuttlers. During a fight between rival gangs, she had kicked a lad as he lay on the ground after being stabbed. In Openshaw, in 1889, a 100-strong gang, including male and female Scuttlers, threw stones at each other. In 1890, following a trial related to the Hope Street and Ordsall Lane feud, a constable was ambushed in what appears to have been a revenge attack against the police. He was knocked to the ground, kicked, bitten and nearly killed by a gang comprising five youths and three young women. During the assault, Annie Tucker battered the policeman a few times with her clog, while Maggie Moffat used her boot as a weapon. Moffat was the sister of Peter, the leader of the Ordsall Lane gang who, just a week earlier, had been given twelve months for his own part in the feud.

In a related case, George White, who had been a witness to the assault on the policeman, found himself the victim of intimidation and harassment intended to deter him from testifying. In one incident, a gang of fourteen-year-old girls, allegedly armed with knives, pursued him through the streets of Ordsall. After taking refuge in his house, the girls stood outside and shouted, "Come out, Totty White, and we'll rip you open."

According to Charles Russell, the Ikes, or Ikey Boys, were the successors of the Scuttlers. The name probably derives from the gang's preference for buying their clothes from Jewish tailors. In Russell's view, this group was a more degenerate development. The Ike didn't do much work and, if he did, it was of a casual nature. Like the Cornermen, he was more of a loafer. Scuttlers had a sense of comradeship and organisation, at least in the sense that they formed gangs. The Scuttlers also had energy and drive, even if it was misdirected into violent pursuits. The Ike was more of a solitary individual and only rarely would he bother to set upon innocent strangers.

Just as Justice Day was believed to have put an end to the High Rip, so Mr Higgins, Q.C., chairman of the Quarter Sessions, was said to have wiped out the scuttling epidemic. In his autobiography, Manchester Police Superintendent James Bent wrote that the sentences Higgins passed were so severe that the violence was effectively stamped out. Nevertheless, in addition to the stick, Bent placed great stress on the carrot, when he revealed his hope that, in the future, education would inspire disaffected Manchester youngsters to aim for "something better".[8]

SCUTTLING WAS ON its way out by the late 1890s. In London, however, another worrying development in youth disorder was about to begin. The term "hooligan" has become part of the modern-day language to denote any young ruffian. However, the label was originally used to refer to a series of gangs who were active in the capital from the late 1890s to around 1910. The term made its brief newspaper debut in an article in the *Daily News* of July 26, 1898, although the origin of the name is uncertain.

Some say that the gang took their name from Patrick Hooligan, a notorious ruffian who had apparently died in prison after murdering a policeman. Others think that the word derives from the Hoolehan brothers, a pair of pugilists. In court, a policeman is supposed to have wrongly pronounced their name as Hooley's gang. Hooligan was also the surname of a fictional Irish family featured in a music hall song of the 1890s, the lyrics of which would make rather a good terrace chant:

> Oh, the Hooligans! Oh, the Hooligans!
> Always on the riot,
> Cannot keep them quiet,
> Oh, the Hooligans, Oh, the Hooligans!
> They are the boys
> To make a noise
> In our backyard.[9]

Whatever the term's origins, many gangs adopted the name all over the capital. The first reported reference to youths calling themselves Hooligans probably occurred on August 19, 1898.[10] A sailor had been beaten and robbed by a group of three youths in Whitechapel. Shortly before the attack, a policeman had noticed the lads looking suspicious and had taken refuge in a doorway where he heard them boasting, "We are the Hooligan Gang."

Hooligans ranged in age between sixteen and twenty-one. Like the Scuttlers, they wore a uniform of bell-bottomed trousers over their boots, a neck scarf and caps, sometimes of velvet or plaid, depending on the particular gang affiliation. Hooligans usually wore their hair in a "donkey-fringe" style. However, for a court appearance, one young trendsetter had his hair closely clipped all over the scalp except for a long piece on the crown, which he pulled forward over his forehead in a version of the Mohican style later popularised by Punk Rockers.

Belts were also worn, for fashion and for fighting. In August 1898, some Hooligans attacked Henry Pearce and William Freeman in Stepney. For weapons, the gang employed thick leather belts studded with sharp brass caps. As if this wasn't sadistic enough, each stud was adorned on each side with pointed bits of wire at intervals of every half-inch. The effect was devastating; Freeman had several teeth smashed. Albert Smith, aged twenty, was found guilty and sentenced to six weeks' hard labour.

Liverpool's Cornermen had burst into media prominence after an August Bank Holiday disturbance in Tithebarn Street. The Hooligans also stormed onto the scene after an August Bank Holiday festival in 1898.

On a particularly scorching holiday, a number of street disturbances and fights resulted in a larger than usual amount of arrests. In a single day, in a court in Marylebone, seventy-seven people were charged with various forms of disorderliness, including assaults, robberies, gang fights, stabbings and vandalism. It was suggested that the heat had led to increased drinking of alcohol, which in turn had sparked the disorder.

On that infamous August Bank Holiday, a group of four lads aged between seventeen and twenty went on the rampage in Marylebone Road, overturning an Italian ice-cream vendor's cart and attacking a park-keeper in Regent's Park. As he was being arrested, one of the gang also kicked and bit a policeman. The lads were described as "larrikins", the Australian term for a hooligan. They were, in fact, members of the "Somers Town Boys", although as they ran across the park the people following them shouted, "Look out for the Hooligan Gang." A policeman stated that the lads were part of a gang of nine or ten youths who had been terrorising Euston Square and Gower Street station.

Hooligan behaviour ranged from childish pranks to fatal violence. They would hang about the streets like the Cornermen, spitting and using bad language, sometimes pushing people off the pavement. Like the High Rip, they would also assault and rob people. In common with the Scuttlers, they would engage in faction fights, battling for street supremacy. While Britain expanded her Empire abroad, through the Boer War, Hooligans were busy carving up their own inner-city territories. Rival gangs often fought against each other, street against street, district against district: for example, the Chelsea Boys versus the Fulham Boys, which reads rather like a football fixture. The football analogy is useful. Like the Cornermen, the Hooligans used their boots as weapons. With the ferocious war cry of "Boot 'em", the gangs would wade in with their feet.

However, in a disturbing development that had no precedent in earlier gang behaviour, one elderly woman was knocked down by a gang and robbed of her bag of shopping, while in a separate incident a seventeen-year-old attacked an old lady and gave her two black eyes. Also unlike their Liverpool and Manchester predecessors, the

Hooligans indulged in wanton vandalism and anti-social behaviour, such as throwing the coloured lights from railways carriages and placing obstacles on the tracks. In the late 1890s, there was also a spate of attacks from bridges across the river. Objects would be thrown and people would be spat at as they emerged from the tunnels.

At first, when the Hooligans battled against each other, they were viewed as a manageable problem, even when weapons were used. However, the situation deteriorated when ordinary, innocent members of the public became targets of the disorder. This echoes the reaction to Liverpool's Cornermen, who were not seen as a major social problem until they had murdered the respectable Richard Morgan. By 1900, a more serious picture of the Hooligans was being painted: "[They] go from bad to worse; they do not starve and they do not work; they hustle and waylay solitary old gentlemen with gold watches; they hunt in packs too large for a single policeman to cope with."[11]

Indeed, as had been the case in Liverpool, there were many assaults upon policemen who had simply been trying to do their duty. If the crowd thought that an unfair arrest was being made or that the policeman was being heavy-handed, there would be cries of "Rescue! Rescue!" In one incident, the police were surrounded by a baying mob of up to 200 ruffians screaming, "Boot 'em", as they separated a brawling man and woman. In Hoxton, a policeman was stabbed to death as he struggled among a crowd of drunks.

In October 1900, a single day's court report listed a catalogue of gang crimes. John Schafer had gone out for a walk and had come home battered and bruised. He told his father that he had been knocked down and kicked by a gang in Bethnal Green. The following day he had to be taken to hospital where he died. The coroner, at the man's inquest, reported an outbreak of violent crime in the city. At Hackney, a man was killed when somebody struck him on the jaw, and a lad was stabbed to death in Hoxton. In Whitechapel, ruffians had set upon George Acton and had beaten him unconscious with heavy sticks. At Southwark, a gang had viciously attacked a publican. All these assaults were seen as the work of Hooligans.

However, such widespread disorder demonstrates that the Hooligans were not a single unified gang, but that they consisted of separate small groups spread across the capital. There were many gangs with memorable names: the "Clerkenwell 'Pistol' Gang", the

"Girdle Gang", named after its leader, Thomas "Tuxy" Girdle, the "Drury Lane Boys", the "Somers Town Boys", the "Velvet Cap Gang" and Poplar's "Plaid Cap Brigade". The latter was said to be one of three major gangs who terrorised the East End of London. In August 1898, a policeman described how they would push people off the pavement and assault them if they complained. As with the High Rip, many people were too afraid to give evidence against the lads, who were aged between sixteen and eighteen. Gang member William Fell repeatedly warned one old gentleman, "You give evidence and your blooming head will be knocked off."

"Tuxy" Girdle was perhaps too old to have been a Hooligan. He was twenty-six and his gang ranged from nineteen to twenty-four years of age. In fact, in court, Girdle's lawyer had objected to his client being labelled a Hooligan. Girdle was part of a large criminal family and ran a couple of brothels, but in the media frenzy that had arisen around hooliganism in autumn 1898, the Girdle boys had been lumped together with the rest of the gangs.

In one incident, two workmen named Clark and Purkiss visited a public house where Girdle was having a drink. Girdle called Purkiss outside and questioned him about where he lived and whether he drank there regularly. The man's friend went outside to see what was going on. Girdle turned to him and said, "You're one of them... You're the bloke I want." Tuxy then punched the man in the face, knocking him to the floor, and raised the war cry, "Come on boys, put the boot in." Eight men rushed out of the alehouse and proceeded to kick the poor man's head in. The victim tried to roll onto his stomach to protect his face, but one man placed his foot on him to keep him on his back where he provided a better target. Purkiss was also badly beaten. Two women shouted "murder" and "police" and the gang ran off. Some were arrested later.

In court, witnesses came forward to speak of the prisoners' good character, even though it was revealed that Girdle had a previous conviction for assault. It seems as though the gang had mistaken the two men for plain-clothed detectives who had been sent to watch one of Girdle's brothels nearby. Thomas Girdle was sentenced to three years and his gang received between twelve and twenty months.

This ungentlemanly behaviour of youth gangs was often seen as un-English or un-British. The press largely viewed Liverpool's Cornermen as an Irish problem, with imported ruffians indulging in the most un-English violent behaviour. Similarly, crime historian Geoffrey Pearson notes that "it was most ingenious of late Victorian England to disown the British Hooligan by giving him an 'Irish' name".[12]

Whenever there was an outbreak of violence, the newspapers looked for analogies with other uncivilised, lawless or primitive places where the situation was just as bad. During the High Rip scare, Liverpool was reported to be as bad as Belfast, Malay or Burma. When the Hooligans arrived, it was felt that parts of London were more dangerous than the remote districts of Calabria, Sicily or Greece.[13]

As with the High Rip scare, newspapers were accused of sensationally highlighting the Hooligans' activities in order to fill up their pages. Just as one of the heads of the police department interviewed by a journalist cast doubts on the existence of the High Rip, so Patrick McIntyre, a former New Scotland Yard detective, who also wrote a crime column, felt that accounts of Hooligan gangs were being blown up as part of "silly season" journalism.[14]

The concern about street crime focused the public's attention on the social conditions of the Victorian underclass. The huge gap between rich and poor was highlighted by the way in which violence against poor people seemed to be ignored, almost permitted, by the authorities, while well-off people had the full protection of the law. After the Tithebarn Street murder, it was argued that if Morgan had been "a Peer or a Bishop" then there might have been no need to debate how best to tackle such brutal crimes.[15] Similarly, the point was made that, if the Hooligans had attacked a cabinet minister: "We should soon hear of some scheme to improve London life."[16]

It seems that the whole issue of gangs and street violence was capable of producing not only horror and revulsion at the brutality of the ruffians but also a degree of social concern over what was happening to the country, and its young people in particular. As the new century dawned, and as the hooligans fought each other on the streets, another ferocious battle was taking place in debating chambers, lecture halls, the pages of periodicals and even parliament itself. In one corner were those supporting the punishment of young ruffians; in the opposite corner were those advocating the social care of disadvantaged youth. This battle, of course, is still being fought today.

CHAPTER 20

Social Reform

AT THE HEIGHT of the Hooligan reign of terror, newspapers printed headlines such as: "Kick a man like a football"; "They play football with a man" – a chilling echo of Richard Morgan's own death. Ironically, it was admitted that the Hooligan could make a good footballer or cricketer.[1] The problem was that the only way the youths could get rid of their high spirits was by rioting and causing trouble. It was suggested that gymnastics, baths, playgrounds, parks and open spaces would do more good for the lads than flogging them.

On the other hand, the East End novelist Arthur Morrison proposed an original solution to hooliganism. He advocated rounding up all the hooligans and putting them in their own town, with a big wall around it. They could then terrorise each other to their heart's content until there was none of them left.[2] Interestingly, government ministers have recently revived the idea. It has been suggested that yobbos and problem families should be lumped together in their own citadels, far away from decent law-abiding communities.

Yet not everybody advocated harsh punitive remedies for criminals. As the nineteenth century progressed, there was a growing body of opinion that favoured alternative solutions for wrongdoing. In direct contrast to the usual sadistic responses to offending, a religious journal viewed the social problem of Liverpool's Cornermen from a Christian perspective.[3] People were urged to act in imitation of Christ, who came "to seek and to save that which was lost". Readers were asked to speak words of sympathy, encouragement and hope to the Cornermen, even to take them to the baker's shop to buy them a loaf of bread. It was pointed out that such benevolence should not be repeated too often, lest the Cornermen became idle through dependence on charity. Yet it was proposed that such kindness might just touch their hearts and help the benefactor gain a good influence over them.

The enlightened view was to improve the person morally from within, through compassion, rather than to regulate the offender from the outside through whipping and incarceration. It was considered wiser to prevent the crime from being committed in the first place than to try to control it afterwards through punishment.

In response to the Tithebarn Street murder, some called for more men of the stamp of the Canon Major Lester and the Rev. Father Nugent, two eminent local clergymen.[4] Today, the responsibility for providing welfare has been largely supplanted by the work of Social Services, but in Victorian times this drive for social action was largely the initiative of such brave and tireless individual reformers.

In addition to being chaplain of Walton Gaol, Nugent was the driving force behind the establishment of numerous refuges, ragged schools, industrial schools and reformatory institutions to help educate children and to keep them clothed, fed and with a roof over their heads. He also formed boys' clubs both to keep children off the streets and to keep them gainfully occupied. His friend, Canon Major Lester, the incumbent of St Mary's Church of England, Kirkdale, from 1855 to 1903, also did sterling work with the Kirkdale Child Charity.

There were appeals for more than church buildings in the town; some argued that in addition to people going to church, the Church itself needed to go to the people. They questioned the hypocrisy of spending time and money converting heathens in far-off lands when Liverpool had its own savages hanging around every street corner. What was needed, it was argued, were workers, teachers and missionaries, such as Nugent and Lester, who would go out onto the streets of Liverpool to do good work, particularly to educate the sons of the Cornermen.

The Hooligan reign of terror also forced people to question the moral condition of their own communities. Similar criticism was aimed at the interest people took in the religious conversion of the barbarians of Sudan while ignoring the wilder barbarians living in their own Hooligan-infested neighbourhoods.[5]

The nineteenth century saw a great deal of effort to reclaim criminals and to help turn their lives around. It was evident to some that the worlds of the miscreant and the respectable citizen were not fixed opposites. Just as Tithebarn Street itself bridged the two worlds of rich and poor, the civilised and the savage, so people themselves could move from one state to the other. The case of Peter Campbell, the hard-working lad who fell in with a bad crowd, is a good example.

Without the safety net of modern-day welfare services, unfortunate and tragic events such as widowhood, unemployment and illness could easily cause Victorian people to drop from a condition of respectability to pauperism rapidly. From there it was all too easy for some of them, out of sheer necessity, to drift into crime.

Another tragic case was that of Alice Morgan, the widow of the man murdered in Tithebarn Street. In September 1876, Mrs Morgan remarried a bargeman named Gracey. Perhaps still devastated by Richard's death, she turned to drink. A week after the wedding, Alice went on the run with her husband's wages, which she admitted to having spent on alcohol. When she returned, she had even sold her wedding ring. Her husband forgave her and took her back, but she went missing on four further occasions. When she returned for yet another reconciliation, her husband refused to let her back on the boat. Alice appealed to the guardians and was given poor relief. Her husband was then arrested and charged with deserting his wife, but when he explained the circumstances of the marriage breakdown to the court, he was informed that he was no longer responsible for supporting his wife.

It seems ironic that, despite calls for public donations to help Mrs Morgan, this respectable woman was eventually reduced to a state of destitution, with as much reliance on alcohol as the very lads who murdered her husband.

Yet it was also believed that the lives of criminals and drunkards could, in turn, be morally transformed through religious instruction, temperance and hard work, by teaching them the virtues of thrift, restraint, responsibility and respectability. There is much written today about the link between drugs and crime. In Victorian times a similar debate centred on the relationship between drink and crime. It was believed that giving up drinking led to self-improvement and self-respect, offering a clear path out of poverty. It was Father Nugent who founded the Catholic Total Abstinence League of the Cross in order to help people turn away from the evils of alcohol.

Yet despite such liberal viewpoints, the old-fashioned remedies to crime were sometimes hard to dismiss. A newspaper correspondent who called for more men of the stamp of Father Nugent nevertheless went on in his letter to call for the public thrashing of criminals to make an example of them. Perhaps it was felt that a belt-and-braces approach to criminal justice worked best.

Another great force for social improvement was education. In 1875, while commenting on the Tithebarn Street murder, a journal correspondent noted a cycle of criminality: as degenerate poor people in Liverpool continued to expand their already large families with more children, it merely perpetuated their lawless lifestyles. These were most likely to be Irish Catholics. It was felt impossible to train their offspring in "any habits of decency and honest labour". It was as if such a population explosion among people divorced from their social and economic responsibilities threatened to overthrow the law-abiding middle-classes. The feared result would be moral collapse.

The correspondent continued, "It is painful to see the flocks of boys and girls about the canal banks stealing coals or anything they can lay their hands on ... forming the predatory herds of the town, while the School Board inspector either does not notice them, or does not know what to do with them if he does."[6]

Truancy is not a new problem. In 1870, education had become compulsory for children aged between five and thirteen, but many youngsters were kept from school by their parents in order to earn money. Around this time, Liverpool ship owner Charles Booth estimated that there were about 25,000 children in the town without either schooling or jobs. Many lived by their wits on the streets. The middle classes saw education as the great hope for these feral children, as it would offer them a chance to better themselves.

After the Tithebarn Street murder, it was hoped that education would rapidly improve the social and moral condition of Liverpool's poor. Judge Mellor, in his address to the grand jury at the beginning of the 1874 winter assizes, recognised that it was still too early to observe any real benefit, but said that he hoped to live long enough to see a marked improvement in children's behaviour as a result of the Education Act.

For many in the slums, however, such hopes were futile. When Michael McLean, the first leader of the High Rip, was hanged in 1884, the point was made: "Had the lad been born in happier circumstances, had he been educated at Eton instead of being left to the schooling of street life, he might have led a forlorn hope and perished in the moment of victory, to the honour of his country instead of her disgrace. The daring and energy which led him on to robbery, murder, and the scaffold, might, if conditions had been happier, have been to that benefit and to that of his fellow men."[7] Sadly, instead of earning valour on some distant battlefield, McLean waged a vicious and disastrous war on Liverpool's streets.

It was felt that what was needed was something to channel the energy of young people: "Here are lads, brimful of animals sprits, absolutely without mental resources, untrained to reflection, thrown together – the worse corrupting the better; and under the circumstances to which we have alluded, we cannot wonder that robbery and violence should be their natural resort."

Education and keeping youths occupied were commonly offered as remedies for crime. Manchester youth worker Charles Russell offered his own solution to the Scuttler problem: "Punish offences against the person as severely as those against property, and try to teach while you are punishing. Make a point of having work ready for them immediately their punishment is over, and watch them in it."[8]

During the height of the High Rip terror, there were renewed efforts to change the behaviour of the gangs. In September 1886, in response to the feature on "Savage Liverpool" in the *Daily Post*, the Liverpool architect and surveyor William Henry Picton wrote a letter to the newspaper offering an explanation of the causes of ruffianism among the young. Picton, the second son of Sir James Picton, was a great advocate of public free libraries, gymnasia and open spaces in the congested slum areas of the city. He felt it was no surprise that bands of high-spirited youths should congregate in the city centre. Picton outlined efforts that were being made to tackle the problem of the High Rip. In particular, he pinpointed the youth work of the Gordon Working Lads Institute in counteracting the influence of the gangs. Picton was Honorary Secretary of the Institute.

A boys' infantry brigade had recently been formed and drill was given three times a week, leading to much improvement in both the boys' manners and discipline. The brigade had begun to march in the neighbourhood, accompanied by their own brass band. The club looked forward to new premises in Stanley Road, where they hoped to reach 500 members. The Institute also gave weekly concerts and "free and easys" where the lads entertained themselves with songs and recitations. Picton appealed for funds to furnish the new building.[9]

Picton laid some of the blame for gang violence on "the sensational stories contained in cheap publications", a reference to the "penny dreadfuls". Picton's letter led to a response from the *Echo* on the same day. The newspaper also felt that lads were influenced by "reading the cheap romantic and pernicious periodicals of the day". Such reading motivated them to join gangs such as the High Rip, where they could act out their violent fantasies. The *Echo*, while not condoning the criminal activities of the High Rip, also felt some pity for lads who were given no chance in life. The paper praised the Gordon Institute for inspiring youngsters to rise above their present level. It was felt to be good social policy to "make the schoolmaster do the work of the policeman".[10]

Other publications also accused penny dreadfuls of being the cause of youth disorder. Society's moral indifference and a lack of police will only aggravated the problem:

> The men comprising these "High Rip" and other gangs are mostly young – many of them mere lads. They have the audacity and inventiveness in evil of a generation nourished upon thieves' literature, if it is permissible to call such garbage literature at all, and their native daring has been encouraged by immunity from interference. They are not taught to feel that their mode of life is a criminal one until some murderous outrage, such as the Tithebarn Street or Blackstone Street case, shocks the community.[11]

The blame for Scuttler violence was also laid at the door of the penny dreadfuls, which were seen to "engender a morbid love of horrors and atrocities".[12] Inevitably, the press also blamed the violent antics of the Hooligans on the malign influence of penny-dreadful literature.

It is ironic that, after the Tithebarn Street murder, it was thought that a lack of education was to blame for the savage nature of children. Yet years later, when young people were starting to become literate, their savagery and delinquency were blamed on reading the wrong sort of literature. Oddly enough, a version of this argument continues to this day with attacks on "video nasties" and violent computer games as causes of juvenile crime.

Fabian activist Sidney Webb blamed hooliganism on youths receiving too much pocket money. Others cited the evils of smoking. In 1901, at St Martin's Town Hall, London, Miss Honnor Morten delivered a lecture entitled "The Hooligan". The Humanitarian League sponsored the event and so the views expressed were a world apart from the usual "hang-'em-and-flog-'em" responses that were printed daily in the press. Miss Morten argued that much of what passed for hooliganism was mere boisterousness and high spirits. She laid the blame for such behaviour on over-stimulation of the child's brain in infancy. This led to a lack of concentration and, later in life, to rowdyism. In true Christian fashion, her solution to hooliganism was "forgiveness".

The Rev. W.D. Morrison saw poor housing and atrocious social conditions as the causes of hooliganism. Mr J. Carvell Williams wrote to the conference to offer his own opinions. He identified faults in the education system, parental neglect and "evil training" as the major contributory factors.

Yet another newspaper correspondent blamed hooliganism on the bad example that prominent members of society, including MPs, were setting by repeatedly breaking the speed limit in their motorcars and then laughing off any fines they had to pay. Under the headline, "How Hooligans are Made", the writer made the point that, given such poor role models, was it any wonder that members of the lower classes also refused to abide by the law when they wished to commit their own crimes?[13]

In 1907, a journal identified the evil influence of ice-cream parlours and fish-supper bars, particularly for their "glitter and ... inducement ... and ... inviting aroma... It is perfectly appalling to think of the moral damage that is being done in these places."[14]

Charles Russell, an expert on Manchester's youth, felt that the gangs formed because lads had nothing else to do, because there was no other form of entertainment. They made war with neighbouring gangs as a means of burning up their surplus energy. The Scuttlers, however, were not young unemployed people who idly loitered around street corners with nothing else to do with their time. Like the

High Rip, for the most part they held down manual jobs and enjoyed a steady wage. Indeed, the employed status of young people was seen by some to be part of the problem. Lads and young women with jobs had a degree of independence and could do more or less what they liked. The parents of delinquent youths dared not come down too hard on them, since they relied on the wages they brought home. This lack of parental discipline in turn led to bad behaviour.

Nevertheless, the idea that the devil makes work for idle hands gained increasing popularity. A whole range of boys' movements, such as the Boys' Brigade and Boy Scouts, sprang up to mould young-sters in a better image. Such organisations offered discipline and moral instruction through exciting physical activities. In *Scouting for Boys*, Baden-Powell estimated that of the two million lads in Great Britain only about half a million could be considered good citizens. The rest were said to be "drifting towards 'hooliganism' or bad citizenship".[15] Baden-Powell felt that his organisation attracted and morally transformed the hooligan type, although there is also plenty of evidence to suggest that lads from the rougher areas rejected such organisations and that they would physically attack a boy scout if they saw one wearing a uniform in the street. The Boys' Brigade often found themselves performing drill under a barrage of bricks and bottles. In April 1891, in north London, a battle between the Brigade and young ruffians was fought outside a drill hall. A Brigade officer ended up knocking out a lad who was causing trouble.

Despite the growth of the youth movement, as the twentieth century progressed gangs continued to exist. The First World War diverted a whole generation of youths into more violent action at the Front. The Hooligans became heroes. On the other hand, it has been argued that the absence of many father figures during the Great War led to a fresh generation of children growing up without fatherly discipline.

The austerity of the 1920s and '30s gave rise to more violent gangs, such as Glasgow's Billy Boys and Redskins and other assorted razor gangs and cosh boys. After the Second World War, the combined influences of greater consumerism, rock 'n' roll music and a newly found financial independence led many youths to become Teddy Boys, followed by Mods, Rockers and Skinheads. Liverpool had its own notorious Peanut and Swallow gangs. With the passing of each decade and the formation of yet another new gang culture, older people habitually take refuge in a nostalgic view that things were better in the past; that violence was rare, that you could leave your front door open. Many identify the abolition of hanging and corporal punishment, together with the abandoning of National Service, as the beginning of the end. The kids now have the upper hand; we are all doomed!

However, we have moved a long way from the Victorian age. The grinding poverty, squalor and atrocious slums have disappeared. We now have new housing estates, health services, social services, youth services, mass education, better working conditions and a more humane penal system – everything that enlightened Victorians thought would eliminate street crime.

And yet still the gangs remain, assaulting, robbing and abusing people. Occasionally they murder innocent passers-by, just like Richard Morgan. Off-licences and fast-food takeaways on every corner have replaced public houses on every corner. The street-corner loafers have become off-licence loafers. Scrounging money for drugs has replaced begging money for drink. "Bucco" caps have become baseball caps.

The question of what to do about street crime is as valid today as it was in Victorian times. The proposed solutions are also as polarised now as they were back then. For some, young people need praise and encouragement to stay on the right path. For others, they deserve censure and punishment when they stray. A pat on the back or a whip across the back? The vital questions remain: more prisons or more leisure centres? More policemen or more youth workers? The debate rages on.

Glossary of Underworld Slang

The following slang derives from the criminal underworld from all over the country, not just Liverpool. The list borrows heavily from James Bent's *Criminal Life* and Kellow Chesney's *The Victorian Underworld*.

Bleeder – Knife
Bonneting – Knocking off a stranger's hat
Buzzing – Stealing, especially picking pockets
Cash carrier – Prostitute's manager, a ponce
Chiv – Knife blade
Chuck – Food
Cockchafer – Prison treadmill
Cop – A victim
Copt – Caught by the police
Cracksman – Safe-breaker
Crapped – Hanged
Crusher – Policeman
Daisy Roots – Boots
Dimmick – Base coin
Donahs – Mistresses of the High Rip
Dose – Stab somebody
Drag (1) – Three-month jail sentence
Drag (2) – Street
Eye me float – Coat
Finny – Five-pound note
Flash house – Public house frequented by criminals
Flimsy – Five-pound note
Flying the blue pigeon – Stealing roof lead
Flying the mags – Pitch and toss
Fusee – Match
Gonoph – Minor thief, inferior pickpocket
Griddling – Begging, peddling, stealing
Haybag – Woman
Heck Heck – Warning, watch out
Highland frisky – Whisky
Jack – Detective
Jerry – A watch
Jerryshop – Pawnbroker
Jimmy Skinner   – Dinner
Jolly – A disturbance, fracas
Judy – Woman or prostitute
Kidsman – Organiser of child thieves
Kynchin lay – Street stealing from children
Larrikin – Australian term for a hooligan
Long-tailed (of banknotes) – Of more than five pounds face value
Mag or *Meg* – Halfpenny
Miseried – Sent to reformatory school

Mouthpiece – Barrister
Nethersken – Low lodging house
Newgate knockers – Heavily greased side-whiskers curling back over the ears
Nicked – Stabbed
Nine moon – Nine months' imprisonment
Nix Nix – Warning, watch out
Purring – Kicking form of fighting
Rasher wagon – Frying pan
Rubs – Years of penal servitude
Ruffles – Handcuffs
Scaldrum dodge– Begging with the aid of feigned or self-inflicted injuries
Scroby – Flogging in prison
Scutch – Thrash, from the act of separating textile fibres by beating them
Shake lurk – Begging under the pretence of being a shipwrecked sailor
Shallow, work the – Beg half-naked
*Shinscrape*r – Prison treadmill
Skilly – Thin gruel. Deriving from the Irish word skillagalle
Slops – Policemen
Smashed – Committed for trial
Snakesman – Agile young thief involved in housebreaking
Snide – Base coin
Snowing – Stealing linen off washing line
Sprat – Sixpence
Stall – Thief's accomplice who impedes pursuit
Suck-crib – Beer shop
Tail – Prostitute
Terrier crop – Short haircut denoting recent spell in prison or workhouse
Tightener – Good meal
Totty – Female prostitute
Translators – Second-hand clothes (especially boots)

References

Preface
1. *Liverpool Daily Post*, September 4, 1886. Hereafter called *Daily Post*.
2. Robert Louis Stevenson, *Strange Case of Dr Jekyll and Mr Hyde* (London, 1886).

Chapter 1 – The Tithebarn Street Outrage
1. *Liverpool Citizen*, May 16, 1888.
2. Quoted in James O'Donald Mays, *Mr Hawthorne Goes to England* (Burley, 1983), p. 59.
3. *Daily Courier*, September 16, 1874.
4. John Ruskin, *Fors Clavigera: letters to the workmen and labourers of Great Britain*, 8 vols (Orpington, 1871–77), letter 49.

Chapter 2 – The Cornermen
1. Eveline B. Saxton, *Rhymes of Old Liverpool*, enlarged edn (Liverpool, 1948), p. 53.
2. *Daily Post*, January 5, 1875.
3. Hippolyte Taine, *Taine's Notes on England*, trans. with an introduction by Edward Hyams (London, 1957), pp. 225–226.
4. *Daily Courier*, January 5, 1875.
5. Figures from P.J. Waller, *Democracy and Sectarianism: A Political and Social History of Liverpool, 1868-1939* (Liverpool, 1981), pp. 23–24.
6. *Daily Post*, September 4, 1886.
7. *Daily Post*, November 10, 1883.
8. *Liverpool Mail*, January 16, 1875.
9. *Plain Talk*, March 1875, p. 2.
10. Hugh Shimmin, *Liverpool Sketches*, 1862, p. 122.
11. *Daily Courier*, August 14, 1874.
12. *Spectator*, August 15, 1874.

Chapter 3 – Manhunt
1. *Daily Post*, August 6, 1874.
2. HO 43/122. National Archives.

Chapter 4 – The Black Assize
1. Tod Sloan, *The Treadmill and the Rope: The History of a Liverpool Prison* (Parkgate, 1988), p. 14.
2. Leon Radzinowicz and Roger Hood, *A History of English Criminal Law and its Administration from 1750* , vol. 5. *The Emergence of Penal Policy in Victorian and Edwardian England* (Oxford, 1990), pp. 678–79.
3. *The Liverpool Weekly Albion*. Quoted in Rob Sindall, *Street Violence in the Nineteenth Century: Media Panic or Real Danger?* (Leicester, 1990), p. 61.
4. *Daily Post*, January 5, 1875.
5. Basil Thomson, *The Criminal* (London, 1925), p. 25.
6. *Liverpool Weekly Albion*, January 9, 1875.

Chapter 5 – Execution
1. *Liverpool Citizen*, May 16, 1888.
2. *The Treadmill and the Rope*, p. 46.
3. Brian J. Bailey, *Hangmen of England: A History of Execution from Jack Ketch to Albert Pierrepoint* (London, 1889), p. 73.

4. *The Treadmill and the Rope*, p. 48.
5. *Liverpool Weekly Albion*, January 9, 1875.
6. *St James Gazette*, August 31, 1892.
7. *Daily Courier*, August 31, 1886. The journalist who reported this, many years after the event, must have been mistaken, for all three hanged men had brothers still alive. None was an only child.

Chapter 6 – Why Was The Murder So Shocking?
1. *Liverpool Daily Albion*, August 5, 1874.
2. *Liverpool Citizen*, May 16, 1888.
3. *Liverpool Journal*, August 8, 1874.
4. *Daily Courier*, January 5, 1874.
5. *Daily Courier*, August 31, 1886.
6. Quoted in Tony Barnes, *Mean Streets: A Journey Through the Northern Underworld* (Bury, 2000), p. 30.
7. *Street Violence in the Nineteenth Century*, p. 64.
8. *Liverpool Weekly Albion*, December 19, 1874.
9. *Liverpool Weekly Albion*, December 19, 1874.
10. *Liverpool Echo*, May 21, 1887. Hereafter called *Echo*.
11. *Liverpool Weekly Albion*, December 19, 1874.
12. *Spectator*, August 8, 1874.
13. *The Porcupine*, August 8, 1874.
14. *Daily Courier*, January 5, 1874.
15. Henry Mayhew, *London Labour and the London Poor, 1861–62*, vol. 2 (New York, 1968), p. 338.
16. *The Times*, December 26, 1874.

Chapter 7 – Senseless Violence
1. *The Porcupine*, May 1875.

Chapter 9 – Sectarian Gangs
This chapter is indebted to Frank Neal's *Sectarian Violence: the Liverpool Experience, 1819–1914* (Manchester, 1988).

1. *Fifty-Two Years a Policeman* (London, 1926), p. 57.
2. *Daily Post*, September 4, 1886.
3. *Echo*, October 21, 1886.
4. Herbert Asbury, *The Gangs of New York: An Informal History of the Underworld* (London, 2002), p. 21.

Chapter 10 – Tiny Terrors and Juvenile Gangs
1. *The Times*, October 10, 1876.
2. *Liverpool Journal*, January 12, 1884.

Chapter 12 – The High Rip Gang
1. *Daily Courier*, August 31, 1886.
2. *Liverpool Citizen*, May 16, 1888.
3. *Evening Express*, February 12, 1885.
4. *Echo*, February 18, 1885.
5. *Daily Post*, November 25, 1884.
6. *Daily Post*, September 4, 1886.
7. *Daily Post*, September 4, 1886.
8. *Daily Courier*, August 31, 1886.
9. *Liverpool Review*, August 28, 1886.
10. *Daily Post*, September 4, 1886.
11. *Liverpool Review*, August 28, 1886.
12. *The ABZ of Scouse* (Liverpool, 1966).

13. *Daily Post*, September 4, 1886.
14. *Echo*, October 2, 1886.
15. Silas K. Hocking, *Her Benny* (Liverpool, 1968), p. 17.
16. *Daily Post*, March 1, 1887.
17. *Daily Post*, September 20, 1886.
18. *Daily Post*, September 4, 1886.
19. *Daily Post*, September 4, 1886.
20. *Daily Post*, September 20, 1886.
21. *Daily Post*, reprinted in the *Echo*, October 2, 1886.
22. *Daily Post*, September 20, 1886.
23. *Liverpool Review*, October 9, 1886.

Chapter 13 – Crimes of the High Rip
1. *Echo*, October 19, 1960.
2. *Daily Post*, December 22, 1885.
3. *Daily Post*, March 1, 1887.
4. *Daily Post*, September 16, 1886.
5. *Daily Post*, September 21, 1886.
6. *Echo*, May 21, 1887.

Chapter 14 – Gang War
1. *Daily Post*, September 4, 1886.
2. *Echo*, November 13, 1886.
3. *Echo*, October 20, 1886.
4. *Echo*, November 13, 1886.

Chapter 15 – Denying the High Rip
1. Anonymous, *The Whitechapel Murders, or The Mysteries of the East End* (London, 1888).
2. *Echo*, October 2, 1886.
3. *Echo*, October 13, 1886.
4. *Echo*, October 14, 1886.
5. *Echo*, October 16, 1886.
6. *Liverpool Review*, September 25, 1886.
7. Quoted in Freddy O'Connor, *A Pub On Every Corner, vol. 4: Scotland Road, Everton, Anfield* (Liverpool, 2001), p. 56.
8. Sir William Nott-Bower, *Fifty-Two Years a Policeman* (London, 1926), pp. 148–49.
9. Reprinted in *Echo*, November 13, 1886.
10. *Echo*, May 21, 1887.
11. *Head Constable's Special Report Book*, October 20, 1886, Liverpool Record Office, 352 Pol 2/11.
12. *Liverpool Review*, November 13, 1886.
13. *Echo*, November 20, 1886.
14. *Daily Post*, March 1, 1887.
15. *Echo*, May 21, 1887.
16. *Liverpool Review*, March 5, 1887.
17. *Street Violence in the Nineteenth Century*, p. 67.
18. *Liverpool Weekly Mercury*, June 2, 1888.
19. *Liverpool Weekly Mercury*, July 21, 1888.
20. *Liverpool Weekly Mercury*, December 29, 1888.
21. *The Times*, December 21, 1897.

Chapter 16 – The Social Causes of Gang Violence
1. *Democracy and Sectarianism*, p. 108.
2. Sir William Nott-Bower, *Fifty-Two Years a Policeman* (London, 1926), pp. 147–48.
3. *The Porcupine*, August 8, 1874.
4. F. Neal, "A Criminal Profile of the Liverpool Irish", *Transactions of the Historical*

Society of Lancashire and Cheshire, vol. 140 (1990), 166.
5. Father James Nugent, *Select Committee on Prisons and Prison Ministries Acts 1870*, Minutes of Evidence, q. 4010.
6. Thomas Burke, *Catholic History of Liverpool* (Liverpool, 1910), p. 37.
7. *Daily Courier, Evening Express*, August 5, 1874.
8. Kellow Chesney, *The Victorian Underworld* (Harmondsworth, 1972), p. 37.
9. Quoted in *Daily Post*, November 24, 1884.
10. *The Times*, January 11, 1875. The letter was reprinted in the *Daily Post* the next day.
11. *Liverpool Weekly Albion*, December 25, 1875.
12. *The Times*, January 11, 1875.
13. *The Times*, October 2, 1876.
14. *Daily Post*, September 4, 1886.
15. Henry Mayhew, *London Labour and the London Poor*, 4 vols, 1862–64. Charles Booth, *Labour and Life of the People in London*, 9 vols, 1892–97.
16. *Daily Post* reprinted in *Echo*, October 2, 1886.
17. Walter Lewin, *Clarke Aspinall: A Biography* (London, 1893), p. 148.
18. *Echo*, November 20, 1886.
19. *Liverpool Weekly Albion*, January 5, 1878.

Chapter 17 – Judgement Day

1. *Punch*, October 3, 1874.
2. *Liverpool Journal* quoted in *Daily Post* August 10, 1874.
3. *Liverpool Town Crier*, December 23, 1874.
4. *Daily Post*, August 6, 1874.
5. *Daily Courier*, August 14, 1874.
6. *Spectator*, January 16, 1875.
7. *The Porcupine*, December 19, 1874.
8. *Spectator*, August 8, 1874.
9. *The Porcupine*, January 9, 1875.
10. Parliamentary Papers (1897), vol. xxxv, Q 12263, T.E. Sampson.
11. *Liverpool Review*, September 4, 1886.
12. *The Porcupine*, January 9, 1875.
13. *Daily Courier*, August 14, 1874.
14. *Liverpool Weekly Mercury*, September 1, 1888.
15. *The Porcupine*, January 9, 1875.
16. *Daily Courier*, January 5, 1875.
17. *Daily Courier*, August 11, 1874.
18. *Daily Post*, March 1, 1887.
19. *Echo*, October 21, 1886.
20. *Fifty Two Years a Policeman*, pp. 149–50.
21. Richard Whittington-Egan, *Echoes* (Liverpool, 2002), p. 71.
22. Arthur Day, *John C.F.S. Day: His Forbears and Himself: A Biographical Study By One Of His Sons* (London, 1916), p. 120. William Nott-Bower, the Head Constable, believes this incident happened in November 1886 and involved 20 prisoners. However, it was more likely to be the May 1887 Assizes, involving only four convicted men.
23. *John C.F.S. Day: His Forbears and Himself*, p. 119.
24. *John C.F.S. Day: His Forbears and Himself*, p. 121.
25. Joseph Collinson, *Facts about Flogging*, rev. edn. (London, 1905), p. 29.
26. *Facts about Flogging*, pp. 29–30.
27. *Fifty-Two Years a Policeman*, p. 151.
28. *Fifty-Two Years a Policeman*, p. 151.
29. *Fifty-Two Years a Policeman*, p. 153.
30. J.D. Crawford, *Reflections and Recollections* (London, 1936), p. 60.
31. *Daily Courier*, November 15, 1886.

Chapter 18 – The Police

1. *Liverpool Mercury*, November 20, 1886.

2. *Liverpool Weekly Albion*, December 19, 1874.
3. *Liverpool Town Crier*, January 16, 1875.
4. *The Times*, January 11, 1875.
5. *Liverpool Journal*, quoted in the *Daily Post*, August 10, 1874.
6. *Daily Post*, January 18, 1875.
7. *Daily Post*, January 18, 1875.
8. *Liverpool Journal*, August 8, 1874.
9. *Liverpool Journal*, August 8, 1874.
10. *The Times*, January 11, 1875.
11. *Liverpool Mercury*, August 5, 1874, *Daily Courier*, August 7, 1874.
12. *Daily Courier*, August 7, 1874.
13. *Daily Courier*, August 11, 1874.
14. *Daily Courier*, August 14, 1874.
15. *Plain Talk*, March 1875, p. 6.
16. *Head Constable's Special Report Book*, Liverpool Record Office, 352, Pol 2/6.
17. *Plain Talk*, March 1875, p. 2.
18. *Street Violence in the Nineteenth Century*, p. 117.
19. *Liverpool Weekly Mercury*, January 12, 1884.
20. *Liverpool Review*, August 28, 1886.
21. *Daily Post*, October 21, 1886.
22. *Echo*, October 19, 1960.
23. *Daily Post*, September 20, 1886.
24. *Echo*, October 21, 1886.
25. *Daily Post*, September 21, 1886.
26. *Echo*, October 15, 1886.
27. *Liverpool Review*, September 4, 1886.
28. *Evening Express*, August 21, 1876.

Chapter 19 – Scuttlers, Hooligans and a Sense of Style

1. *Plain Talk*, March 1875, pp. 1–2.
2. *Daily Post*, December 22, 1885.
3. Charles E.B. Russell, *Manchester Boys: Sketches of Manchester Lads at Work and Play*, 2nd edn (Manchester, 1913), p. 51.
4. A. Devine, *Scuttlers and Scuttling: Their Prevention and Cure* (Guardian Printing Works, 1890), p. 7.
5. Andrew Davies, "Youth Gangs, Gender and Violence, 1870–1900", in Shani D'Cruze (ed.), *Everyday Violence in Britain, 1850–1950: Gender and Class*, Women and Men in History (Harlow, 2000), pp. 70–85, p. 73.
6. *Plain Talk*, March 1875, p. 1
7. "Youth Gangs, Gender and Violence, 1870–1900".
8. James Bent, *Criminal Life: Reminiscences of Forty-Two Years as a Police Officer* (London, 1891), p. 226.
9. *Music Hall Theatre Review*, August 26, 1898, quoted in Geoffrey Pearson, *Hooligan: A History of Respectable Fears* (London, 1983), reproduced with permission of Palgrave Macmillan.
10. *The Times*, August 19, 1898.
11. *The Times*, October 30, 1900.
12. *Hooligan: A History of Respectable Fears*, p. 75, reproduced with permission of Palgrave Macmillan.
13. *The Times*, October 30, 1900.
14. *South London Chronicle*, August 6, 1898.
15. *Spectator*, August 8, 1874.
16. *Reynolds Newspaper*, August 28, 1898.

Chapter 20 – Social Reform

1. *The Times*, October 30, 1900.
2. Arthur Morrison, "Hooligan", *Pall Mall Magazine*, vol. 23, 1901.

3. *Plain Talk*, March 1875.
4. *Daily Courier*, August 11, 1874.
5. *Reynolds Newspaper*, August 14, 1898.
6. *The Porcupine*, January 9, 1875.
7. *Daily Post*, September 4, 1886.
8. *Manchester Boys*, p. 51.
9. *Daily Post*, September 6, 1886.
10. *Echo*, September 6, 1886.
11. *Liverpool Review*, September 4, 1886.
12. *Scuttlers and Scuttling*, p. 5.
13. *The Times*, July 28, 1903.
14. Quoted in Harry Hendrick, *Images of Youth: Age, Class, and the Male Youth Problem, 1880–1920* (Oxford, 1990), p. 130, by permission of Oxford University Press.
15. R.S.S. Baden-Powell, *Scouting for Boys* (London, 1908), pp. 339–40.

Bibliography

Victorian Newspapers and Journals
Catholic Times
Daily Courier
Daily Telegraph
Evening Express
The Liverpool Citizen
The Liverpool Daily Albion
Liverpool Daily Post
Liverpool Echo
The Liverpool Journal
Liverpool Mail
Liverpool Mercury
Liverpool Review
Liverpool Telegraph and Daily Shipping and Commercial Gazette
Liverpool Town Crier
The Liverpool Weekly Albion
Liverpool Weekly Mercury
Plain Talk
Police Gazette
The Porcupine
Punch
Reynolds Newspaper
St James Gazette
The Saturday Review
Spectator
The Times

Books and Journal Articles
The ABZ of Scouse, Liverpool: 1966.
Anonymous, *The Whitechapel Murders, or The Mysteries of the East End,* London: G. Purkess, 1888.
Asbury, Herbert, *The Gangs of New York: An Informal History of the Underworld*, London: Arrow, 2002.
Baden-Powell, R.S.S., *Scouting for Boys*, London: Horace Cox, 1908.
Bailey, Brian J., *Hangmen of England: A History of Execution from Jack Ketch to Albert Pierrepoint*, London: W.H. Allen, 1989.
Barnes, Tony, *Mean Streets: A Journey Through the Northern Underworld*, Bury: Milo Books, 2000.
Bennett, Canon, *Father Nugent of Liverpool*, Liverpool: The Liverpool Catholic Children's Protection Society, 1949.
Bent, James, *Criminal Life: Reminiscences of Forty-Two Years as a Police Officer*, London: Heywood, 1891.
Burke, Thomas, *Catholic History of Liverpool*, Liverpool: C. Tinling, 1910.
Chesney, Kellow, *The Victorian Underworld*, Harmondsworth: Pelican, 1972.
Collinson, Joseph, *Facts about Flogging*, Rev. ed, London: A.C. Fifield, 1905.
Crawford, J.D., *Reflections and Recollections*, London: Marchand Press, 1936.
D'Cruze, Shani (ed.), *Everyday Violence in Britain, 1850–1950: Gender and Class*, Women and Men in History, Harlow: Pearson Education, 2000.

Davies, Andrew, "Youth Gangs, Masculinity and Violence in Late Victorian Manchester and Salford", *Journal of Social History* (Winter 1998).

Day, Arthur, *John C.F.S. Day: His Forbears and Himself: A Biographical Study By One Of His Sons*, London: Heath Cranton Ltd, 1916.

Devine, A., *Scuttlers and Scuttling: Their Prevention and Cure*, Manchester: Guardian Printing Works, 1890.

Glasgow, Gordon H.H., "Clarke Aspinall: Liverpool Borough Coroner, 1867-1891", *Lancashire History Quarterly*, vol. 3, no. 1 (March 1999), 14-19.

Head Constable's Special Report Book. Liverpool Records Office.

Hendrick, Harry, *Images of Youth: Age, Class and the Male Youth Problem, 1880-1920*, Oxford: Clarendon Press, 1990.

Hocking, Silas K., *Her Benny*, Liverpool: Gallery Press, 1968.

Holloway, Henry, *An Echo from Prison: or My Mother and I,* Manchester: J. Heywood, 1877.

Humphries, Steven, *Hooligans or Rebels?: An Oral History of Working-Class Childhood and Youth, 1889-1939*, Oxford: Blackwell, 1981.

Lewin, Walter, *Clarke Aspinall: A Biography*, London: Edward W. Allen, 1893.

Mayhew, Henry, *London Labour and the London Poor*, 4 vols, 1862-64, New York: Dover Publications, 1968.

Mays, James O'Donald, *Mr Hawthorne Goes to England*, Burley: New Forest Leaves, 1983.

National Archives, HO 43/122.

Neal, F., "A Criminal Profile of the Liverpool Irish", *Transactions of the Historical Society of Lancashire and Cheshire*, vol. 140 (1990), 161-199.

Neal, Frank, *Sectarian Violence: The Liverpool Experience, 1819-1914,* Manchester: Manchester University Press, 1988.

Nott-Bower, Sir William, *Fifty-Two Years a Policeman*, London: Edward Arnold, 1926.

Nugent, Father James, *Select Committee on Prisons and Prison Ministries Acts*, 1870, Minutes of Evidence, q. 4010.

O'Connor, Freddy, *Liverpool: Our City, Our Heritage*, Liverpool: Bluecoat Press, 1990.

O'Connor, Freddy, *A Pub On Every Corner, vol. 4: Scotland Road, Everton, Anfield*, Liverpool: Bluecoat Press, 2001.

Pearson, Geoffrey, *Hooligan: A History of Respectable Fears*, London: Macmillan, 1983.

Priestley, Philip, *Victorian Prison Lives: English Prison Biography, 1830-1914*, London: Pimlico, 1999.

Radzinowicz, Leon and Roger Hood, *A History of English Criminal Law and its Administration from 1750*, vol. 5: *The Emergence of Criminal Policy in Victorian and Edwardian England*, London: Stevens, 1986 (reprinted by Oxford: Clarendon Press, 1990).

Ruskin, John, *Fors Clavigera: Letters to the Workmen and Labourers of Great Britain*, 8 vols, Orpington: Allen, 1871-77, letter 49.

Russell, Charles, E.B., *Manchester Boys: Sketches of Manchester Lads at Work and Play*, 2nd edn, Manchester: Manchester University Press, 1913.

Saxton, Eveline B., *Rhymes of Old Liverpool*, enlarged edn, Liverpool: *Daily Post*, 1948.

Shimmin, Hugh, *Liverpool Sketches*, 1862.

Sindall, Rob, *Street Violence in the Nineteenth Century: Media Panic or Real Danger?*, Leicester: Leicester University Press, 1990.

Slemen, Tom, *Wicked Liverpool*, Liverpool: Bluecoat Press, 2001.

Sloan, Tod, *The Treadmill and the Rope: The History of a Liverpool Prison*, Parkgate: Gallery Press, 1988.

Stevenson, Robert Louis, *Strange Case of Dr Jekyll and Mr Hyde*, London: Longmans Green, 1886.

Taine, Hippolyte, *Taine's Notes on England*, translated with an introduction by Edward Hyams, London: Thames and Hudson, 1957.

Thomson, Basil, *The Criminal*, London: Hodder and Stoughton, 1925.

Vauxhall Community Archives Project, *Old Vauxhall: A Miscellany of Local History*, 1994.

Waller, P.J., *Democracy and Sectarianism: A Political and Social History of Liverpool, 1868-1939*, Liverpool: Liverpool University Press, 1981.

Whittington-Egan, Richard, *Echoes*, Liverpool: Bluecoat Press, 2002.